REASONABLE CHILDREN

REASONABLE CHILDREN

Moral Education and Moral Learning

Michael S. Pritchard

 University Press of Kansas

Published by the University Press of Kansas (Lawrence, Kansas 66049), which was organized by the Kansas Board of Regents and is operated and funded by Emporia State University, Fort Hays State University, Kansas State University, Pittsburg State University, the University of Kansas, and Wichita State University

Library of Congress Cataloging-in-Publication Data

Pritchard, Michael S.
    Reasonable children : moral education and moral learning / Michael
S. Pritchard.
        p.   cm.
    Includes bibliographical references and index.
    ISBN 0-7006-0796-X (cloth)   ISBN 0-7006-0797-8 (pbk.)
    1. Moral education.   2. Critical thinking in children.   I. Title.
LC268.P72   1996
370.11'4—dc20   96-25633

British Library Cataloguing in Publication Data is available.

Printed in the United States of America

10 9 8 7 6 5 4 3 2 1

The paper used in this publication meets the minimum requirements of the American National Standard for Permanence of Paper for Printed Library Materials Z39.48-1984.

To Gabe and all the children
from whom we've learned so much

Contents

Preface

Can children be reasonable? On such questions I am what children's writer and illustrator William Steig calls a "hopist." That is how he described himself when asked by a television interviewer whether he were an optimist or a pessimist about the future. On the topic of this book, a pessimist would insist that children cannot be reasonable. They are too impulsive. They lack education and experience. Besides, reasonableness is rare even in adults. An optimist would say either that children actually are reasonable or that becoming so is readily within their reach. A hopist attempts to avoid being overwhelmed by the evidence either way. Instead, he or she clings to the hope that children can be reasonable and sets about seeing what can be done to help bring this possibility into reality.

In any case, what follows are some of my hopist reflections on the prospects for helping children develop their capacity to be reasonable. To the pessimists, I note that if we are to have any hope that children will end up as reasonable adults, we need to attend carefully to those aspects of childhood that hold out some prospect for such an outcome. To the optimists, I offer a word of caution. "Reasonableness" is not an all-or-nothing concept. There are degrees of reasonableness. I have no interest in trying to convert children into adults. But I am interested in the extent to which children, as children, can be reasonable, and I am interested in the bearing this possibility might have on their becoming reasonable adults.

This book explores some ways in which we might help children become more reasonable. For the schools to do well in this endeavor, it is necessary for them to treat children as already capable of some degree of reasonableness even when they first enter school. In Chapter 1, I explain what I mean by "reasonableness," especially in the context of morality. Chapter 2 adapts the Hastings Center's well-known goals and objectives for teaching ethics in higher education to moral education in the schools. As Chapter 3 will make clear, I believe a key to promoting the reasonableness of children is providing them with opportunities to develop their philosophical abilities. In this regard my thinking is especially indebted to the pioneering work of Matthew Lipman and others associated with the Institute for the Advancement of Philosophy for Children, as well as the writings of Gareth Matthews on children's potential for philosophical thinking. Chapters 4 and 5 discuss the recent concern with critical thinking in the schools and suggest ways in which critical thinking might be linked to moral education. Special attention is given to science education. Chapters 6–8 address a variety of concerns about the role of schools in enriching the moral education of children. There are concerns about moral authority, indoctrination, relativism, the relationship between church and state, the role of the family, and, most important, the role of teachers. A basic theme running through these chapters is that it is quite appropriate for the public schools to help students develop their capacities for reasonableness but that doing so calls for empowering rather than indoctrinating children. Chapter 9 discusses how empowered children might proceed on their own, but in ways that are mutually respectful and supportive.

It is important not to exaggerate my intentions for this book. There is a great deal of concern about the moral development of children today. National surveys consistently show that the vast majority of adults in our society favor some sort of moral education in the schools—but they do not all have the same thing in mind. For many, the most important concern is to shape the character and conduct of children. These people are concerned about violence, drugs, sexual behavior, and so on, and those are important concerns. But it is not my aim to present a prescription for solving society's ills—not even those of its children. I certainly hope that what I offer will contribute to dealing effectively with these problems, but my concern is with educational methodology and content. The schools should not be expected to solve society's problems alone. The schools play a necessary but a limited role—an educational one. That is my focus.

In some respects this book picks up where my *On Becoming Responsible* (University Press of Kansas, 1991) left off. It brings together that work with work I have been doing for the past fifteen years in Philosophy for Children. In reviewing an early draft of *On Becoming Responsible*, Gareth

Matthews suggested I add a chapter on moral education, and I used a small section of the final chapter to address moral education explicitly. However, my basic response to Matthews's suggestion was that an adequate treatment of moral education would go well beyond anything I could take up in *On Becoming Responsible.* At the same time, it was evident to me that much of my work in Philosophy for Children informed what I would say about moral education were I to take up Matthews's suggestion in a full-scale way. This is what I have done in this book.

I wish to thank Gareth Matthews for the wise advice he has given me over the years and for directing a wonderful National Endowment for the Humanities Summer Seminar in 1985 on The Philosophy of Childhood. Participating in that seminar was a special privilege. I also wish to thank Matthew Lipman, Ann Margaret Sharp, and so many others for introducing me to the extraordinary work of the Institute for the Advancement of Philosophy for Children (IAPC) at Montclair State University. Through my association with IAPC I have had the distinct pleasure of meeting and learning from educators around the world who are dedicated to the idea that philosophy is for children as well as for adults. Finally, of course, I thank all of the wonderful children who over the years have shared their thoughts with me, thereby convincing me that this book was worth writing.

Earlier versions of portions of various chapters have appeared elsewhere. Several chapters draw from my now out-of-print *Philosophical Adventures with Children* (Lanham, Md.: University Press of America, 1985). I thank the publishers of the *Denver University Law Review* for permission to include sections of my "Families, Schools, and the Moral Education of Children" (vol. 69, no. 3, 1992) in different chapters. I also thank the publishers of *Europe, America, and Technology: Philosophical Perspectives* (Netherlands: Kluwer Academic Publishers, 1991) for permission to include sections of my "STS, Critical Thinking, and Philosophy for Children."

My hope is that this book will be read by not only those already intrigued by the philosophical thinking of children but also by teachers and parents who are looking for ways to encourage children to develop potential for reasonableness. Reasonableness alone cannot ensure that children will successfully negotiate their way through the moral challenges they face now and will encounter later. But it surely should help.

1

Reasonable Children

The eighteenth-century Scottish philosopher Thomas Reid held that there is a strong analogy between bodily development from infancy to maturity and the development of the powers of the mind.[1] Although both are "the work of nature," both may be greatly aided or hurt by education.[2] Thus, a natural process is not an inevitable one. We can help or hinder it. Even more, our own natural development requires careful nurturing and education.

As for bodily development, Reid says: "It is natural to a man to be able to walk, or run, or leap; but, if his limbs had been kept in fetters from his birth, he would have none of those powers."[3] However, these activities require little, if any, direct instruction. One might think that in the absence of fetters, walking, running, and leaping will inevitably emerge. But, of course, they will not. Food and sustenance are also necessary, and the particular manner in which one walks, runs, or leaps may be patterned after other people.

Development of the powers of the mind seems to present much more difficult challenges to caregivers. Here, some sort of formal education seems needed, especially in societies that have complex social, political, and economic institutions. The ability to read or write, for example, is not as easily acquired as the ability to walk, run, or leap. The intelligent exercise of such abilities is even more difficult to acquire. Hence, we have schools.

Nevertheless, Reid's analogy is quite useful. By emphasizing that the development of the powers of the mind is a natural process, Reid directs our attention to the natural capacities of children, not merely the educational environment surrounding them. Instead of regarding children as "empty vessels" to be filled, we need to consider what they may al-

1

ready have to contribute. At the same time, by pointing out that children are vulnerable and need our assistance, Reid invites us to consider our responsibilities in helping them develop their powers of mind.

As Reid realizes, helping children develop their powers of mind is a serious and challenging responsibility. Although most children learn to walk—if not run and leap—quite easily, Reid does not think children fare nearly as well with regard to reasoning abilities. The power of reasoning "appears not in infancy. It springs up, by insensible degrees, as we grow to maturity. But its strength and vigour depend . . . upon its being duly cultivated and exercised."[4] Reid takes a rather dim view of how most fare in this regard. He complains that most adults are "sunk in gross ignorance of things that are obvious to the more enlightened and fettered by errors and false notions, which the human understanding, duly improved, easily throws off."[5]

Reid's concern is echoed in today's complaints that the schools are paying too little attention to helping children develop their critical thinking abilities. Of course, this is not the only complaint leveled against the schools, as many decry what they take to be the public schools' abandonment of moral education. For some, these complaints may seem quite distinct, perhaps even in conflict with each other. Critical thinking may be feared as potentially undermining moral values. Certain moral values, some will say, must simply be inculcated and not questioned. My own view is that the kind of critical thinking the schools should help children develop has important implications for their moral education. This kind of critical thinking is quite compatible with a solid commitment to moral values that can be appreciated by everyone; it is also compatible with children maintaining commitment to moral values not shared by everyone. The idea that enables us to see how critical thinking and moral education can successfully be linked together is *reasonableness*.

REASONABLENESS AND RATIONALITY

I first offer a few remarks about what I take reasonableness to be. I make no attempt to define "reasonable," or related concepts (such as "unreasonable"). As terms of appraisal, they are somewhat contestable concepts, and they are open-ended enough to defy definition in terms of necessary and sufficient conditions. Nevertheless, it is possible to give a rough demarcation of what I have in mind. I am concerned mainly with how appraisals of reasonableness might be applied to persons, their beliefs, attitudes, actions, and decisions, but such appraisals can also be applied to policies, practices, and processes used by deliberative bodies and the like.

It should be noted at the outset that reasonableness is not to be equated with rationality. Someone can be unreasonable without necessarily being irrational. A selfish person may (unreasonably) insist on taking more than his or her fair share, likely at the expense of others. Yet from the standpoint of self-interest, this is not necessarily irrational. A person may make excessive (unreasonable) demands and yet not be irrational. A person might deliberately ignore evidence contrary to his or her favored view, be unwilling to reason with others about an issue, or refuse to listen to others' points of view without being irrational, but we may regard such behavior as unreasonable.

At the same time, reasonableness is itself a form of rationality. It places a premium on supporting one's beliefs and actions with reasons, and these reasons acquire their respectability in a public arena rather than simply in private reflection. Finally, even if sometimes it can be rational to be unreasonable, it is still rational to be reasonable in such circumstances as well.

Thus, I think of reasonableness as typically having *social* features that distinguish it from other forms of rationality. The title of this book, *Reasonable Children,* was chosen with this point in mind. The emphasis is on children thinking together rather than alone. In any of its forms, rationality includes the ability to engage in skillful reasoning. However, as Laurance J. Splitter and Ann M. Sharp point out, reasonableness includes much more:

> Reasonableness is primarily a social disposition: the reasonable person respects others and is prepared to take into account their views and their feelings, to the extent of changing her own mind about issues of significance, and consciously allowing her own perspective to be changed by others. She is, in other words, willing to be reasoned with.[6]

Splitter and Sharp connect this conception of reasonableness with two other observations. First, reasonableness in the classroom is best promoted by encouraging active listening and dialogue, thus promoting a community of inquiry.[7] Second, reasonableness goes some way toward bridging the gap between thought and action. As Splitter and Sharp put it, "We would not describe as reasonable someone who is able to formulate good judgments yet cannot, or consistently does not, put those judgments into practice."[8]

In its typically ironic way, the comic strip *Calvin and Hobbes* nicely illustrates the contrast between rationality and reasonableness. As all faithful readers know, Calvin is a highly imaginative six-year-old boy. His closest companion is Hobbes, his stuffed tiger. One episode finds Calvin reflecting on the fact that Moe, the local bully, has stolen his toy truck:

> Should I steal it back? I know stealing is wrong. But *he* stole it from *me*, and if I *don't* steal it back, Moe will just keep it. And that's not fair.[9]

It is noteworthy that Calvin is talking to himself. Not even Hobbes is present. Calvin continues:

> They say two wrongs don't make a right. But what are you supposed to do then? Just let the biggest guy make his own rules all the time? Let might make right? . . . That sounds reasonable.

Previous episodes have made it quite clear that Moe has no interest in Calvin's moral musings. Realizing this, Calvin stops trying out his ideas on Moe and unhappily draws his conclusions. In other contexts, "sensible," "prudent," or "wise" might be substituted for Calvin's "reasonable," but Calvin has chosen just the right word to give this episode its ironic edge. He would like Moe to "listen to reason" but realizes this desire is hopeless. What Calvin does not seem to realize is that he, too, lacks reasonableness.

This point is evident in the awkward passes at moral reasoning Calvin frequently makes. For example, he complains to Hobbes that people are too self-centered, adding that "the world would be a better place if people would stop thinking about themselves and focus on others for a change."[10] Hobbes slyly asks, "Gee, I wonder who that might apply to?" Calvin replies, "Me! Everyone should focus more on *me*."

Noting that many people lack principles, Calvin proudly proclaims that he is unwaveringly committed to one principle: "Look out for number one."[11]

In his relentlessly self-centered way, Calvin often seems on the threshold of moral insight. Although he never quite succeeds, he is dissatisfied with the full consequences of his thinking. Frustrated by the notion that might makes right (at least insofar as it works to his disadvantage), he realizes he does not have the strength or cleverness to stop Moe from acting as if might does make right. Calvin concludes that given Moe's imperviousness to the sorts of reasons he offers, the best practical strategy is to let him have his way. Moe will be satisfied only on his own terms—and these terms are strictly *his*, not *theirs*. In short, Moe is unreasonable. So, Calvin asks what it is reasonable to do in the face of the unreasonableness of another, more powerful, person.

Calvin is learning the hard way what might happen to him if others also live by the principle "Look out for number one." When Moe picks him up by the scruff of the neck, Calvin retorts, "Let go of me, ya big galoot! Why don't you pick on somebody your own size?" Raising his fist, Moe replies, "They'd hit back." Smarting from Moe's blow, Calvin comments, "I guess that has a certain unethical logic to it."[12]

Calvin is again on the edge of a moral breakthrough. He sees that logic and ethics do not necessarily go hand in hand. Despite Moe's questionable ethics, Calvin sees him as rational—and successfully so. To avoid concluding that Moe is also reasonable, Calvin must take another step. He needs to adopt a social standard, but one that he can apply to himself as well as others, and he balks at the fully reciprocal attitude that such a step requires. Faced with the unfortunate repercussions his pronouncements sometimes have, Calvin nevertheless stops short of seeing that he needs to change. Instead, he unhappily revises his assessment of what it is in his best interests to do. "Reasonable" for him is still confined to the prudential.

REASONABLENESS AND MORALITY

W. H. Sibley's "The Rational Versus the Reasonable" provides a useful account of what is needed.[13] Insofar as I am rational, Sibley says, I must be willing to consider all factors relevant to my circumstance, including likely consequences for others. But, he notes, there is an important difference between taking into account how one's own interests might be affected by what happens to others and regarding the interests of others as important in their own right. A prudent egoist (like Moe) will be concerned about the former but not the latter.

What if one wishes to be regarded not merely as rational but also as reasonable? Sibley points out that in a nonmoral context, there may be no significant difference. Someone's investment, he suggests, may turn out badly, but we might nevertheless agree that it was a reasonable risk and that reasonable precautions were taken. Here both "rational" and "reasonable" basically mean "prudent." But reasonableness in a moral context requires more:

> If I desire that my conduct shall be deemed *reasonable* by someone taking the standpoint of moral judgment, I must exhibit something more than mere rationality or intelligence. To be reasonable here is to see the matter—as we commonly put it—from the other person's point of view, to discover how each will be affected by the possible alternative actions; and, moreover, not merely to "see" this (for any merely prudent person would do as much) but also to be prepared to be disinterestedly *influenced,* in reaching a decision, by the estimate of these possible results. I must justify my conduct in terms of some principle capable of being appealed to by all parties concerned, some principle from which we can reason in common.

Sibley's account calls for several comments. First, it is clear that from a moral point of view a reasonable person tries to be responsive to the perspectives of others, which minimally requires trying to understand what those perspectives are while noting significant differences from one's own. That this is not an easy task for young children is evidenced by Jean Piaget's work in cognitive development.[14] Although Piaget seems to underestimate younger children's capacity to engage in non-egocentric thinking, getting beyond egocentric thinking is especially difficult in social relations, particularly for those with limited experience.[15] However, it seems only fair to add that this is a lifelong struggle. Adults, too, are susceptible to a great deal of egocentric thinking. (One of my favorite illustrations: I once spent a fair amount of time trying to explain to a class the role of egocentricity in the early stages of Lawrence

Kohlberg's theory of moral development. A student then announced that she thought she understood what is meant by "egocentric." Pleased, I asked her to explain. She smilingly replied, "You find Kohlberg's work interesting. So you assume we do too.")

Second, Sibley's reasonable person not only tries to understand what matters to others but also is prepared to be influenced by this understanding. Of course, even those who make use of their understanding of others' perspectives for manipulative or exploitative purposes can be said to be influenced by that understanding. Clearly this is not what Sibley has in mind, for he refers to being disinterestedly influenced, which requires respecting others, acknowledging that their interests matter too, and trying to justify one's behavior by appealing to principles or considerations from which all can reason in common.

Third, reasonable people remain open to the possibility that their favored conceptions may require alteration or revision. Ronald Dworkin provides a good illustration of what this might involve:

> Suppose I tell my children simply that I expect them not to treat others unfairly. I no doubt have in mind examples of the conduct I mean to discourage, but I would not accept that my "meaning" was limited to these examples, for two reasons. First, I would expect my children to apply my instructions to situations I had not and could not have thought about. Second, I stand ready to admit that some particular act I had thought was fair when I spoke was in fact unfair, or vice-versa, if one of my children is able to convince me of that later; in that case I should want to say that my instructions covered the case he cited, not that I had changed my instructions. I might say that I meant the family to be guided by the *concept* of fairness, not by any specific *conception* of fairness I might have had in mind.[16]

It should be noted that Dworkin is not inviting just any kind of challenge to his conception of fairness. Presumably it will have to be one capable of *convincing* him that he was mistaken, which implies that the challenge is accompanied with good reasons. Thus, both parent and child are subject to the constraints of reasonableness. Like any parent, Dworkin would like to believe that the examples of unfairness he has in mind at any given time are reasonable. But he is not willing to hold this belief in the face of convincing reasons to the contrary. As a reasonable parent, he is open to the possibility that he might be wrong about some of his examples. To deny this possibility (and reject evidence to the contrary) is to be willing to be wrong twice—and to wish that for his child as well.

An important implication of Dworkin's view is that we should not expect reasonable people always to agree with one another. There are many reasons why this is not a realistic expectation. There may be some disagreement or confusion about just what certain principles or concepts mean (e.g., fair, greater good, safe, health, well-being), as well as about how they apply to particular circumstances. Not only are the relevant moral concepts somewhat open-ended, but they also sometimes conflict with one another, requiring judgment about the relative weight they should be given. There may be disagreement about facts and about inferences made from facts (e.g., there may be disagreement about the chemical properties of asbestos in the schools, as well as about the long-term risks to those exposed to it). There may be differences in personal values (e.g., some may prefer reading novels to watching television, playing sports to walking in the woods, living in the city to rural life, and so on). Although reasonable people can be expected to reject many interests as unacceptable (e.g., those violating basic considerations of respect and regard for the well-being of others), this leaves much about which to differ. Furthermore, likemindedness is no aim of reasonableness. The ability to accept, or at least tolerate, differences is itself a mark of reasonableness.

REASONABLENESS AND THE BURDENS OF JUDGMENT

John Rawls refers to factors that explain reasonable disagreement as sources of the "burdens of judgment."[17] Complex judgment is required in order to assess and balance our various ends; to evaluate our common practices and institutions; to determine relevant evidence and assess the weight of relevant factors; to apply indeterminate concepts in hard cases; and to take into account the impact of our total experiences, which obviously differ widely among persons. Given limited resources, as well as the limited capacities of institutions in any given time or place, not all important values can be equally served. Nevertheless, Rawls says, all of this is compatible with people justifiably regarding each another as reasonable. We should not expect conscientious, reasonable people to agree on all important issues, even after extensive, open discussion. Rawls's point is that reasonableness must acknowledge the burdens of judgment—not simply because they exist but also because they are "of first significance for a democratic idea of toleration."[18]

It is important not to confuse what Rawls calls the burdens of judgment with a general skepticism about the truth of our judgments. Although people may reasonably disagree about many matters, Rawls notes that it does not follow that none of the conflicting views is true (or that all of them are true). Nor does it follow that no views are unreasonable. Rather, Rawls's intent is only to emphasize the difficulty of determining what should count as the best judgment.

Max Black makes a similar point.[19] Although we may be able to ascertain that some actions or judgments are more reasonable than others, "we are very seldom able to choose a single action as uniquely reasonable."[20] Black refers to appraisals of reasonableness and unreasonableness as *dianoetic* appraisals. Such appraisals are called for when there is some element of uncertainty (which, Black says, is most of the time): "The natural habitat of 'reasonable' is a situation in which a task is to be performed, with the outcome still in doubt."[21] To call something "unreasonable" is to suggest that although there are supporting reasons, those reasons are weak or insubstantial. Dianoetic appraisals, Black says, are comparative and typically less than conclusive. In contrast, to call something "irrational" is more like making a diagnosis of the pathological. As R. S. Peters says, an irrational belief or action flies in the face of what are considered to be conclusive reasons against it.[22]

REASONABLENESS AT WORK

Although reasonable people often disagree with each other, sometimes quite deeply, and appeals to reasonableness seldom settle matters conclusively, we nevertheless prize reasonableness in group deliberation, negotiation, and in forming and implementing social policies. The ability of diverse individuals to come to reasonable agreement was nicely illustrated by the National Commission for the Protection of Human

Subjects of Biomedical and Behavioral Research, charged in 1974 to make recommendations about ethical constraints in research. Albert Jonsen and Stephen Toulmin describe the committee in this way:

> The eleven commissioners had varied backgrounds and interests. They included men and women; blacks and whites; Catholics, Protestants, Jews, and atheists; medical scientists and behaviorist psychologists; philosophers; lawyers; theologians; and public interest representatives. In all five commissioners had scientific interests and six did not.[23]

Although the commission eventually issued the widely influential *Belmont Report,* initially it was stymied by the deep philosophical and religious differences among its members.[24] However, when members shifted their attention to particular examples of research, they discovered substantial points of agreement, enabling them to articulate three basic areas of ethical concern: respect for persons (not treating subjects merely as means to the ends of research, respecting their autonomy and the importance of informed consent); beneficence (maximizing benefits and minimizing harms to research subjects); and justice (especially in regard to the selection of research subjects).

Realizing the complexity and difficulty of some cases, as well as possible differences among reasonable persons, the *Belmont Report* wisely says:

> Three principles, or general prescriptive judgments, that are relevant to research involving human subjects are identified in this statement. Other principles may also be relevant. These three are comprehensive, however, and are stated at a level of generalization that should assist scientists, subjects, reviewers and interested citizens to understand the ethical issues inherent in research involving human subjects. These principles cannot always be applied so as to resolve beyond dispute particular ethical problems. The objective is to provide an analytical framework that will guide the resolution of ethical problems arising from research involving human subjects.[25]

The *Belmont Report* is a good example of the results of reasonableness at work. It also provides a model for the reasonable work of others. Following the guidelines of the *Belmont Report,* institutions that use federal grants to fund any of their research now have policies concerning appropriate and inappropriate research involving human subjects. They also have committees that review research proposals for compliance with the policies. Committees are typically designed to have representative membership and include researchers and nonresearchers, as well as members who are not affiliated with the institution sponsoring the research. Representative membership can be expected to contribute to the reasonableness of a committee's recommendations.

However, members themselves need to be reasonable, as well as representative, persons. What marks of reasonableness might we look for in potential members? Preeminent features might include the ability and disposition to:

- seek relevant information
- listen and respond thoughtfully to others
- be open to new ideas
- give reasons for one's views
- acknowledge mistakes and misunderstandings
- compromise (without compromising personal integrity).[26]

Equally important are items that should *not* be on such a list. We should not expect reasonable persons to:

- feel a need always to agree with other committee members
- lack deeply held beliefs and convictions that may differ fundamentally with those of others
- be willing to change virtually any belief or conviction, however deeply held
- insist that they are necessarily right and others wrong
- insist on having their own way.

Although not complete, these considerations provide a rough picture of the sorts of dispositions and tendencies that characterize reasonable people. Furthermore, they also provide an outline of those qualities the schools might hope to encourage in students as they move from childhood toward adulthood.

Of course, reasonableness and unreasonableness are not our only terms of appraisal, and reasonableness cannot stand alone as a virtue.

Our values have many different sources, and there is great diversity among them, both between persons and within the same person. Not all values are specifically moral values, and there is no reason to insist on uniformity across persons. But even within morality there may be many different ways of satisfying plausible criteria for being a well-developed, moral person, and reasonable people might well disagree about some of the criteria. Nevertheless, the range of possibilities is not limitless. It is important to recognize and be supportive of the earliest appearance of those cognitive and affective capacities that are essential to the development of well-developed, moral persons; whatever else is emphasized, those capacities that contribute to reasonableness need special attention.[27]

REASONABLENESS, EGOCENTRICITY, AND EMPATHY

We might wonder what the future holds in store for young Calvin. Already into his school years, he seems precocious in many respects. He is able to talk about his thoughts and feelings at a level well beyond his years. Many may think of him basically as an articulate representative of the thoughts, feelings, and actions of his peers. Amusing as Calvin's candid reflections are, they reveal that something is seriously missing— something we should hope is present to some degree in real children his age. If schoolchildren really are as self-interested and egocentric as Calvin, this should cause us real concern. Imagine Calvin as an adult. He seems well on his way to becoming a full-blown egoist. The lessons he is learning seem to be lessons more in prudence than morality. He learns that people like Moe are to be feared rather than reasoned with.

Consider this lesson from Hobbes. Calvin says:

> I don't believe in ethics any more. As far as I'm concerned, the ends justify the means. Get what you can while the getting's good— that's what I say! Might makes right! The winners write the history books! It's a dog-eat-dog world. So I'll do whatever I have to and let others argue about whether it's "right" or not.[28]

At this point Hobbes shoves Calvin from behind into a mud puddle. Outraged, Calvin shouts, "Why'd you do THAT?!?" Hobbes smilingly replies, "You were in my way. Now you're not. The ends justify the means." What does Calvin learn from this? He retorts, "I didn't mean for *everyone*, you dolt! Just *me*." As an egoist finding his way about the world, Calvin may learn to keep some of his innermost thoughts about ethics to himself, but there is little evidence that he is about to undergo a moral conversion. What Calvin needs is a change of heart, not simply further understanding of reciprocal treatment. His rational powers need to be supplemented by something else if he is to be moved in the direction of reasonableness as a social virtue. The worry is that incorrigible as he seems to be, it may be too late for Calvin.

Fortunately, there is considerable evidence that very young children, even infants, have empathic concerns that are not wholly self-interested or egocentric.[29] What are some of these signs? Educational psychologist William Damon suggests that we look at children's empathy in the context of sharing.[30] The practice of sharing, he notes, begins as soon as children interact with one another. Often this begins before they are two years old. The problems of distributive justice young children learn to deal with are based on the same sorts of considerations that take on their more complex forms in adult life. Even preschoolers connect sharing with features of fairness such as equality, merit, and benefiting those suffering from disadvantages.

Damon cites five basic social and emotional sources of young children's sharing: (1) children approaching each other through their common interest in toys and other objects; (2) their deriving pleasure "through the symmetrical rhythm of turn-taking with toys and other objects"; (3) urgings of parents and peers to share when possible; (4) children's natural empathic responses to other children who want to share or take a turn, especially when adults help them understand that excluded children will be unhappy; and (5) wanting playmates to reciprocate.[31] Especially as children move into the school years, their conceptions of sharing and fairness take on increasingly sophisticated dimensions. However, for Damon, the fourth factor, children's natural empathic responses, is the most crucial for morality, "since developmentally it is the first step towards the major reasoning and behavioral systems soon to follow."[32]

Although even children under two years of age can respond in empathic and supportive ways to the distress of others, these early manifestations of empathy are only precursors of moral response. According to Damon, "It is around the child's fourth year that the combination of natural empathic awareness and reasoned adult encouragement leads the child to develop a firm sense of obligation to share with others."[33] As with adults, this sense of obligation competes for attention with self-interest, and there often is a gap between thought and action. However, Damon concludes, at this point the child has internalized the notion that sharing is obligatory in social relationships, and sharing is now viewed in terms of right and wrong.[34]

There are two especially noteworthy features of Damon's account. First, when it comes to sharing, children's sense of right and wrong is significantly grounded in their capacity for empathic response. Insofar as this has a distinctively moral cast, empathic response involves both understanding how others might feel and being moved by this understanding to share. Someone like Moe can perhaps understand that keeping Calvin's truck makes him unhappy, but he does not care. But, for all of his moralistic machinations, it is not clear that Calvin has the requisite empathic capacities either.

However, if Damon is right, most children entering school are more developmentally advanced than Moe and Calvin, which leads to the second noteworthy feature of Damon's account. In addition to the importance of empathic capacities, he emphasizes "*reasoned* adult encouragement" (emphasis added). This is not simply a matter of adults having reasons for encouraging sharing; it involves sharing those reasons with children. If the role of adults were simply to assert their authority or inject fear, it would not much matter whether their encouragement was reasoned or arbitrary. So, what Damon is really emphasizing here is children's capacity to engage in reasoned thought.

It is precisely the combination of children's capacities to empathize and engage in reasoned thought that constitutes their potential for reasonableness. Whatever we might say about Calvin and Moe, if Damon is right, the early elementary-school years are critical to the moral development of children. Furthermore, they enter with certain moral dispositions already in place, and they are ready, if not eager, to exercise and further develop their moral muscles. How the schools might constructively respond to this readiness is the topic of the next chapter.

2
Aims and Goals of Moral Education

It is often asked whether morality can be taught. In higher education this question is commonly converted to the question of whether students might learn anything by studying morality.[1] If we think instead of children studying morality, our attention shifts to students actively striving to develop and refine their abilities to think through moral concerns. This, at any rate, seems to have been the consensus view of a large and diverse group of educators brought together by the Hastings Center some years ago to discuss the appropriate goals and objectives of teaching ethics in higher education.[2] What I hope to show in this chapter is that these same goals and objectives are suitable even at the elementary-school level.

A SET OF GOALS AND OBJECTIVES

The Hastings Center group agreed on five major goals and objectives for ethics courses in higher education.[3] They should:

1. Stimulate the moral imagination of students
2. Help students recognize moral issues
3. Help students analyze key moral concepts and principles
4. Elicit from students a sense of responsibility
5. Help students to accept the likelihood of ambiguity and disagreement on moral matters, while at the same time attempting to strive for clarity and agreement insofar as it is reasonably attainable.

Intended for college-age students, this set of goals presupposes that students are not moral neophytes. Students are regarded as a basic resource in the sense that they are assumed already capable of moral imagination (which needs further stimulation), already capable of understanding moral issues (even though they sometimes need help recognizing their presence), already possessing moral concepts and principles (which need more careful analysis), already having a sense of responsibility (which can be further activated by studying ethics), and already somewhat experienced at attempting to negotiate unclarities and disagreements. Seriously pursued, these goals can be expected to enhance the capacity for reasonableness in students as they encounter moral issues surrounding them.

Just as it is presumed that college students have some basic logical sensitivities and abilities prior to taking their first college course in logic, it is presumed that college students have some basic moral sensitivities and abilities. If this could not be presumed, one might ask, how could one even begin to teach a course in ethics? But, it might be thought, matters are quite different at the precollege level, especially in the elementary schools where such presumptions have no place. Particularly at the elementary-school level, moral education is commonly regarded as a matter of "instilling" or "implanting" moral values. However, this view underestimates the already considerable moral abilities children typically have by the time they enter school.

As I will now try to show, the Hastings Center goals are suitable for elementary-school students as well as college students. Of course, adjustments for the more limited understanding and experience of young children must be made, but enhancing the capacity for reasonableness is as realistic an objective for young children as for college students. In fact, insofar as children's capacity for reasonableness is neglected, we should lower our expectations for the reasonableness of college students.[4]

It should not be supposed that the five goals identified in the Hastings Center study can be pursued separately, one at a time. Stimulating the moral imagination, for example, can lead us to analyze key moral concepts or principles. Analyzing key moral concepts or principles can help us recognize hidden moral issues, and it can also stimulate the moral imagination to think of new possibilities. Such analysis can also reveal ambiguities and important disagreements. A sense of responsibility might be encouraged merely by pursuing the other four goals. Thinking about what our responsibilities are can help us recognize hidden moral issues, stretch our moral imagination, disclose uncertainties about how far our responsibilities extend, and so on. The same examples and exercises that serve one goal may serve the others as well. Nevertheless, it is important to see these goals as distinct, though complementary, aspects of moral education.

One effective way to stimulate the moral imagination is through stories. For example, what child has not had serious thoughts about being brave—whether this involves putting one's head under water for the first time, going to the dentist, speaking in front of an audience, standing up to a bully, or staying home alone for the first time?

Frog and Toad also wonder about bravery.[5] Here is how Arnold Lobel's "Dragons and Giants" begins:

> Frog and Toad were reading a book together. "The people in this book are brave," said Toad. "They fight dragons and they are never afraid." "I wonder if we are brave," said Frog. (42)

How can they tell if they are brave? Toad suggests two conditions that must be met: They must do the sorts of things brave individuals do, and they must not be afraid when they do them (or at any other time). But they discover that telling whether these two conditions are met is not easy:

> Frog and Toad looked into a mirror. "We look brave," said Frog. "Yes, but are we?" asked Toad. (42–43)

So Frog and Toad set out on an adventuresome hike. They begin climbing a mountain. They come upon a dark cave:

> A big snake came out of the cave. "Hello, lunch," said the snake when he saw Frog and Toad. He opened his wide mouth. Frog and Toad jumped away. Toad was shaking. "I am not afraid!" he cried. (45)

As if to prove their fearlessness, Frog and Toad continue climbing. Then they hear a loud noise and see large stones rolling toward them:

> "It's an avalanche!" cried Toad. Frog and Toad jumped away. Frog was trembling. "I am not afraid!" he shouted. (47)

They reach the top of the mountain, only to find themselves under a shadow cast by a hawk. They jump under a rock. After the hawk flies away, Frog and Toad scream out, "We are not afraid!" At the same time they begin running as fast as they can back to Toad's house. After arriving safely, Toad says, "Frog, I am glad to have a brave friend like you." Frog replies, "And I am happy to know a brave person like you, Toad" (50). Then Toad jumps into bed and pulls the covers over his head. Frog jumps into the closet and shuts the door. The story concludes: "They stayed there for a long time, just feeling very brave together" (51).

What should the reader conclude? Were Frog and Toad brave? Remember, Frog and Toad set down two conditions for bravery. First, they had to do the sorts of things brave individuals do. Climbing the mountain and not turning back seem to be the right sort of things, although running back home and hiding may raise some doubts about just how brave they were. The second condition, doing these things without being afraid (in fact, never being afraid), seems to fare much worse. After all, Toad shook, Frog trembled, and they both ran down the mountain as fast as they could and hid under covers and in the closet. How can they say they were not at least a little bit afraid? And doesn't that spoil their bravery?

But, a young reader might say, they did do some things that they had been afraid to try before. That must have taken at least a little bravery. Still, another young reader might reply, they shook and trembled and ran home and hid, so they must have been afraid. Yes, another reader replies, but weren't some of the things they did really dangerous? "Hello, lunch," said the snake. Was that just a bluff? Wouldn't even a brave frog have reason to fear such a snake? What else could Toad do—stay for lunch? But, the first reader counters, Toad didn't just run away—he *shook*. We adults might now recall Aristotle's distinction between bravery and foolhardiness, a distinction that makes fear an integral part of bravery. Further, Aristotle distinguishes bravery from cowardice. What if Toad had not moved, we ask. Aristotle might say that he was either foolhardy (lacking proper fear) or cowardly (paralyzed by fear).

Can young children appreciate these distinctions? One way to find out is to try some variations on the Frog and Toad story, which invites children to analyze key moral concepts. Suppose that Frog and Toad are next time accompanied by some other friends, say Turtle and Mouse.[6] This time when the snake says "Hello, lunch," neither Turtle nor Mouse move. Turtle does not move because he has fallen asleep inside his shell while they have paused in front of the dark cave. He is awakened by the snake saying "Hello, lunch." But he simply thinks they are being invited to lunch and decides he would rather extend his nap instead. Mouse does not move because he is too terrified. Does it matter how Frog and Toad behave? Suppose Toad quickly runs to safety, but Frog first yanks on Mouse's tail to get him to move to safety. Was Turtle brave because he was not afraid of Snake? Was Mouse brave because he did not move? Who was more brave, Frog or Toad? Do we have to suppose that Frog was not afraid when he stayed to help Mouse?

We usually think that being brave is a good thing. Is it? Why? Is it better to be brave and fearless than brave and fearful? Arnold Lobel does not complicate his story by directly raising such questions. Frog and Toad present themselves in such a way that the young reader is invited to challenge their claims to be brave. But it is only a short step from this to questioning Frog and Toad's early characterization of bravery as requiring fearlessness. If bravery is indeed a desirable quality, then reflecting on what it means to have it can be a valuable exercise—one that calls on the use of reason, and one that may contribute to a person's reasonableness in both attitude and behavior.

Frog and Toad think of bravery in terms of physical courage. However, there are other forms of bravery, too, such as moral courage. For example, in Judy Varga's *The Dragon Who Liked to Spit Fire,* Darius the friendly dragon is banished from the king's castle after accidentally setting fire to the royal banners.[7] Although forbidden from ever seeing little Prince Frederic again, Darius later saves Frederic from a wild boar. This action might be regarded by readers as another instance of physical bravery, but since Darius acts contrary to the king's orders, it also seems to be an instance of moral courage.

The king provides an even clearer instance of moral courage. He has to summon up the courage to admit he was mistaken about Darius:

> The king cleared his throat three times. He did not know how to begin, for kings don't like to admit they are wrong. But he was a very just king, so he cleared his throat a fourth time. "It is rather nice to have a dragon around the castle," he said. "Frederic could never have a better, more faithful friend than Darius." He took off his own medal and hung it on the little dragon's neck. (25)

Admitting that one has made a serious mistake sometimes requires as much courage as facing physical dangers bravely.

Other Frog and Toad stories invite young readers to reflect. "A List" humorously portrays Toad compiling a "List of things to do today," only to become frozen into inaction because his list is carried away by the wind. Toad does not chase it down because that is not something on his list of things to do. This story raises questions about rational planning. Can one ever expect to be able to list everything one might need to do? Should one even try? How is it reasonable to proceed when unexpected events interfere with planned events?

"The Garden" addresses both the virtue of patience (waiting for seeds to grow into flowers) and the irrelevance of many of our well-intentioned efforts to help other things grow. "Cookies" is a delightful story about willpower: "trying hard *not* to do something that you really want to do" (35). If Frog and Toad give away all their cookies to the birds, does this show that they now have the willpower not to eat any more cookies? Or do they have to be able to resist eating cookies while they still have some within reach? Once again, young readers are invited to analyze an important moral concept, willpower. Do Frog and Toad really have lots and lots of willpower after they give the cookies to the birds? Is Frog and Toad's strategy reasonable, even if it does not actually exhibit willpower? Here is another possible strategy. Frog and Toad could keep on eating cookies until they feel sick (something Frog offers as a reason for stopping now). Then they could resist eating more cookies even if several were left. Of course it would no longer be true to say that they really want to eat more—and they would not have to try hard at all not to eat them. Would this be a reasonable strategy?

Some might want to say that Frog and Toad use a reasonable strategy for dealing with situations in which they do not have willpower: if the temptation is too great, remove it. But are there times when it might be really important to be able to do better than this—that is, to be able to resist cookies even when they are within reach and you really do want another one? What if you cannot really get rid of what you want (e.g., they are not your cookies to give away to the birds, or every time you try to get rid of a tempting something, more of it shows up)? Is it important to have willpower in situations like that?

The last story in *Frog and Toad Together*, "The Dream," is quite interesting from a developmental standpoint. Since Lobel's stories are in the

I CAN READ series, the primary audience constitutes an age range (four–eight) that Jean Piaget and Lawrence Kohlberg would say is dominated by egocentric thinking.[8] If they are right, most of the intended audience will fail to grasp much of what "The Dream" is about. Toad dreams that as he becomes more and more impressed with himself, Frog gets smaller and smaller. "Why do you think Frog gets smaller and smaller?" we might ask a four-year-old. One possible answer is that this is how Frog seems to Toad in the dream—and this is because Toad keeps "puffing himself up" in comparison to Frog:

> "Frog," cried Toad, "can you play the piano like this?" "No," said Frog. It seemed to Toad that Frog looked even smaller. "Frog," cried Toad, "can you do tricks like this?" "No," peeped Frog, who looked very, very small. "Frog, can you be as wonderful as this?" said Toad as he danced all over the stage. There was no answer. Toad looked out into the theater. Frog was so small that he could not be seen or heard. [Toad dreams he is spinning in the dark, shouting] "Come back, Frog. I will be lonely." "I am right here," said Frog. Frog was standing near Toad's bed. "Wake up, Toad," he said. "Frog, is that really you?" said Toad. "Of course it is me," said Frog. "And are you your own right size?" asked Toad. "Yes, I think so," said Frog. Toad looked at the sunshine coming through the window. "Frog," he said, "I am so glad that you came over." "I always do," said Frog. (55–60)

Toad seems to have learned much from this dream. Can a four-year-old? Seemingly, no, if the estimation of developmental psychologists such as Piaget and Kohlberg is correct, for Toad has learned something about immodesty, loneliness, and friendship that he could not appreciate if he were trapped totally within an egocentric perspective.[9] But Toad can appreciate this, and many of his four-year-old friends probably can, too.

Although not written for a young audience, J. D. Salinger's short story "Down at the Dinghy" provides a poignant example of a four-year-old recognizing a moral issue that only moments earlier he failed to notice.[10] Lionel is upset and tells his mother he is going to run away:

> "Well, will you tell me from there why you're running away?" Boo Boo asked. "After you promised me you were all through?"

A pair of underwater goggles lay on the deck of the dinghy, near the stern seat. For answer, Lionel secured the headstrap of the goggles between the big and the second toes of his right foot, and, with a deft, brief leg action, flipped the goggles overboard. They sank at once.

"That's nice. That's constructive," said Boo Boo. "Those belong to your Uncle Webb. Oh, he'll be so delighted." She dragged on her cigarette. "They once belonged to your Uncle Seymour."

"I don't care."

"I see that you don't," Boo Boo said. Boo then takes a small package from her pocket. "This is a key chain," she says, "Just like Daddy's. But with a lot more keys on it than Daddy's has. This one has ten keys."

Lionel leaned forward in his seat, letting go of the tiller. He held out his hands in catching position. "Throw it?" he asked. "Please?"

"Let's keep our seats a minute, Sunshine. I have a little thinking to do. I *should* throw this key chain in the lake."

Lionel stared up at her with his mouth open. He closed his mouth. "It's mine," he said on a diminishing note of justice.

Boo Boo, looking down at him, shrugged. "I don't care."

Lionel slowly sat back in his seat, watching his mother, and reached behind him for the tiller. His eyes reflected pure perception, as his mother had known they would.

"Here." Boo Boo tossed the package down to him. It landed squarely on his lap.

He looked at it in his lap, picked it off, looked at it in his hand, and flicked it—sidearm—into the lake. He then immediately looked up at Boo Boo, his eyes filled not with defiance but tears. In another instant his mouth was distorted into a horizontal figure-8, and he was crying mightily.

Salinger's little episode cries out for analysis. Just what is Lionel's perception? Is it that one bad turn deserves another—and that this is best accomplished by the wrongdoer administering self-punishment? Has Lionel engaged in a bit of Golden Rule reasoning, or is this a misreading of the Golden Rule, since it is not clear that anyone is being done unto as they would have others do unto them? However Lionel's reasoning is to be characterized, it is clear that by appreciating a perspective other than his own, he learned a lesson in responsibility (eliciting a sense of responsibility). It also seems clear that this lesson will not be lost on many young children who hear such a story.

Lionel seems to be expressing some sort of recognition of the moral importance of reciprocity which adults know is a very complex area of moral life. To what extent are children capable of appreciating such complexities? Lionel seems to have begun to catch on to some of it at age four. What is it reasonable to expect a bit later down the road? Some years ago I had the privilege of participating in a forty-minute discussion of just such matters with a group of ten-year-olds. I began the discussion by reading an episode from Matthew Lipman's children's novel *Lisa*.[11] Timmy accompanies Harry to a stamp club meeting at which Harry trades stamps with other children. Timmy is deliberately tripped by a classmate as he and Harry are leaving the classroom. Timmy immediately knocks his classmate's books off his desk and runs out of the room. Later, as Harry buys Timmy an ice cream cone, Timmy comments, "But I had to get even. I couldn't get away with it, tripping me like that for no reason" (11–13).

Harry is perplexed by all these examples. Is it right to retaliate against someone who trips you? How is this like or unlike a fair exchange of stamps? If someone does you a favor, should you return the favor someday? The ten-year-olds with whom I shared the story were eager to help sort out these matters. They discussed at great length possible alternatives to Timmy's retaliation (thus exercising moral imagination). One boy challenged the basic idea of "getting even" (analyzing key moral concepts): "Sometimes you do need to get even. Well, actually there's no such thing as even, because then he'll get even." Having raised the problem of what it means to "get even," he went on to distinguish between *wanting* to do something (strike back) and *having* to do it.

Several children suggested ignoring the offender as a tactic for discouraging him (since he would have failed to get the desired response from the victim). Pressed by the example of an offender who stays on the attack, a girl said: "If he were to, like Emily said, chase after you and hit you or something like that, then you defend yourself. I mean, maybe then you've got to get him back. Not really get him back, but you have to defend yourself and hit him if he's hitting you." Thus a basic distinction was made between trying to get even ("get him back") and self-defense. Further, the children distinguished both of these ideas from attempting to teach someone a lesson. Finally, they carefully distinguished exchanges involving harms from exchanging favors, insisting that the Golden Rule applies in the latter cases but not the former.

Although this discussion was limited to problems that are familiar to children, the ten-year-old participants uncovered an impressive variety of considerations that need to be brought to bear on those problems. I have often asked myself what other kinds of considerations adults might wish to bring up in that context; I always come up empty. Furthermore, the principles and concepts discussed by the children serve adults rather well when applied to analogous problems in adult life.

In between Arnold Lobel and J. D. Salinger's fictional four-year-olds and my actual group of ten-year-olds are many actual examples of six- to eight-year-olds displaying readiness for serious moral reflection. For example, philosopher Clyde Evans reports a discussion he once had with a group of kindergartners and first graders about the following dilemma:

A father has promised to take his daughter to the carnival on her seventh birthday. Just before arriving at the ticket window the father discovers he has forgotten his wallet, and there is not time to return home for it. The sign says that children under seven get in at half-price. The father counts the money in his pocket and realizes that if his daughter lies about her age, there will be enough money to get them into the carnival and go on some rides. If she tells the truth about her age, there will be enough money to get into the carnival but none for any rides. He leaves the choice up to her.[12]

As might be expected, the children had divided opinions. A boy said that lying in this case might lead the girl to become a habitual liar. Others replied that this was just one little lie. Then came a response in the form of a striking analogy, as Evans reports:

The first boy then provided further support. He said that lying is just like pollution. To say that it's only one little lie is like saying it's only one little candy wrapper. But all the little candy wrappers add up. The first thing you know you have a big pollution problem. Likewise, the first thing you know you'll have a big lying problem.[13]

This is an impressive instance of analogical reasoning. It may be just a reiteration of the first worry—that the girl might become a habitual liar—but the pollution analogy suggests another angle. One person habitually dropping candy wrappers is not going to result in a big pollution problem. But *everyone* (or lots of people) dropping candy wrappers (popcorn boxes, soda cans, and so on) might. Attention now shifts from what one person does to a kind of act performed by everyone ("What if everyone did that?")—that is, attention now shifts to the collective consequences of many people telling lies.[14]

Gareth Matthews reports this example:

Ian (six years old) found to his chagrin that the three children of his parents' friends monopolized the television; they kept him from watching his favorite program. "Mother," he asked in frustration, "why is it better for three children to be selfish than one?"[15]

This question would be a challenge for any adult. Matthews decided to write a little story around Ian's comment and present it to a group of eight- to eleven-year-olds.[16] The lively discussion that followed elicited comments about the inconsiderateness of the three visiting children, the desirability of working out a solution that would satisfy all four children, the importance of respecting people's rights, and how one might feel if one were in Ian's place. Matthews then outlined a possible utilitarian analysis: "What about this argument, that if we let the three visitors have their way, three people will be made happy instead of just one?"[17] One boy replied, "It's not really fair if three people get what they want and leave one person out. That one person will feel very hurt." This statement was followed by children's comments about very specific considerations, such as the types of television programs involved and relationships among the children (e.g., relative ages, whether they are siblings, friends, or strangers). In short, by examining various possibilities, the children tried to work out a reasonable resolution of a very difficult problem.

Ian's question, like many other questions children will eagerly discuss if given the chance, may not readily lend itself to a solution that all reasonable people will agree upon. One mark of reasonableness is recognizing that this is so in a way that does not destroy mutual inquiry, which is why the Hastings Center group of educators emphasize a fifth goal of ethics in higher education: Helping students learn to accept ambiguity and disagreement while at the same time continuing to try to reduce it through further attempts to clarify ideas and to engage in reasonable discussion.

Children's discussions make clear the importance of this fifth goal. I will give an extended illustration. As noted in Chapter 1, William Damon emphasizes the central role that sharing plays in the development of children's sense of fairness. However, there are other, equally fundamental aspects of children's notions of fairness. Whenever they first appear, and whatever might account for their emergence, it is clear that such notions are robustly present in ten-year-olds. This was certainly evident in the group of fifth grade students with whom I met once a week in an after-school Philosophy for Children program hosted by a local library.[18] From everything I was able to determine, the discussions we had were very unlike their usual school experiences to that point.[19] Near the end of one of our forty-five-minute sessions I asked the group what they thought fairness is.[20]

What is fairness? Most adults would readily acknowledge that fairness is not just one thing. It could be treating equals equally, not discriminating against others, providing equal opportunities, providing people fair compensation for their services, avoiding biased judgment, considering all sides of an issue, taking turns, returning favors, sharing responsibilities and burdens. The list could go on. Whether there is some common core linking these samplings is a matter of philosophical debate. However this debate might be resolved, it seems clear enough that the question "What is fairness?" requires a complex answer. In fact, the question is so difficult that most find it easier to approach it somewhat indirectly by first considering its contrary—namely, "What is *un*fairness?"

Given all these complexities, we might well doubt whether a group of ten-year-olds could make much headway with the question of what fairness is. Certainly not many would expect such a group, in the space of a just few minutes, to show much awareness of the nuances and subtleties that make the question so challenging for adults. More likely, most might expect simplistic answers that betray quite limited experiences with issues of fairness. This, in any case, was my fear.

My first surprise came when a boy named Larry began the discussion by asking, "Can we say what *un*fairness is?" My next surprise was the first example of unfairness he selected. It was not an example of shar-ing. Instead, he recalled a passage from Matthew Lipman's *Harry Stot-tlemeier's Discovery* that we had read together several weeks earlier.[21] Here is the passage to which Larry referred:

> The bell was about to ring, and the two monitors were still stand-ing at the door. Both boys were large and rather heavy, and they decided to tease Fran by not giving her much room to pass. Maybe she thought they did it because she was a girl, and most likely she thought they did it because she was a girl and black, too, but she didn't care for that kind of teasing, and she pushed them out of her way. Mrs. Halsey turned around just in time to see what Fran had done, and she spoke to Fran very sharply about it.

This passage does not say anything about the fairness or unfairness of what took place. In subsequent passages, neither Fran nor her friends say anything about the fairness or unfairness of what happened to her. Furthermore, this was not a topic of our earlier discussion of the chap-ter in which the passage occurs. Yet, this was the first example of unfair-ness that came to Larry's mind.

Larry explained that the teacher was unfair because she did not allow Fran even to say, "Well, they wouldn't—they wouldn't move out of my way. So, I pushed them. And they're always bullying me. So, I pushed them out of the way so I could get into the room." Instead, Larry con-cluded, the teacher simply corrected Fran and made her go sit down. It should be noted that Larry selected only one of several ways in which the episode about Fran raises questions about fairness.[22] He focused on taking into account all relevant facts, rather than the unfairness of block-ing Fran's way or discrimination against her because she is a girl and is black. Andy agreed, adding: "Fairness is getting the facts and getting both sides. If somebody's in a quarrel or something, and all mad at each other, they should get the facts and get the whole story instead of just sit there and say. . . ." Rick continued for Andy, " 'You're in trouble for that, and you're in trouble for that, and you're okay, because you didn't do nothing.' "

Soon Rick commented that "fairness" has several meanings, and he gave some examples in rapid-fire. One was a teacher publicly praising a student who has done poorly and criticizing one who has done very well. Another concerned buying an ice cream cone for someone: "Hey kid, I got chocolate ice cream, and you get the vanilla." "I don't like vanilla; I like chocolate." "I don't care. I bought it. I'll give you what I want." Finally, Rick offered a personal example of fairness. Whenever he and his sister have to share something like a candy bar, his mother has one person cut pieces while the other gets to choose first. But, not satisfied that he had provided the full range of examples, Rick concluded, "And there's just really a lot of meanings."

How many different kinds of examples had Rick mentioned? He agreed with Larry and Andy that fairness requires getting as complete a picture as possible of the relevant facts. He thought it unfair to deliberately misrepresent the facts about someone, either to that person's benefit or detriment. He thought it unfair for a person who is sharing something to do so only in terms of what he or she wants, without taking into consideration what others might want. A fair procedure for sharing, Rick offered, is to have the person who divides something get the last piece.

Others joined in the discussion. Once again Rick insisted that fairness has several meanings. Finally he burst out, "Mr. Pritchard, who thinks of these questions? They've always got a two-way answer to them!" This comment was a philosopher's delight. Rick frequently made such remarks, showing his sensitivity to the philosophical nuances of the topics being discussed. Although some fifth graders might not enjoy such conversations, Rick and his friends seemed to welcome the challenge.

Noelle continued: "I think unfairness is, let's say, somebody throws a snowball at you, and you'll get—you'll be the one to get in trouble because, let's say, somebody threw a snowball, I turned around and bent over to pick it up, and I'm the one who had it in my hand." Mike commented, "You could have said you didn't throw it." "Yes," Noelle replied, "but what if the teacher didn't believe me?" Imitating the teacher, Rick joined in, "You had it in your hand. Even if you drop it, it's throwing snowballs."

I suggested that Noelle's situation was like Fran's: "Somebody did something to her, and then she did it back. But they only saw her. They didn't see the first part." Actually, Noelle's example was significantly different from Fran's situation. Fran had retaliated, whether justifiably or not. The unfairness in Noelle's example seems to be that of accusing someone basically on circumstantial evidence. Of course, Rick's last comment raised the question of intent. Why did Noelle have the snow-ball in her hand? But, Noelle might rejoin, is it fair to punish her for intent alone? And what evidence is there that she was actually going to throw it?

Rick picked up on Noelle's concern about being punished on the basis of circumstantial evidence alone. His next example focused on long-term rather than immediate consequences of wrongdoing, consequences that he apparently felt were unfair:

> My Mom said that, you know, I used to be the kid who lied because I was afraid when I was young that I'd get a spanking. But now I've stopped lying for about two years now, and my Mom still doesn't believe me. And each time she goes, "You're still lying." She'll never believe me anymore. She always says, "It's 6 to 1, it's 6 to 1 and half a dozen of the other"—to say it's both our faults when I don't do nothing.

Is it fair for Rick's mother to think he is lying simply because he used to when he was younger? One notion of fairness insists that each alleged instance of wrongdoing is to judged in and of itself, which may be Rick's view. Is it not unfair to hold him responsible for something he did not do, regardless of whether he had lied about such things in the past? However, Mike offered another perspective: "Rick, but you've earned that responsibility. You lied when you were young. If you never started lying, your mother would have believed you all the time." Others added, "I lied all the time, and I got it, you know." "Yeah, me too." "I mean, it stinks now."

Is it unreasonable for those who have consistently lied to others to be presumed guilty of lying even when they are not? Can it be argued that the liar deserves his or her fate—or at least that he or she must "earn" the right to be regarded as having credibility? Or is it reasonable to expect someone who has repeatedly been lied to now to believe the liar? These are vexing problems for adults as well as children.

Sissela Bok explores the tendencies adults have to rationalize lies without adequately taking into account the harms they cause others as well as their own credibility.[23] In her efforts to urge us to be more reflective about the value of truthfulness, she offers a justificatory standard that she calls the "test of publicity": If a lie is justified it should be able to meet with the approval of a group of representative, reasonable people, who need to be representative to ensure inclusion of the perspectives of those who could be seriously affected by the lie. As reasonable people, those who represent these different perspectives take seriously into consideration the perspectives of others as well. They also consider long-term as well as short-term consequences, including how valued practices and institutions can be harmed by widespread lying. Taking all these matters into consideration is not easy. Even considering how a lie might affect only the liar and someone to whom it is told is challenging. When more than two parties need to be considered, or social practices and institutions, the task can become quite complicated.

Of course, it would be an exaggeration to suggest that the level of reflection of a group of ten-year-olds can match what Bok is recommending. However, once we subtract for differences in background and experience, parallels between the thoughts of these children and the kind of careful reflection advocated by Bok are undeniable. Their brief discussion provides substantial evidence that young children can be highly motivated to discuss fairness in terms of requirements of reasonableness; and the subtle twists and turns of their discussion show that they can do this very well.

It is not an exaggeration to suggest that ten-year-olds are capable of significant philosophical thinking. The previous discussion shows children addressing fundamental questions about what fairness and unfairness are, presenting a variety of examples that reveal the complexity of conceptual analysis required, and self-consciously reflecting on the nature of what they are doing. The ability of children to engage in serious philosophical thought is still not widely appreciated. But, as I hope to show in the next chapter, tapping the philosophical abilities of children, even as they enter school, has much to offer their moral education.

3
Philosophy for Children

When I took my first course in philosophy as a college sophomore, I was warned by a friend that philosophy is a very difficult subject. Students were advised to wait until at least their sophomore year, and the vast majority simply avoided the subject entirely. Some fifteen years later another friend asked me if I thought that elementary school children might benefit from studying philosophy. I was somewhat embarrassed to confess that I had never seriously entertained this question. Like nearly everyone else, I simply assumed that the study of philosophy should begin at the college level. Then I was introduced to Harry Stottlemeier, and I learned why my assumption was fundamentally mistaken. In this chapter I attempt to show that philosophical inquiry should have a place in the schools long before college.

HARRY STOTTLEMEIER

Harry Stottlemeier is the fictional creation of philosopher Matthew Lipman, director of the Institute for the Advancement of Philosophy for Children (IAPC) at Montclair State College in Upper Montclair, New Jersey. Since the mid-1970s, Harry and his fifth grade friends have introduced thousands of actual elementary- and middle-school children to the study of philosophy. In fact, Harry is celebrated worldwide; Lipman's ninety-six-page novel *Harry Stottlemeier's Discovery* has been translated into fifteen languages.[1] Since the publication of *Harry*, IAPC has published novels and accompanying classroom materials for the entire K-12 curriculum.

Initially skeptical, I have long since been persuaded that young children are, indeed, capable of significant philosophical thinking—and that the schools should do much more than they presently are to foster such

31

thinking. Gareth Matthews (*Philosophy and the Young Child*, 1980; *Dialogues With Children*, 1984; and *The Philosophy of Childhood*, 1994) has amply illustrated the natural place philosophical thinking occupies in early childhood. In fact, he indicates that he first became interested in exploring the philosophical thinking of children as a means for persuading his college students that philosophy is not such a strange, alien subject as they suppose—by showing them that although philosophy might now seem strange to them, it is likely that there was a time in their lives when philosophical curiosity was as natural as anything else.

Although doubters remain, there has been ample documentation over the last couple of decades that schoolchildren are quite capable of engaging in serious and sophisticated philosophical enquiry.[2] However, even if this capability is acknowledged, we can still ask why the schools should pay it any particular attention. The curriculum, educators might object, is already overcrowded. How can room be found for yet another subject? Besides, philosophy is a "troublemaker." After all, wasn't Socrates tried for believing in false gods and corrupting the youth of his day?

The first objection is practical, and it should not be underestimated. However, there is no point in addressing it if objections of the second sort carry the day. Is philosophy basically just a "troublemaker," or does it have an important contribution to make to the education of our children? Lipman and others contend that it does have an important contribution to make. Their answer goes well beyond the contribution philosophy can make to fostering critical thinking, but here I will focus primarily on this aspect of their answer. As for whether philosophy is a troublemaker, it is, but this is an inherent risk of any program that is serious about promoting critical thinking. So the real issue is whether the schools should encourage critical thinking. If the answer is yes, then the only remaining question is how this task is best accomplished. Lipman argues that here philosophy shines and that, therefore, the schools should find a place for philosophy even if it puts a squeeze on some other parts of the curriculum.

Lipman contends that not only do elementary-school students find philosophical topics intensely interesting, but they also can begin to make sense of their educational experiences as a whole once they are encouraged to inquire philosophically about the kinds of thinking processes they actually employ both in and out of school. They wonder, guess, speculate, hypothesize, doubt, puzzle, infer, question, form beliefs, and so on. In Philosophy for Children programs, students wonder about what wondering is, how planning is different from guessing, how doubting is related to believing, and so on. In short, they think (reflectively) about thinking, the novelty of which is aptly captured by Harry Stottlemeier in one of his school essays:

THINKING

> To me the most interesting thing in the whole world is thinking. I know that lots of other things are also very important and wonderful, like electricity, and magnetism and gravitation. But although we understand them, they can't understand us. So thinking must be something very special. . . . In school, we think about math, and we think about spelling, and we think about grammar. But who ever heard of thinking about thinking? If we think about electricity, we can understand it better, but when we think about thinking, we seem to understand ourselves better.[3]

In the space of ninety-six pages, Harry and his friends discover on their own, and in their own terms, many of the basic concepts and rules of Aristotle's syllogistic logic. They apply these concepts and rules in the classroom, on the playground, and within their family lives. They also discuss such heady philosophical questions as whether thoughts are real, what the mind is, whether everything has to have a cause, and what fairness is. Throughout the story the children develop a concern to think impartially (look at all sides of issues and not jump to conclusions), to think consistently (avoid self-contradiction), to work out the implications of statements, to give reasons for what they think rather than simply assert opinions, and to examine assumptions.

A crucial feature of the novel is that the children themselves initiate inquiry rather than depend on adults always to set the agenda. The students do not see themselves as empty vessels into which information is to be poured. Neither do their teachers. Slowly the reader sees the classroom converted into what IAPC programs call a "community of inquiry." In such a learning environment each student is regarded as having the potential to make an important contribution to the discussion. Students are pressed to give reasons in support of whatever they say and to evaluate the views of others. However, mere put-downs, insults, and disrespectful behavior in general are discouraged.

One thing that becomes evident to the children in *Harry*—and to readers of the story—is that even those whose thinking is logically flawed may have something important to contribute. When we ask how someone arrives at even an obviously incorrect answer, we see that he or she is not simply mistaken. Near the end of *Harry*, as the children are reflecting on the kind of thinking they have been doing in their rather unusual classroom, Lisa recalls a poem her father read to her:

> It said the thoughts in our minds are like bats in a cave, and these ideas go flying about blindly, keeping within the walls. But then, in the last line, the poem says that every once in a while, "a graceful error corrects the cave."[4]

Just such an error is illustrated at the very outset of the novel when Harry is asked by his science teacher, "What is it that has a long tail and revolves about the sun once every 77 years?" Harry couldn't remember that it is Halley's comet, but he knew that his teacher had just said that all planets revolve around the sun. So he guesses, "A planet?" This is greeted with derisive laughter from his classmates. Harry doesn't let his embarrassment at giving the wrong answer to an easy question discourage him from trying to figure out how he had gone wrong. He discovers that he had converted "All planets revolve about the sun" to "All things that revolve about the sun are planets." He converts several more sentences, each time discovering that what began as true became false. He then forms a hypothesis: When you turn sentences around, they are no longer true.

Excited at this discovery, Harry shares it with his friend Lisa and offers to demonstrate it with any example she might present to him. Lisa's very first example puts a dent in Harry's hypothesis. She offers a counterexample: "No eagles are lions." However, by the end of chapter 1, Harry and Lisa formulate a more complex hypothesis: When a sentence beginning with "all" is reversed, it is no longer true; but when a sentence beginning with "no" is reversed, it stays true. Later the children in the novel try to figure out why "all" and "no" sentences behave in this way—and why anyone should care about such things.

Harry has some very special features that may take the unsuspecting adult reader by surprise. First, although *Harry* is intended to help students develop and refine their logical thinking, the logic is not presented didactically. Instead, the children are permitted to discover rules of logic much as a scientist might go about testing a hypothesis, including making false starts and confronting initial disappointments. Second, *Harry* deliberately has its characters make logical mistakes that are not corrected anywhere in the story. Thus, readers are invited to join the quest with Harry and his friends, rather than have everything worked out neatly for them. Third, and as a consequence of both of these points, the children in *Harry* and in the classroom are credited with having logical abilities. Their abilities are challenged and stretched rather than "implanted" through didactic instruction. This kind of respect for children as competent inquirers also characterizes the extensive workbooks that accompany each of the novels in the IAPC programs.

GETTING STARTED

Allowing children to discover things on their own can reap rewarding dividends. For example, fourth graders have no difficulty at all finding exceptions to Harry's hypothesis that sentences beginning with "all" are no longer true when reversed. A favorite example is "All tigers are tigers." Another is "All rabbits are hares." During one session I had with a lively group of fourth graders, a student offered his classmates this example: "All answers have questions" and "All questions have answers." It might be tempting for a teacher to object that these sentences are not of the "right sort." Harry's sentences are all of the variety "All ... are ... ," whereas these sentences have the form "All ... have. ..." But the students can rightly reply that Harry never qualified his statement in this way. His statement was a very general one about sentences beginning with "all."

Another temptation might be to "stick to task," thanking the student for an interesting example and asking if anyone else has an example. But in a philosophy class such an example can provide an occasion for an exciting digression. Fortunately, I had the presence of mind to encourage this group of fourth graders to talk a bit about whether they thought both sentences were true. They insisted that "All answers have questions" must be true since we would not call something an answer unless it were an answer *to a question*. But "All questions have answers" provoked a barrage of challenges:

- How many grains of sand are there on earth? [Answer: Just count them. Reply: The wind will blow them around and we'll count some more than once.]
- How many grains of sand are there on all the planets? [Answer: Maybe *we* can't count them, but there is an answer anyway.]
- How many trees are there on earth? [Answer: It might take a long time to count them, but there's an answer. Reply: By the time we finish counting them, some trees would have died and others would have started to grow.]
- Did God make time begin? [Student correction: *If* there is a God, did He make time begin? (A potential "troublemaker.")]
- Does space have limits? [A stopper.]
- Will time end? [Offered with an impish grin, betraying the student's sense that this was *the* stopper. He noted that if time does end some day, no one will be able later to confirm this. But he may also have been puzzling about the meaningfulness of the question—what could it mean to say that time will end?]

Thus, in the space of just a few minutes this group of fourth graders moved from logic to metaphysics—on this, my first visit to their class.[5]

It is remarkable how quickly young children can convert seemingly innocuous questions into issues of philosophical importance. During my yearlong sessions with an after-school library group of fifth graders, I typically read a paragraph or two from *Harry* or another children's story (such as Frank Baum's *Ozma of Oz*). For example, in one brief passage in *Harry*, Lisa agrees with Harry that while all cats are animals, not all animals are cats.[6] Still, she says, "in make-believe they can be. I can imagine what I please, and when I do, Harry's rules won't apply."

I asked the group to imagine a world in which all animals are cats. Then, to have us test Lisa's claim about the logic of make-believe, I asked Jeff, "In a world in which all animals are cats, would you be a cat?" Jeff grinned and replied, "In my case, no, because I'm not an animal. But in Mike's case, yes, because he is an animal!" After their laughter died down, the group launched a forty-five-minute discussion that not only questioned Lisa's claim that Harry's rules do not apply in make-believe but also explored questions about the logic of classificatory schemes, concluding with a serious discussion of what it is to be a person. What follows are some of the highlights of the session.

The discussion began with several students attempting to work out the implications of "All animals are cats." Chip provided the most thorough taxonomy:

> Suppose we had a family tree or something. You'd have the group of, let's say, animals. . . . There's many groups of types of animals, right? There's mammals, amphibians, reptiles. Then you branch off again. This branches off into types of mammals. Now you have to name different types of mammals—whales, dolphins, porpoises, and people. You see, you have to separate things. You have to have names for different groups.

This comment prompted questions about why things have more than one name (e.g., mammal, tiger). Chip and several others thought that noticing that things have more than one name paves the way to the conclusion that people are also animals (i.e., a subgroup of the larger group). But Jeff offered stiff resistance to this conclusion:

> We don't say, "Hey, you animal, come over here." If you see a person crawling on the floor, you don't say there's an animal crawling on the floor. You don't say, "Hey, mammal, come over here" to a whale, do you? You say, "Hey, whale, come over here," don't you?

It was clear that Jeff still was not willing to concede that people are animals. But Chip had a ready challenge:

> *Chip.* What are we, then? What are we?
> *Jeff.* People.
> *Chip.* Jeff, what are people? Just tell me, what are people? You can't answer that, can you?
> *Jeff.* Yes, I can.
> *Chip.* What are you?
> *Jeff.* A person.
> *Chip.* What's a person?
> *Jeff.* A living somebody.

Chip. A living somebody could be a whale.

Jeff. I said *somebody,* not an animal.

This statement prompted Chip to suggest that Jeff's view was prejudiced. I asked him what he meant by prejudiced. He replied that Jeff
"thinks he's better than any other animal." Chip himself characterized
people as animals but "a type of smarter animal." Jeff replied that he
was not saying people are better than animals, only different.

Mike agreed with Jeff, adding: "If it's a person, you say 'some*body.*' If
it's an animal you say, 'some*thing.*' Somebody is human. Somebody is a
human body." Undaunted by Jeff and Mike's reply, Chip repeated his
taxonomy: "There's living life, okay? Then you branch off from there.
. . . Now you go to the animals and branch off—mammals, amphibians,
reptiles, and whatever there is. Then you branch off and you have all
these special humans." Chip asked Jeff if he agreed so far. Indicating he
knew where this was leading, Jeff replied that he was not going to
change his mind: "I'm not an animal. I'm a person. And I'm going to
stay that way." In response to Chip's statement, "You're a type of animal," Jeff replied, "I'm not going to walk up to Dr. Jekyll and say, 'Hey,
change me into an animal!' "

A frequent employer of analogical reasoning, Amy gave the discussion a new twist:

People are a type of animal, like a bird is. That's different than like
an elephant is. A bird's different than an elephant, and we're different than a bird. Mike says we don't call our dog a person or
somebody. But someone might be real close to their pet and consider it part of the family.

These comments prompted a very interesting exchange between Jeff and
Amy:

Jeff. Okay, Amy says if you've got a close, close pet, we'd call it
part of the family. You could call it part of the family, but it isn't.
Your Mom didn't have the dog as a baby. If the dog's part of the
family, you'd be a dog, too.

Amy. You might have adopted an Indian boy and you might not
be an Indian.

Jeff. But that Indian boy is a person.

Amy. You might adopt a dog, like you do a person.

As the session came to a close, it was obvious that no consensus was about to be reached, but this did not seem to bother the students. A few moments earlier Larry had asked, "I want to know why everyone's getting so huffy about a little subject." Rick replied, "We're thinking! That's what we're here for." As the students were leaving one of them commented, "If we want to, we could argue for hours!" Another replied, "For days!" They might have meant simply that they could go on arguing just for the sake of arguing. However, when we met the following week, it was clear that more than arguing was going on.

When I entered the room, the students were already heavily engaged in a discussion of whether people are animals. Looking up from an encyclopedia, Penny said they discovered that it said humans are animals. Rather than settling the issue, this statement generated a discussion of whether everything in the encyclopedia is known to be true. Emily commented: "Some things we're not sure of; and the encyclopedia could put down every word about how the solar system was formed, and it would probably say there was big dust that spun around like a top. But we're not sure about that. And, so, that could be wrong." I asked whether in that case the encyclopedia will say, "We're not sure." Mike replied, "It'll say 'hypothesis'—which is a guess." Kurt added, "It'll say we're not sure yet."

Most of these students seemed quite content to pursue questions vigorously and thoughtfully without feeling the need to bring everything to closure. However, Jeff usually found it difficult to accept this uncertainty. After two lively sessions about the relationship between the mind and the brain, he pounded on the table and demanded, "What's the answer, Mr. Pritchard? Tell us what the answer is!" Our group had a reunion three years later and again when they were nearing the end of high school. Both times the students recalled the mind/brain discussions, and on both occasions Jeff indicated that he wanted to be told what the answer was.

Perhaps Jeff's desire for closure reflected what he had grown accustomed to in his regular classes. At our final reunion I asked the group if they had been able to pursue in their classes any of the kinds of questions we had discussed some years before. Their responses closely matched that of two students at another high school. Philosopher Martin Benjamin introduced his son David and David's friend Jeremy Scott to *Harry Stottlemeier* when they were fifth graders. Here is what they later said as tenth graders:

> In high school there is a common system of "learning" that goes something like this: listen, take notes, memorize, and regurgitate facts. Each high school subject seems to show the world through a distinct window unconnected to the windows presented by other classes.[7]

This passage is from their review of Thomas Nagel's *What Does It All Mean?* As tenth graders they approached David's father and said they wanted to read some philosophy again. In contrast to what they found in their high school, they say of Nagel's little book:

> Philosophy, on the other hand, attempts to look through all windows at once. The method of reasoning we acquired through *What Does It All Mean?* is not introduced in high school. We feel that a high school philosophy course would benefit interested students. Not only does philosophy deal with abstract concepts, but it also is concerned with everyday decisions. As we reached high school age, we realized that we were facing some difficult problems involving ethics and justice. Philosophy encouraged us to gain a better understanding of these questions and to reach an objective position, on which we might base our actions.[8]

It should be noted that what these two students claim to have gained more than anything else from their study of philosophy is a method of reasoning rather than a particular set of answers. The opening words of their review are instructive:

> The wise guru, who has obtained all knowledge and a complete understanding of the world, sits atop a misconception. People have long believed that the final ending point of knowledge is the guru's peak. They think that from the guru's mountain-top, with complete knowledge, the world can be simplified and viewed clearly and accurately. We have found that high school reinforces this fantasy.

Thomas Nagel's short introduction to philosophy, *What Does It All Mean?* made us see that as you obtain more knowledge, you find that there is more knowledge to be obtained. Answering questions brings about more unanswered questions, and thus a point of complete and final knowledge cannot be reached.[9]

This endless quest for knowledge was not a cause of despair for these two young philosophers. They found reading Nagel's little book thoroughly enjoyable. They close their review with an enthusiastic endorsement of their most recent philosophical excursion:

Philosophy would help high school students to link and understand their knowledge. The guru may understand his knowledge, and he may in fact be a wise man, but in believing that he knows all, he lacks the open-mindedness and critical questioning we discovered through philosophy.[10]

SELF-KNOWLEDGE

David Benjamin and Jeremy Scott suggest that aided by philosophical reflection high-school students may gain a better understanding of both the nature and limits of their knowledge, thus enabling them to approach learning in a more open-minded, critical manner. Challenged by the problems of ethics as high-school students, they wanted to revisit philosophy. Evidently something they recalled from their fifth grade exposure to *Harry* made them want to turn to philosophy for help. Perhaps they recalled having conversations something like the one I observed in John Foster's combined fifth and sixth grade class some years ago.[11]

The class began with a reminder of the closing words of Harry Stottlemeier's essay on thinking: "When we think about thinking, we seem to understand ourselves better." John Foster then asked his students what they thought about Harry's conclusion:

Mary. Well, thinking is—well, maybe the way you might understand yourself is because thinking is kind of part of you in a way.

Tammy. You get to thinking about yourself and trying to become mature; and you get to know more things about your life.

Hilary. If you think about yourself—like, if you think about how you think, you might find out what kind of personality you have by your thoughts—how you think.

Jeff. Like Hilary said, if you think about what you think, and if you think you did it wrong and you can think of others ways, and if you think you have a bad personality, then you can change it.

Mary. [Thinking about thinking] just makes you think I guess, and it's like you think out in every direction; and you just don't think at one angle.

Foster then asked the first of a series of questions about self-knowledge. Suppose you met someone walking down the street who looked just like you. Would you think that person was you?

Preston. No, you wouldn't really think it was you because he'd have a different personality—he'd think differently.

Jim. It's like, your personality is one—it's the only one in the world. And it's you, and you use that every day. And it's—it's—it can't be duplicated.

Several students supported Preston and Jim's view that each person is unique in some way. If there are no obvious physical differences, there still would be some differences in personality.

Foster shifted the question: "Let's say your friend was walking down the street and *he* saw this person. Would that friend maybe mistake that person as being you?" Again the students stressed the importance of personality and interests. They agreed that a friend might mistake that person for you if the person were viewed from a distance. But having a conversation with the person, they felt, would enable the friend to resolve the confusion.

So, the students seemed to be saying, although there could be circumstances in which even friends might mistakenly identify look-alikes with us, we will not make this same mistake about ourselves. How is it, John Foster next asked, that we are so sure who we are? David answered, "By your shoes, or your pants, or how your face looks, or how your hair looks." He paused a moment, perhaps realizing that these criteria might not settle the matter, since these are the same criteria available to a friend who might confuse you with someone else. He added, "Or your emotions."

David may have thought that each of us has access to our own emotional life in a way that others do not: I know my emotional life by experiencing it. However, as several students had already suggested, I can only infer yours by talking with you, observing your behavior, attempting to read your facial expressions, and so on. So, in some sense, I have firsthand acquaintance with who I am and therefore cannot be mistaken about who I am. But some students were not satisfied with this:

> *Mary.* I have something to say. Sometimes some people, they don't even know who they are. Maybe the way they look, they can see themselves. But maybe through everything they've gone through, or something like that, they really haven't experienced themselves at all.

Mary's comment moved the discussion to another level. We may know our names, how old we are, where we live, and even that we are different from others no matter how much we look like them, but we still may be confused about who we are in a deeper sense. Jim picked up on this:

> *Jim.* I think we know who we are. Like I know who I am and you know who you are. But I don't think we really know ourselves deep down. Like maybe we're nice people and we don't know deep down how angry we can get at people, and violent or something.

Tammy brought up another set of considerations. Not only do we want to be certain sorts of persons, but others want us to be certain sorts of persons, too—and these expectations may clash in ways that result in personal confusion about who we are:

> *Tammy.* I feel that you really do know deep down inside who you are, but sometimes you can't be what they would like. . . . But if you don't like your life then sometimes you get confused—the kind of personality you are not.

Very likely, Tammy was expressing concern about adult expectations from children, although that may not be all she had in mind. Children are also concerned about how they are regarded by their peers, as Jeff and Rich's follow-up comments make clear:

> *Jeff.* If some people say you're a kook or something, and you ask your friends, "Do you think I'm a kook or do you think I'm normal?" and if they say yes, then it would be sort of different and you'd be confused and you wouldn't know what you were.

Rich added that if you are not really sure whether or not you are a "kook," asking someone would not really help. What might he have had in mind? We may be so certain of some things about ourselves (for example, that we are not "stupid") that the opinions of others cannot create self-doubt. However, in some respects, we may think that what we are depends on what others think of us. Thus, I may believe that whether or not I am a "kook" depends on how others see me; and I may not know how to regard myself until I know how others regard me. Furthermore, others may be reluctant to be candid with me about how they, or others, regard me. So, Rich might ask, what good does it do to ask others whether you are a "kook"? (Recall advertisements about bad breath: "Even your best friend won't tell you.")

The problem of coping with conflicts between what we might want to be and what others might want us to be was pursued further:

> *Becky.* Some people—kids—they don't act like they want to. Like, they want to please their mother, but then their personality wants them to be something else.
>
> *Foster.* So, you're saying that some mothers may want you to be a certain way, and you may be that way to please them; but that may not be the way you really are?
>
> *Becky.* Or *want* to be.
>
> *Mary.* Somebody may tell you what you're going to be, but just to please them you want to be that way. But then that person is making you. That person is molding you in what that person wants you to be, not what you want to be. So, you're really not—you're really not yourself.

Hababa added that one must have the inner strength to resist such efforts by others if one is not to end up being just the kind of person others are trying to mold. Rich pointed out that in an effort to impress others, people who are uncertain of themselves sometimes act foolishly or try to act like someone else. Hababa replied that if we are confident of who we are, we do not have to prove ourselves to anyone. Mary supported this idea but added a significant qualification:

> It's kind of like what Hababa said. You don't have to prove it to anybody. The only person you *have* to prove it to is yourself—that you're the person that you want to be. You have to prove it to yourself, not anyone else.

Recall that this portion of the class discussion began with John Foster's question about how it is that we are so sure who we are. However, it did not take the students long to challenge the assumption that we are so sure. After suggesting that some people might not know themselves all that well, the students shifted the discussion to some subtly value-laden concerns. The statement "The only person you *have* to prove it to is yourself—that you're the person that you want to be" is fundamentally a statement of personal responsibility, of accountability to oneself.

"Proving to yourself" who you are is not a matter of gathering conclusive evidence about your personal identity. Rather, for these students it seems to be a matter of self-determination—perhaps even in the face of external pressures to be a different kind of person than one really wants to be. To say that one *has* to be self-determining in this way is not to say it is inevitable that one will be. The students had already pointed out that some people do allow themselves to be "molded" by others. To say that one *has* to be self-determining, then, is to ascribe a special responsibility to each of us.

Of course, these comments about self-knowledge and personal responsibility mark only the beginning of philosophical inquiry into areas of great complexity and importance. But it cannot be doubted that these fifth and sixth graders made an impressive start, and it is clear that the issues they raised were of special significance to them. Furthermore, it was not just a handful of students who participated in the session. Nor were they handpicked, "gifted and talented" students. This was an ordinary classroom of twenty-five students, and by the end of the session the vast majority of them had contributed something to the discussion.

PIXIE: AN EXTENDED ILLUSTRATION

In Chapter 2 I showed through the use of a variety of illustrations that the Hastings Center goals and objectives can be applied to elementary-school moral education as well as to college level courses in ethics. Here I will try to show that an entire IAPC Philosophy for Children program can be adapted to the Hastings Center objectives. I have selected IAPC's *Looking for Meaning* program, which uses the *Pixie* novel.[12] This is a reasoning and language arts program that is designed to sharpen thinking skills by applying reasoning to ideas that are of interest to children. Intended primarily for third and fourth grade children, the program emphasizes thinking skills that focus on ambiguities, relationships, similes, analogies, and rules. As in all IAPC programs, the classroom is characterized ideally as a community of inquiry in which children are encouraged to engage in discussion with others, supporting their own ideas with good reasons and responding thoughtfully to ideas that may differ from their own.

Since neither the word "moral" nor any of its close cognates is conspicuous even in the teacher's manual, the *Looking for Meaning* program may seem an unlikely resource for moral education. However, it is no more necessary to use such words in order to encourage moral reflection than it is to use the word "philosophy" to encourage philosophical reflection. Instead, children can be invited to think about ideas such as sharing, taking turns, fairness, right and wrong, promising, lying, friendship, teasing, kindness, unkindness, being helpful or unhelpful, and so on. These are all central ideas in the moral life of children. Furthermore, there are capacities and skills that may contribute to moral development even when they are not specifically directed to moral concerns as such. For example, the capacity for empathic understanding, a crucial element in moral education, can be nurtured (or thwarted) prior to the emergence of specifically moral concepts in very young children.[13] Developing the general disposition to seek good reasons for one's ideas can also contribute to developing reasoning skills essential to moral reflection. More specifically, developing the general skills of analogical reasoning is invaluable for moral reasoning. The *Looking for Meaning* program has very rich offerings in all of the above, which can be shown by discussing how this program might satisfy the Hastings Center objectives.

As we have seen, one effective way to stimulate the moral imagination is through stories. *Pixie*, of course, is a fictional story. Told in the first person, it invites children to join Pixie in her frequent flights of imagination. Whether the issue is about the relationship between Pixie and her leg (How can I be awake when my leg is asleep?) or if something is right or wrong (Could it be that some things are neither right nor wrong?), Pixie's attitude is one of puzzlement and wonder. This attitude is infectious, no doubt resulting in most children feeling by page 11 that older sister Miranda is the unusual one, not Pixie:

See, that's the big difference between Miranda and me. She never sees anything as a problem! It's not that she thinks she knows all the answers. It's just that she isn't even *interested* in the questions!

Pixie's questioning attitude opens her to new possibilities, moral or otherwise. However, Pixie is also portrayed as needing imaginative prodding herself. When the class is asked to think of a mystery creature to look for on the zoo trip, Pixie suggests that Tommy pick a unicorn for his creature. She comments:

I don't know why I did it. I wasn't trying to be mean. I just wanted to have some fun. I mean, Tommy teases me sometimes, so I thought this time I'd tease him. (p. 15)

She then gleefully thinks to herself, "Wait 'til he tries to find a unicorn in the zoo. Oh, I'd love to see his face when he finds out there's no such animal!" Perhaps later, when she experiences somewhat similar disappointment about her own choice, Pixie will ask herself whether she may have gone too far with her teasing. She may then puzzle more generally over when teasing is merely fun and when it is mean, or at least her readers might.

In any case, Pixie's friends Brian and Isabel exhibit moral imagination in helping Pixie cope with her disappointment. Seeing (perhaps empathically) how unhappy she is, they seek ways to make her feel better.[14] Brian suggests that since she selected "mammal" as her mystery creature, she saw more examples of her creature than anyone else. Unconsoled, Pixie thinks her mystery creature "turned out to be practically nothing at all—just the name of a class, and not something warm and furry, with a wet nose and soft brown eyes" (p. 67). Isabel tries another, more successful, tack and suggests that Pixie can still make up a very good mystery story.

Pixie then comments that this suggestion was nice of Isabel, because it did shift Pixie's attention away from her disappointment and toward the task of writing the story. But what about Brian? Was it nice of him to try to help, even though it actually didn't seem to help? Pixie does not say. Still, readers might wonder why Pixie bothers to mention Brian's attempt to be helpful, and they might wish to discuss the entire episode. After all, Isabel is Pixie's best friend. Brian, on the other hand, has just begun talking with others. What has happened that explains Brian's willingness to talk after remaining silent so long? Is he now Pixie's friend? Why?

The same example can be used to help children recognize moral issues. When Pixie recounts teasing Tommy about selecting a unicorn as his mystery creature, children can be invited to discuss whether this is just good fun or whether it is mean or cruel. Pixie herself suggests that it is possible to cross the line from one to the other. Is there a problem here? Children may suggest related examples that indicate that teasing can go too far and that we need to think carefully about other people's feelings. Later, when Pixie experiences her disappointment, children can be invited to reconsider what Pixie did to Tommy.

Whether we are adults or children, moral issues do not come to us with the announcement, "Attention, this is a moral issue." It may be only after harm is done, only after we find ourselves facing a difficult decision because of an unfortunate earlier decision, or only after we are faulted by others that we recognize what was at stake morally. Throughout *Pixie* readers are given opportunities to identify and think through moral issues that can easily go either completely unnoticed or only partially recognized.

Again, there is no need to assume that the concept "moral" is to be a topic of discussion in moral education. Thus, the task of helping students recognize moral issues need not result in labeling situations as "moral" (or "immoral").[15] Instead, issues can be seen as those concerning what is fair/unfair, selfish/unselfish, honest/dishonest, right/wrong, good/bad, kind/unkind, and so on.[16] Readers of *Pixie* will have some familiarity with all of these concepts and probably very strong ideas about many of the situations in which they might be used. *Pixie* and the teacher's manual take advantage of this familiarity and invite children to think more deeply and more clearly about these concepts and principles that might be associated with them (such as various renderings of the Golden Rule). The manual, for example, provides discussion plans on treating a person as a person (p. 47); sharing (p. 59); what does "right" mean? (p. 62); accepting help and asking for help (p. 80); getting even (p. 81); staring (p. 103); excuses and reasons (p. 118); when is a reason a good reason? (p. 121); rules (pp. 233–35, 247); teasing (p. 242); anticipating the consequences of what we do (p. 243); should the way we treat others resemble the way we would like them to treat us? (p. 244); not doing something you want to do (p. 312); breaking a promise (p. 312); and what is a promise? (p. 313).

Each discussion plan in the manual is prompted by an episode in *Pixie*. Pixie often uses concepts in a provocative way. For example:

> I didn't tell Miranda either. Just because she's my sister, and she's two years older than I am, and we share the same room, I don't have to tell her *everything*!
>
> Besides, does she ever show me that book she's always writing things in? And does she let me stand around and listen when her friend, Sue, comes over? All that whispering and giggling they do!
>
> Right in front of me she'll say to Sue, "Wait a minute, I've got to get rid of my kid sister." Oh, I can't tell you how much I *hate* her when she does that. (p. 9)

Just these few lines raise questions about sharing, secrecy, privacy, hatred, treating others as they treat you, and treating someone as a person. Many of these ideas come up later in the teacher's manual (but could be discussed now, as well).

Here is the discussion plan to go along with this episode (*Looking for Meaning*, p. 47):

DISCUSSION PLAN: Treating a person as a person

Is it treating a person as a person if:

1. you keep staring at that person?
2. you talk about him as if he weren't there, right in front of him?

3. you put him in a garbage can when you are finished talking to him?
4. you interrupt him whenever he begins to talk?
5. you answer him politely when he asks for directions?
6. you show him that you are interested in what he thinks and his reasons?
8. you never do anything without first asking him what to do?
9. you let him do all your thinking for you?
10. you change the subject whenever he disagrees with you?

These are questions the children are invited to discuss rather than questions to which the teacher is expected to provide answers. This does not mean that there are no right or wrong answers, better or worse answers, or the like. Rather, the aim is for the children themselves to try to answer these questions, supporting their answers with the best reasons they can muster. This approach has three important features. First, it places responsibility squarely on the children's shoulders. Second, it acknowledges that they have the ability to give these questions their thoughtful consideration. Finally, it shows respect for them as thinkers, thus treating *them* as persons. Of course, questions 8 and 9 indirectly raise precisely these three concerns for the children answering them.

The manner in which the *Pixie* program is used in the classroom is a good illustration of how a sense of responsibility can be encouraged in children. As we have seen with the discussion plan on treating a person as a person, students are given the responsibility to think through the questions on their own and make a serious effort to answer them responsibly. The confidence and respect accorded them is likely to have a positive effect in this regard.

Further, of course, many of the topics for discussion themselves focus explicitly on different aspects of responsibility: responsibility for the consequences of what we do, for the harms we may cause, for helping others, for giving and keeping our word, and so on. Again, discussion plans concentrate on questions with which students can be expected to have some familiarity. For example, here is part of a discussion plan on helping (*Looking for Meaning*, p. 80):

DISCUSSION PLAN: Accepting and asking for help
Who should you help? Who should you accept help from?

1. Should you help a classmate think up a topic for a paper?
2. Should you let someone copy your homework?
3. Should you let someone see the paper you're working on?
4. If your best friend wants to copy from your paper, should you let her?

These are issues many students will already have had to deal with in one way or another. They may have been given explicit answers by teachers and school authorities. It is much less likely, however, that students will have been given any opportunity in school to discuss the underlying values at stake. In fact, it is not unusual to find college freshmen who have never had a serious discussion of what plagiarism is, how it can be avoided, and why it poses a special problem. Yet, as many so painfully learn, they will be held responsible for violations.

Many adults are uncomfortable with ambiguity. Pixie seems to delight in it. On the very first page of *Pixie* we find Pixie saying:

> I can cross my legs and walk on my knees. My father says I act like I'm made of rubber. Last night I put my feet around my neck and walked on my hands!
> No, you can't cross your legs *and* put them around your neck at the same time! One or the other, but not both! What do you want to do—turn yourself into a pretzel?

Pixie uses ambiguity here, as well as elsewhere, for humor. She also seems to take special pleasure in using the same word in different contexts that give it different meanings, sometimes even in the same paragraph. ("Wait your turn," says Amanda. Pixie replies, "Turn that water down!" [(p. 11].) Despite continual shifts in meaning, for the most part Pixie seems to be in charge of the language she uses. Yet, even she occasionally needs help—for example, when her confusion about "mammal" results in disappointment at the zoo. (She sees tigers, lions, chimps, and giraffes. But where are the mammals?) However, such occasional setbacks do not seem to diminish Pixie's enthusiasm for language or her openness to multiple meanings. In fact, she takes special delight in the strikingly different interpretations of her mystery story as told by her classmates in the last chapter. No doubt all of this adds to the richness of her world.

At the same time, ambiguity and vagueness can pose moral problems, especially when they are connected to moral disagreement. What, for example, does it really mean to treat people equally? One mark of reasonableness is recognizing even thoughtful people may not agree on answers to such questions. In the discussion plan about treating persons as persons, the last question asks whether it is treating a person as a person if "you change the subject whenever he disagrees with you." This action is an attempt to avoid conflict by avoiding the issue. It is not at all clear that attempting to ignore points of disagreement with one another is "treating a person as a person." Matters about which people disagree often are matters about which they feel very strongly and which may even bear marks of their distinctive identities as persons. However, *Looking for Meaning* and the other IAPC programs suggest another way of dealing with disagreement—namely, openly discussing it and trying to come to terms with it.

HELPING CHILDREN BECOME MORE REASONABLE

The *Looking for Meaning* program's contribution to the moral education of children builds on the already rather well-developed rational and moral abilities of its readers. It is important to keep this in mind for two reasons. First, it reinforces the educational point that children who read and discuss *Pixie* should not be regarded as "empty vessels" into whom moral values must be poured (a form of moral indoctrination). They are active inquirers, ready and willing to offer their own rendering of the issues at hand. Second, a moral point that follows from the first, to fail to respect these capacities in children is to fail to respect children as the moral agents they are.

The *Looking for Meaning* program legitimates for children the pursuit of questions of meaning in the supportive environment of the classroom. Matthew Lipman and Ann M. Sharp point out the benefits for children:

> The children who read *Pixie* together in the classroom will recognize Pixie's puzzlement as akin to their own and will be delighted by that recognition. They will also identify with Pixie's insistent curiosity and *search for reasons*. Unreasonable as Pixie often is, one

discovers in her, despite many backslidings, a *desire to be reasonable,* and a *desire that other people be reasonable too.* This is again something which young readers will acknowledge as linking them affectionately to Pixie.[17]

As I suggested in Chapter 1, reasonableness is a *social* virtue. It is marked by a willingness to reason *with* others and to subject one's reasoning to sharable standards. It might seem that Pixie resists this sharing. After all, *Pixie* is written in the first person. Isn't this just another example of an egocentric child explaining the world from *her* point of view, only at greater length than is usually the case? To draw such a conclusion, however, is to miss the major thrust of her story. Pixie's story is about her struggles to understand relationships—but not just relationships among concepts (and the meaning of "relationship" itself). She is equally interested in understanding relationships among persons. She puzzles about her relationship with her sister, the significance and variety of social rules, the meaning of friendship, and most puzzling of all, why she talks almost continuously while Brian remains silent. Finally, her story comes to a climax when she recounts how her classmates supported her while she was ill. At this point what she finds most striking is how they took her mystery story and retold it in several delightfully different ways. Thus, she felt joined with them even as they obviously differed from her. This final, affectionate challenge to egocentricity can be seen as a crucial step in the direction of Pixie's greater reasonableness— perhaps even a step in the direction of a kind of wisdom.

4

What Is Critical Thinking?

In their playful, teasing ways, the children in *Pixie* are developing and exercising critical thinking abilities. For example, they sort out meanings, classify, explore relationships (causal, logical, part-whole), play with ambiguities, employ similes and metaphors, engage in analogical reasoning, generalize, compare and contrast, and offer counterexamples. Critical thinking skills are a central feature of the entire K-12 IAPC program, which is in keeping with what one would expect from any educational programs that provide space for philosophical thinking. However, whether or not some such space will be provided by advocates of critical thinking very much depends on what they take critical thinking to be. In this and the next chapter I argue for a view of critical thinking that embraces both philosophical and moral reflection.

There is widespread agreement among educators that we need to do a much better job of helping students develop their critical thinking abilities. Many cite lowered scores on standardized reading and math tests as evidence of this need. Others simply note their students' difficulties in engaging in thoughtful, reflective discussion and in writing organized, well-argued essays. It might be thought that these two kinds of supporting evidence should point educators seeking to improve critical thinking in the same direction. Perhaps they should, but, in fact, they do not. Beneath the surface of agreement about the need for critical thinking are striking differences about just what critical thinking is. Leading advocates of critical thinking acknowledge that without at least a rough consensus on what critical thinking is, confusion about what is needed and what might count as educational success or failure in this regard is inevitable.

WHAT IS CRITICAL THINKING?[1]

Robert Ennis offers the following succinct definition of critical thinking: " 'Critical thinking,' as I think the term is generally used, means *reasonable reflective thinking that is focused on deciding what to believe or do.*"[2] This definition has several virtues. First, it is concise. Second, it identifies reflection as a key ingredient. Third, by emphasizing reasonableness, it suggests that critical thinking is not a solitary activity. Although those who exercise critical thinking can be said in an important sense to think for themselves, this does not mean that they think by themselves. To say that someone is reasonable is to say that he or she is someone with whom one can reason. The open-mindedness that this requires does not exclude having settled beliefs and commitments, but it does imply an openness to new perspectives and a willingness to listen to and possibly learn from others. Fourth, the definition does not exclude creative thinking: "Formulating hypotheses, alternative ways of viewing a problem, questions, possible solutions, and plans for investigating something, for example, are all creative acts that come under this definition."[3]

Nevertheless, Ennis's definition may focus too narrowly on deciding what to believe and do. Critical thinking also can be used to make sense of what we read, see, or hear and to make inferences from premises with which we may disagree or about which we have no particular view. This can be seen most readily in deductive inference. Consider the example: All rodents are rabbits. Mickey Mouse is a rodent. Therefore, he is a rabbit. This is a valid deductive inference. *If* rodents are rabbits and Mickey Mouse is a rodent, then necessarily he is a rabbit. But reasoning in this way does not necessarily help one decide what to believe or do, although it does exemplify a fundamental type of reasoning.[4]

One use of deductive reasoning is to determine what someone else's statements mean or imply, even if one's own beliefs are quite unrelated. For example, consider the following pair of sentences discussed in E. D. Hirsh's *Cultural Literacy*:

1. Three turtles rested *beside* a floating log, and a fish swam beneath them.
2. Three turtles rested *on* a floating log, and a fish swam beneath them.[5]

Hirsh reports that experiments indicate that subjects presented with the first sentence consistently, but mistakenly, recalled their original sentence to be:

3. Three turtles rested on a floating log, and a fish swam beneath *it*.

Subjects who were originally presented with the second sentence did not recall their sentence as:

4. Three turtles rested beside a floating log, and a fish swam beneath *it*.

Understanding the differences among these four sentences, including the inferences that can or cannot be made from the original pair, requires critical thinking. But the primary focus is on understanding meanings rather than on deciding what to believe or do.[6] What is true about the meanings of sentences also applies to interpreting the meanings of extended discourse, whether spoken or written.

Matthew Lipman's characterization of critical thinking emphasizes judgment rather than decision-making.[7] Of course, judgment informs decision-making. But, more than this, Lipman says, to judge is to judge relationships, whether invented or discovered. Relationships, he says, are meanings, so "great orders or systems of relationships constitute great bodies of meaning."[8] The development of critical thinking, then, involves the improvement of judgment. Noting an etymological link between "critical" and "criteria," Lipman suggests that we think of critical thinking as involving judgments based on criteria, or reasons.

Criteria can themselves be appraised in terms of what Lipman calls "megacriteria," such as reliability, relevance, strength, coherence, and consistency.[9] In contexts where expertise is appropriate, reliable criteria will have a high level of acceptance among the community of experts. In any case, critical thinking operates in a social context rather than in isolation from others. The reflective model of critical thinking that Lipman proposes is, he says, "thoroughly social and communal."[10] This model does not ignore or suppress differences. On the contrary, critical thinking, for Lipman, is characterized as "thinking that (1) facilitates judgment because it (2) relies on criteria, (3) is self-correcting, and (4) is sensitive to context."[11]

Ennis's taxonomy of critical thinking skills actually comes much closer to Lipman's fuller characterization than his initial definition of critical thinking suggests. For example, Ennis's list includes dispositions to seek clear statements of questions, to be open-minded, to seek as much precision as the subject permits, to think in an orderly manner, and to be sensitive to the feelings and level of understanding of others. It also includes abilities such as focusing on the context of an argument, detecting unstated assumptions, clarifying arguments, making inferences from premises, and interacting with others in a reasonable manner.

The contrast between Ennis's initial, concise definition of critical thinking and his more comprehensive taxonomy of skills, abilities, and dispositions illustrates a danger. As Ennis observes, critical thinking is commonly associated with problem-solving. But exclusive focus on his concise definition may encourage some to construe this association too narrowly. As I will argue later, highly developed critical thinking frequently poses more questions than answers. It opens up new avenues for inquiry and, in this sense, is as creative as it is critical, which is not to deny the value of critical thinking in problem-solving. However, problem-solving does not always involve critical thinking, and the exercise of critical imagination sometimes creates more problems than it solves, thus opening the door to new avenues of inquiry.

The open-endedness of critical thinking—indeed, its penchant for challenging comfortable assumptions—may cause a worry: If we encourage children to be critical thinkers, will we be encouraging them to be radically skeptical, if not cynical? Some might prefer Ennis's brief definition of critical thinking to Lipman's more expansive characterization because the short definition emphasizes *deciding* what to believe and do, whereas Lipman emphasizes the *skeptical* function of critical thinking.

However, Lipman's critical thinker exercises what he calls "cautious skepticism," rather than radical skepticism. In areas that call for critical thinking, judgments are made *provisionally,* not *determinatively.*[12] As Immanuel Kant says, "A provisional judgment is one by which I suppose that there are more grounds *for* the truth of something than against it, that these grounds, however, do not suffice for a *determinate* or *definitive* judgment by which I decide straightaway for the truth."[13] Provisional judging is therefore a consciously problematic judging. In contrast, a radical skeptic "renounces all judging, whereas the true philosopher, when he has not yet sufficient reasons for holding something to be true, merely suspends his judgment."[14]

The point of making provisional judgments, says Kant, is to seek more determinate grounds for judgment:

> Provisional judgments may therefore be regarded as *maxims* for the investigation of a matter. One could call them also *anticipations,* because one anticipates the judgment on a matter before one has the determinate judgment. Such [anticipatory] judgments thus have their good use, and it would be possible even to give rules on how to judge an object provisionally.[15]

Such rules, presumably, serve as criteria for forming good judgments, thereby guiding critical thinking. As Ennis's more elaborate characterization of critical thinking makes clear, any reasonably comprehensive list of guideposts for critical thinking is bound to be lengthy.

So, to minimize misunderstanding, it is perhaps best not to rely heavily on a concise definition of critical thinking. A few years ago the American Philosophical Association's Committee on Pre-College Philosophy sponsored a project to determine if expert consensus could be reached on what critical thinking is, how it might be assessed, and what forms of instruction should be used.[16] A core group of forty-six panelists used the Delphi Method of striving for consensus.[17] After several rounds of reviewing one another's reflections, the panelists arrived at a consensus statement about critical thinking and the ideal critical thinker:

> We understand critical thinking to be purposeful, self-regulatory judgment which results in interpretation, analysis, evaluation, and inference, as well as explanation of the evidential, conceptual, methodological, criteriological, or contextual considerations upon which that judgment is based. CT is essential as a tool of inquiry. As such, CT is a liberating force in education and a powerful resource in one's personal and civic life. While not synonymous with good thinking, CT is a pervasive and self-rectifying human phenomenon. The ideal critical thinker is habitually inquisitive, well-informed, trustful of reason, open-minded, flexible, fair-minded in evaluation, honest in facing personal biases, prudent in making judgments, willing to reconsider, clear about issues, orderly in complex matters, dili-

gent in seeking relevant information, reasonable in the selection of criteria, focused in inquiry, and persistent in seeking results which are as precise as the subject and the circumstances of inquiry permit. Thus, educating good critical thinkers means working toward this ideal. It combines developing CT skills with nurturing those dispositions which consistently yield useful insights and which are the basis of a rational and democratic society.[18]

We might wish for a more concise statement, but it is unlikely that anything less complex than this can guard against serious misunderstanding. Even this statement requires several pages of interpretation in the report. Without repeating those details, I will simply assume that the report provides a reasonably good approximation of what critical thinking is. Examining the question of how critical thinking might be assessed will illustrate just how complex any reasonably comprehensive notion of critical thinking is.

ASSESSING CRITICAL THINKING

Since the trend toward lower scores on standardized reading and math tests has precipitated much of the concern about critical thinking, improved performance on these tests might be used as a criterion of success. In addition, several standardized critical thinking tests are currently available.[19] These tests have several virtues. They can test a variety of critical thinking skills in a short period of time. Machine gradable, the results are quickly and efficiently available. The same tests can be widely administered and are uniformly graded. Thus, representative samples of large populations are easily attainable, and reliable comparisons are readily available. In short, standardized tests are cost- and time-effective and quite amenable to scientific analysis. At the same time, multiple-choice tests are not well suited for assessing students' critical thinking abilities in dealing with ethical and value issues, particularly those that raise broad-scale concerns that require the comparison and integration of various perspectives.

The validity of test results depends on the extent to which the tests actually test for critical thinking. Quite apart from the problem of assessing critical thinking in regard to ethical and value issues, there are other serious problems with multiple-choice tests. Briefly put, good critical thinkers are problem creators as well as problem solvers. In particular, they may create problems for multiple-choice tests, thereby creating problems for themselves. Their critical thinking may actually lower their scores. A more careful construction of items can reduce this problem, but often at the expense of reducing a test's value as a measure of *critical* thinking. I will now try to substantiate these claims with examples.

Consider the following problem:

> 20 is to 30 as 10 is to:
> (a) 5; (b) 10; (c) 15; (d) 20; (e) 25.[20]

If John selects 15 for his answer, does he display critical thinking skills? Not necessarily. It depends on how he arrived at his answer and perhaps on why he rejected the other answers. Suppose his thinking went like this: "This is obviously a question about ratios. I've seen problems like this before. 20 is 2/3 of 30. 10 is 2/3 of 15. So, 15 is the right answer." What is it that led John to view the problem as one about ratios? If this occurred to him only because of its familiarity (and perhaps someone telling him that he could be expected to be tested on ratios), problem-solving skills were used; but it is not clear that any critical thinking was required.

Suppose Amy selects 20 as her answer, an answer frequently selected by teachers to whom I present this problem. She reasons, "In each case the difference between the first and second number is 10." She might not have noticed that 20 is 2/3 of 30. Instead, she might simply have noticed that 30 is 10 greater than 20. Is this answer wrong? It might well be marked wrong on a standardized test. Although 20 may not be the answer the test maker had in mind, this does not settle the question of whether 20 is an acceptable answer.

Neither John nor Amy seems to have relied heavily on critical thinking in coming up with an answer, although we might give Amy the edge in creative thinking. Mark, on the other hand, circles *both* 15 and 20 (clearly unacceptable on standardized tests). He does this because he thinks both answers are acceptable, depending on how the question is taken, and as a way of indicating that the question lacks precision. This response does exemplify an important critical thinking skill, as does his refusal to opt for one "best" answer. Many teachers commenting on this problem suggest that since the test makers probably had 15 in mind as the correct answer, they should not have included 20 as a possible choice. Their objection is that this is a poorly constructed problem. So let us replace "d) 20" with "d) 30."

Susan now answers, "I think that 20 is to 30 as 10 is to 10." On the face of it, this answer seems so absurd that we might suspect that Susan either is not taking the question seriously or she needs a math lesson. However, she explains, "If you add 10 to each of the second numbers the first number will be 1/2 of the second new number." Anyone who can offer this explanation clearly has some understanding of ratios. But obviously not everyone who understands ratios will take such an imaginative approach to the problem. Suppose Susan now playfully adds: "I see that 15 would work. But so would 10. I chose 10 because it wasn't so obvious. I had to think harder to come up with that answer. I like challenges. Besides, it was supposed to be a problem, wasn't it?" Here we can see critical imagination at work—but only because Susan is given an opportunity to explain her thinking.

To prevent clever responses like this from ruining a test (or Susan's score), we might drop "b) 10" from the possible choices and replace it with "b) 60." Now the problem reads:

20 is to 30 as 10 is to
(a) 5; (b) 60; (c) 15; (d) 30; (e) 25

Cathy now says: "I think 20 is to 30 as 10 is to 5. If you add 20 to each of the second numbers, the first number will be 2/5 of the second." She adds: "Of course, 25 could be right, too. After all, 20 is smaller than 30 and 10 is smaller than 25. 30 and 60 would work, too. Besides, if you add the difference between the first and second number to the first number and put the new first number over the second number, the answer will always be 1. So, any positive integers could work!" Cathy may strike us as simply too clever at this point, but when great mathematicians and philosophers like Newton and Leibniz (inventors of the calculus) were children, they might have struck their elders as too clever as well. They would probably have had great fun with this kind of problem, a warm-up exercise for more challenging number games.

However, for testing purposes it might seem desirable to forestall answers like Cathy's by stating the problem more precisely. Here is an attempt:

This is a problem in ratios. Consider 20/30. If 10 is the numerator, what denominator should be selected if the ratio is to match 20/30? (Note: Do not add or subtract from the denominators.)
(a) 3; (b) 7; (c) 15; (d) 23; (e) 31

We could also add, "No clever answers allowed," which might stifle even a Newton or a Leibniz. Unfortunately, it will also stifle critical and creative thinking. No doubt creative and critical thinking are required in constructing such a problem, but answering it requires no more critical or creative thinking than exemplified by John and Amy in answering the original problem.

Of course, we do want students to be able to understand and solve problems with ratios. But we should also want them to detect ambiguities, explore alternative ways of solving problems, and at least occasionally come up with unconventional answers. The problem is that a standardized multiple-choice test may actually suppress these responses. Unconventional responses do not pay; they may even have punishing consequences.

This difficulty is not confined to mathematical problems. In fact, it is compounded by differences in the backgrounds of students. Robert Ennis gives several illustrations. For example, he discusses Item 6 on the widely used Watson-Glaser Critical Thinking Appraisal:

Description:
Mr. Brown, who lives in the town of Salem, was brought before the Salem municipal court for the sixth time in the past month on a charge of keeping his pool hall open after 1 a.m. He again admitted his guilt and was fined the maximum, $500, as in each earlier instance.
Item:
6. On some nights it was to Mr. Brown's advantage to keep his pool hall open after 1 a.m., even at the risk of paying a $500 fine.[21]

The choices are "true," "probably true," "insufficient data," "probably false," and "false." "Probably true" is the keyed answer. Ennis points out that a more experienced student might select "insufficient data" on the grounds that not enough information is provided to determine probabilities. Like Cathy, this person might think of a variety of possible explanations that, based only on the information given, seem equally probable (or improbable). However, a less experienced student might select "probably true" because he or she "has learned in civics class that people often find it profitable to violate the law and pay the resulting fines, but that fines of that magnitude would deter someone unless it were to the person's advantage to be an offender."[22]

Ennis's response to this kind of problem is twofold. First, in constructing his Cornell critical thinking tests he has tried to restrict the items to areas in which background differences are least likely to result in different choices. Second, to resolve the problem of differentiating between students whose responses differ only in degree of probability, Ennis asks only in which direction, if any, the evidence points. However, he reports that interviews with those who have taken the test show that his efforts have not been wholly successful. Both test makers and test takers may have unstated, implicit background beliefs that influence outcomes; and evaluators may not be in a good position to take these into account.

The obstacles presented by unstated background beliefs are especially troublesome for problems requiring students to identify unstated assumptions. Ennis analyzes another Watson-Glaser item:

"I'm travelling to South America. I want to be sure that I do not get typhoid fever, so I shall go to my physician and get vaccinated against typhoid fever before I begin my trip."
Proposed assumption:
Typhoid fever is more common in South America than it is where I live.

The keyed answer says that this assumption is necessarily made. Ennis points out that a student may reason that it is possible that typhoid fever is more common where the speaker lives but more serious in South America, either because of climate differences or less adequate medical facilities.

As stated, this problem poses even greater difficulties. The reader is asked what the *speaker* is assuming, not what the *reader* would be assuming if he or she made the statement. So, what matters is not what actually is possible concerning typhoid fever, but what the speaker might *believe* is the case. Not only are the reader's background beliefs at issue, but also those of the imaginary speaker—about whom no background information is given. Perhaps, the reader might conjecture, the speaker is worried about getting typhoid fever *before* leaving, realizing that this would interfere with taking the trip. For all we know, the speaker may not even be thinking about the possibility of contracting typhoid fever in South America. (Depending on where the speaker lives, it is even possible that a rash of typhoid fever has broken out, and residents have been encouraged to get vaccinated to reduce the chances of coming down with the fever. Are we to assume that the speaker is from the United States, for example?)

Even questions that do not seem to pose special problems of background assumptions can prove unreliable. Ennis cites this example from the New Jersey Reasoning Skills Test:

> Josie said, "This paper must have been written by a boy, because the handwriting is so bad." Josie must be assuming that
>   a. some boys have poor handwriting.
>   b. only boys have poor handwriting.
>   c. all boys have poor handwriting.

Given only these choices, presumably "b." is the keyed answer. But Ennis points out that a careful thinker might leave the item blank because none of the answers seems right. This person could reason, "Josie might think that there are probably girls somewhere who have poor handwriting—just not here." It might be replied that this is carrying matters too far, that if Josie's statement should be taken as elliptical for a restricted class of boys and girls, so should the answers (e.g., "all boys [in Josie's class] have poor handwriting"). But even if this point is conceded, there is another problem. Josie says that the handwriting is *so* bad, but the choices refer to *poor* handwriting. Josie might have to assume that only boys write *so* poorly, but this assumption hardly entails that only boys write poorly.

Ennis concludes that given all the problems with multiple-choice critical thinking tests, we should not expect good critical thinkers to agree on all test items. However, the *best* critical thinkers, he suggests, will agree at least 85 percent of the time. This is a useful suggestion, but it is not clear that it will help us interpret the test results of particular individuals. When evaluators assume there is one preferred answer for each item, apparently we must concede that many of even the best critical thinkers will have several items marked wrong. Good critical thinkers can be expected to miss even more, so some (perhaps many) good critical thinkers may end up with lower scores than average critical thinkers. This may happen to even some of the best critical thinkers. But if multiple-choice tests provide the only basis for assessing critical thinking, there will be no way to correct for this distortion.

Ennis suggests essay tests as an alternative to standardized multiple-choice tests. Essay tests allow students to explain their answers. Although he rejects John McPeck's dim view of general critical thinking courses, Ennis does agree with two of his suggestions about critical thinking tests. McPeck suggests that "the answer format permit more than one justifiable answer" and evaluators should recognize that "good answers are not predicated on being right, in the sense of true, but on the quality of justification given for a response."[23]

Ennis notes that these two suggestions call for essay tests that must be graded by human experts rather than computers, which poses serious practical problems.[24] First, it is time-consuming. Ennis estimates that trained evaluators can grade at the rate of approximately six minutes per essay, which means it would take fifty hours to grade 5,000 tests. Second, a large pool of evaluators would have to be trained to operate at such a level of efficiency. Third, it is no easy matter to provide assurance of interrater reliability, even if doubts about the validity of the test itself are removed.

Although the idea of essay testing is gaining more adherents, as Ennis points out, this mode of testing is not widely used. But even if it were, additional means of assessment seem necessary. An essay is a "one shot" affair; students write their essays and evaluators read them. Further insight into students' critical thinking can be obtained through discussion, allowing students opportunities to respond to criticism by elaborating on points inadequately developed, indicating how they may have been misunderstood, showing a willingness and ability to change their views in light of challenges, and so on. Ennis suggests two ways such further assessments may be possible. One is through classroom observation, particularly in classes that foster serious discussion among the students. Another is through personal interviews. The first may involve radical reconstruction of the classroom. The second is, again, very time-consuming. Both raise serious questions about interrater reliability.

The fact that methods of evaluation that go beyond standardized multiple-choice tests pose serious problems is not an argument against developing and refining these methods. However, it is clear that at present we do not have much reliable data at the national or state level on the effectiveness of various critical thinking programs. At best, the data we have is incomplete. In addition, insofar as it is based exclusively on multiple-choice testing, it may be seriously distorted.

Worse, many schools today are under pressure to *prove* that they are improving student performance. The common standard of proof is improved scores on standardized tests at the national or state level. This encourages "teaching to the test" or, at the very least, teaching in such a way that students are more likely to get the one "correct" answer. I still vividly recall our daughter Susan, then eleven years old, declaring at the dinner table, "You can't get away with being philosophical in school." One of her supporting examples was from her advanced mathematics class. She was asked to provide the next three numbers in the series 1, 4, 9, 16, . . . She correctly supplied 25, 36, 49. Then Susan's teacher asked her *how* she figured out the answers. Susan explained that she noticed that the differences between numbers in the series were 3, 5, 7, 9, and so on. As she put it, "For each new number, the difference between it and the one before it is 2 more than the difference between that number and the one before it. So each time I just added 2 more than I did the last time." Susan's teacher replied, "That's wrong. You are supposed to square the numbers, starting with 1."

Susan knew how to square numbers, but she also wanted to know why her method would not be right as well. That was the question she asked me, not her teacher. As we drove off to soccer practice, we worked through some of the numbers in our heads. The results of each method matched perfectly up to 12 x 12. When I hesitated to check on how much 13 x 13 is, Susan said, "That's all right, we never have to go past 12 x 12 anyway." She was catching on! What difference did it make if we were not able to carry the process any further? And what difference did it make that neither of us could at the time explain *why* the numbers always match?

Of course, there are teachers who welcome responses like Susan's. Shortly after presenting this example to a group of teachers, I received a very instructive letter from a member of the audience. Acknowledging that math teachers in the lower grades often are not mathematicians, George Christoph added:

No true mathematician would have passed up the chance to prove to your daughter the correctness of her hypothesis. If, in the words of Alfred North Whitehead, "Mathematics is the search for patterns," then surely the discovery of alternative explanations should be a cornerstone in the cognitive growth of a youngster.[25]

Then he presented the following elegant proof:

No. of term	Pattern	Increase over previous No.
1	1	—
2	4	3
3	9	5
4	16	7
5	25	9
n	n^2	$2n-1$

difference added	to	previous term	=	pattern
$(2n-1)$	+	$(n-1)^2$	=	n^2
$2n-1$	+	n^2-2n+1	=	n^2
		n^2	=	n^2

Students with some background in algebra should have little difficulty with this proof. Another approach to the problem is suggested by Socrates in Plato's *Meno*.[26] There Socrates tries to demonstrate that an untutored slave boy can "recollect" certain properties of squares and squaring. First we draw a square. Then we draw a square whose sides are twice the length of the first. The area of the second can be seen to be four times that of the first. That is, four squares the size of the first can be put together to form the second (see Figure 4.1). Now make a square whose sides are three times the length of the first (see Figure 4.2). This time we can see that the total area equals that of nine squares the size of the first. If we make the next square have sides four times the length of the first, we can see that the total area equals sixteen squares the size of the first. (see Figure 4.3). A pattern can now be discerned. Think of adding squares the size of the first one. The second square is formed by adding three more. The third square is formed by adding two more than that (five) to the second. The fourth square is formed by adding two

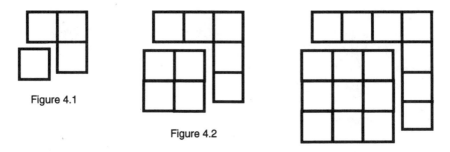

Figure 4.1

Figure 4.2

Figure 4.3

more than the number added to form the third (adding seven rather than five). And so on. Successively larger squares are formed by adding two more than were added to the one just before it: 3, 5, 7, 9, and so on. If this pattern is followed, the resulting square will represent the length of a side squared.

Susan's teacher may have had very good reasons for not wanting to discuss Susan's alternative method. It might have been particularly important to emphasize squaring at that moment. Or, like me, her teacher might not have known at that time why Susan's method also worked. Still, Susan felt rebuffed and unsatisfied. Although she persisted awhile with me, she soon followed the pattern of most students. This situation was just one more lesson in meeting the expectations of teachers. If the reward for coming up with an alternative, if unconventional, method is simply being told that one is mistaken, it does not pay to be very imaginative.

Thus, critical and creative thinking are rather easily discouraged. Encouragement can be quite difficult, especially when doing so requires an unexpected digression from the lesson plan for the day. As already noted, teachers are placed under strictures of accountability. They are told they must make plans, stick to them, and produce measurable results. Some years ago I met with a group of fifty elementary-school teachers to discuss the potential that children have for engaging in philosophical discussion. I showed a videotape of a conversation I had with a group of fifth graders. I begin by asking the students if they believe that computers can think. The main topic of conversation is about relationships between minds, brains, and machines. At one point in the discussion several students reflect on what it might be like to be a cat (a possible intermediary between humans and the nonsensate). For me, a philosopher, the highlight of the discussion was when one of students said we cannot know what it is like to be a cat because if you became a cat for a day, you would only think like a cat. To suppose that you might then say "Oh, this is what a cat feels like" is to fail to take the experiment far enough because "if you do that, you don't know what it feels like because you're still kind of feeling part of a human."

How did the teachers respond to this videotape? Several wanted to know if I often permitted "digressions" like the discussion of what it is like to be a cat. Others commented that they hardly ever have time to allow digressions from lesson plans. Ironically, my audience consisted exclusively of teachers in a program for "gifted and talented" students. If these teachers are not receptive to "digressions," what might be expected from ordinary classrooms?[27]

At every level it seems that there are serious obstacles to encouraging thoroughgoing critical thinking. Although there is much that conspires against it, what is needed is some space for what Floyd Dell calls "idle curiosity." Here is how he characterizes it:

> *The Philosopher.* When Newton looked at his famous apple was there anyone there who said, "Now, Newton, look at this apple, I say! Consider the apple. First, it is round. Second, it is red. Third, it is sweet. This is the Truth about apples. Now let me see if you have grasped what I have told you. What are the three leading facts about apples? What! Don't you remember? Shame on you! I fear I will have to report you to the mayor!"—did anything like that happen?
>
> *The Teacher.* Newton was not a child.
>
> *The Philosopher.* You should have talked to Newton's family about him. This is just what they said he was! . . . Was Newton busy when he lay down under that tree? Did he have an appointment with the apple? Did he say he would give it ten minutes, and come again the next day if it seemed worthwhile? What is disinterested curiosity, in plain English?
>
> *The Teacher.* Idle curiosity, I fear.[28]

FROM IDLE CURIOSITY
TO MORAL REFLECTION

As a way of stimulating discussion I have often presented students with brainteasers, the solution to which require us critically to examine the assumptions we are making. My initial examples might be viewed as falling under the rubric "idle curiosity." However, as will become apparent later, the distance from such examples to those that stimulate moral reflection is remarkably short.

Although sometimes we do need to take things for granted, there are other times when critically examining our assumptions is necessary if we are to handle problems adequately. Here are some examples:

Problem 1. A crime has been committed. There are three, and only three, legitimate suspects: Adams, Baker, and Carr. You know that either Adams or Baker is guilty, but not both. You know that either Baker or Carr is guilty, but not both. Who is guilty?

Problem 2. One of four girls has emptied the cookie jar. Each makes a statement, but one and only one of their statements is true. Here's what they said:

Alice. Betsy did it.
Betsy. Martha did it.
Barb. I didn't do it.
Martha. Betsy lied when she said I did it.

Who emptied the cookie jar?

Problem 1 seems easy enough at first glance. Nearly everyone (adults or children) thinks that it must have been Baker. But, as some students point out, this assumes that the crime was committed by only one person. If we cannot make this assumption, we cannot conclude anything more than either Baker did it alone, or Adams and Carr did it together.

Problem 2 is more complex, but many quickly conclude that Barb must have done it. But can we assume that Betsy was *lying* when she said that Martha did it? What if Betsy mistakenly believed that Martha did it? Then she would not be lying, and Martha's statement would be false; so Alice would have emptied the cookie jar. Although this example has the same frustrating indeterminacy as the first one, it provides an occasion for discussing the concept of lying (a sometimes tricky concept itself).

It might be thought that such examples do more harm than good, suggesting to children that some problems cannot be solved without more information (like good science problems?). But notice that good, solid logic reveals in both cases that we are stuck with two possibilities instead of one definite answer. It is deductive logic combined with a critical examination of assumptions. So some things are quite definite, even though the final answer is not. Only *un*critical thinking permits a final resolution. A steady diet of such irresolution might encourage cynicism, but a few examples should encourage just the sort of "troublemaking" we should expect from critical thinkers. From the indeterminacy of these examples, students might then be encouraged to go on to discuss what further information could help resolve these cases.

Of course, sometimes examining assumptions helps us solve problems. Here is an example:

Problem 3. Take 6 toothpicks of equal length. Without having any toothpick cross any other one, form 4 triangles with equal sides.

This problem can be solved only if we think in three dimensions. Most of us try to arrange the toothpicks on a plane, a two-dimensional surface. A pyramid with a triangular base easily solves the problem. Until students see this, they will be totally frustrated in trying to find a solution. Teachers who want to challenge their students but at the same time enable them to come up with a *partial* solution, might prefer this problem:

MY MOM AND DAD TOLD ME THAT THERE ARE MORE THAN FOUR WORDS IN THIS PARAGRAPH THAT READ THE SAME WHEN REFLECTED IN A MIRROR. BUT THERE MUST BE A SECRET CODE, BECAUSE I CAN FIND ONLY FOUR.

MOM, A, A, and I all work. So everyone can get off to a good start. Many suggest DAD, but others quickly point out that D gets reversed when held up to a mirror. The key assumption that gets in the way of solving the problem is that the puzzle must be held right side up. But nothing says you cannot turn it upside down. CODE works when that assumption is challenged. Students can then be asked why this is so and whether they can think of other words (not in the puzzle) that would work.

Many students like brainteasers like this. In fact, one class would not let me leave until we had run over our scheduled time by thirty minutes. After I had presented my examples, several students challenged me with examples of their own. For example, change "IX" to the number "6" by drawing only one line. I assumed that I had to come up with either "6" or "VI." After it was obvious I was getting nowhere, one of the students came to the board and gleefully wrote "SIX."

Many teachers apparently enjoy sharing brainteasers with their students. Some asked me if I had any more I could leave with them. My fear is that for many students brainteasers are just that—challenging but self-contained exercises in "thinking," a source of amusement but little else. However, when discussing the importance of critically examining our assumptions, they can take on broader significance. In such a context, not only are students trying to solve a challenging puzzle, but they are also reflecting on how they ought to think about problems. That is, they are thinking about their own thinking processes, an important part of critical thinking.

Actually, it is only a short step from seemingly self-contained brainteasers to puzzles about assumptions that clearly have broader implications. A student presented me with just such an example during one of the first sessions I had with a fifth grade class. This example is familiar to old Archie Bunker fans:

> A father and a son are involved in a car accident. Both are seriously injured and require surgery. The doctor enters the room where the boy is and says: "I cannot operate on this child. He is my son." How is this possible?

Students not familiar with the story frequently come up with ingenious answers. Perhaps the doctor is the boy's stepfather, or perhaps the injured father is the boy's stepfather. Or perhaps one of the fathers is a godfather. Or perhaps the injured father is a priest. When this puzzle was first popularized many years ago on the television program "All in the Family," the intended solution occurred to relatively few people—

males or females, adults or children. A sign of some social progress is that today's elementary-school children are much more likely to suggest that the doctor is the boy's mother.

What does this last example illustrate? The session focused on the importance of critically examining assumptions when trying to solve puzzles. The puzzles I offered ranged from innocuous detective stories to geometric puzzles. The student offered an example that addresses a serious social problem, stereotyping. It is also another illustration of hasty generalization. So, by moving us to the social arena, the student opened up the possibility of exploring another area in serious need of critical reflection. Since the assumptions we make about social and professional roles take form rather early in life, exposing them to critical examination should not wait until adulthood.

It should be added that it is not clear to what established precollege discipline this kind of problem belongs. This raises the more general question of where critical thinking might best fit into the schools' curricula, which is the topic of the next chapter.

5
Critical Thinking in the Schools

If we agree that something needs to be done to improve the critical thinking of children, how is this to be accomplished in the schools? On the one hand, a standard view of many who advocate improving critical thinking is to introduce special courses on critical thinking. On the other hand, there are those, like John McPeck, who believe that such courses are seriously misguided; critical thinking instead should be infused in specific disciplines already in place.

McPeck's argument starts from the premise that all *thinking,* critical or otherwise, "is always about some particular thing or subject (let us call this thing X), and that it therefore makes little or no sense to say 'I teach thinking *simpliciter,*' or 'I teach thinking in general but not about anything in particular.' "[1] He concludes:

> Those committed to the standard approach purport to teach courses in critical thinking *simpliciter,* and it doesn't matter what the subject may be about. In my view, this borders on being an absurdity, because there are almost as many ways of thinking as there are things to think about. To claim to teach critical thinking *in general,* even about mundane "everyday problems," is to make promises which cannot be kept.[2]

McPeck's view has two parts, only one of which need be challenged by those favoring separate critical thinking courses. One part is that it is essential that critical thinking be presented within the already existing disciplines in the schools. McPeck's opponents need not challenge this premise. In fact, they should not. There is a need for critical thinking in history classes, in literature classes, in sciences classes, and so on. Advocates of separate critical thinking courses cannot sensibly claim that such courses in and of themselves can take care of the critical think-

74

ing needs in the various disciplines. But McPeck's argument has a second part—viz., that critical thinking courses, as such, do not significantly contribute to developing critical thinkers. He does not deny, however, that critical thinking in one area may carry over to another:

> It is possible that there may be some common elements in the various tasks requiring reasoning, but a little reflection suggests that the *differences* among the kinds of reasoning are far greater, and more obvious, than whatever they may have in common. After the fact, a logician might want to describe some inference by an historian as "inductive," as he might also describe some mathematician's or astronomer's inference as "inductive," but this logical nomenclature is merely a handy *theoretical* (or formal) *description* of the two inferences.[3]

McPeck contends that empirical studies that have tried to discover if there are "transfer-of-training" effects have come up virtually empty. This result, he says, is what common sense would predict and fits nicely within his own conception of critical thinking. He adds, "But the Informal Logic Movement, by contrast, continues to press for its small bag of tricks (e.g., the fallacies, etc.) to make one a critical thinker in any area no matter what the subject matter."[4]

This second part of McPeck's argument calls for several comments. It might be noted first that his broadside against the "Informal Logic Movement" commits two fallacies in the logician's "small bag of tricks." One is the fallacy of "poisoning the well" by substituting pejorative language ("small bag of tricks") for argument. A more serious fallacy here is the "straw man" fallacy of ignoring an opponent's actual position and replacing it with an easily criticizable misrepresentation of the position. As already noted, those who support critical thinking courses cannot sensibly deny the need for critical thinking in already established courses. There is also no reason for them to suppose that critical thinking in those courses is simply a reiteration of what students learn in a critical thinking course. No one can be a critical thinker in an area about which he or she knows little. However, this does not mean that the critical thinking dispositions and skills that are refined in a critical thinking course cannot assist one's critical thinking in other courses.

McPeck seems to believe that there is only a loose relationship between induction in history and induction in science, and at certain levels this is undoubtedly true. However, hasty generalization, ignoring unfavorable evidence, and trying to construct a coherent explanation from bits and pieces of evidence seem to have a great deal in common across disciplines. Methods of verification, falsification, and hypothesis construction may have much in common as well. Ironically, the more McPeck stresses how little different subject areas have in common in regard to critical thinking, the less critical thinking is likely to be encouraged about relationships among these areas. This situation can only exacerbate the problem of an already fragmented curriculum that makes it difficult for students to make sense of their educational experiences as a whole.[5]

It will hardly do for McPeck to cite the lack of empirical evidence of "transfer-of-training" effects from one discipline to another. Both McPeck and his opponents decry the lack of critical thinking in the schools. Common sense would predict a strong correlation between low-level critical thinking and low-level transfer of training, which is the expected consequence of rote learning in particular disciplines that lack mechanisms for critical self-appraisal. Given the low-level critical thinking that McPeck and his opponents claim is prevalent in the schools, it is no wonder that there is little evidence of transfer of training. His hypothesis cannot be tested until the level of critical thinking is significantly raised. Pointing this out is yet another exercise in the kind of critical thinking that McPeck apparently confines to the logician's "little bag of tricks."

On the face of it, McPeck's extreme position seems implausible. For example, the logically flawed processes of hasty generalization and stereotyping cut across a variety of disciplines, even though full understanding of particular examples may often require background in the specific discipline within which they occur. The employment of concepts and principles of critical thinking that cut across the disciplines can aid students not only in thinking critically *in* particular disciplines, but also *between* them. Many problems that call for critical thinking lie between disciplines, at least as they are traditionally conceived. For example, at the adult level, within what disciplines do questions concerning the appropriate use of high technology lie? Physics? Chemistry? Engineering? Biology? Medicine? Economics? Political Science? Anthropology? Religion? Philosophy? And which disciplines at the precollege level are helping to prepare our children to address these questions as they move from childhood to adulthood?

However, we need not frame the question about the place of critical thinking in "either/or" terms. Critical thinking courses can be valuable in their own right. But they will mean little unless critical thinking is encouraged in the already established disciplines as well. It might be argued that everything that can be accomplished in a critical thinking course can be incorporated within particular disciplines. As a practical proposal, this approach seems an unlikely prospect. There is little reason to think that sufficient time will be taken in particular disciplines to attend to not only the critical thinking needs peculiar to a given discipline, but also to relationships among the disciplines and to everyday life as well. A course in critical thinking cannot do all of this either. However, contrary to McPeck's worries, advocates of separate critical thinking courses can agree.

Although McPeck's argument against separate critical thinking courses fails, there is a practical argument that must be taken seriously: the problem of finding space within an already crowded curriculum for yet another course. Some, such as Matthew Lipman, argue that philosophy deserves a regular place in the K-12 curriculum, which is the approach of the IAPC programs. If philosophy were given its own space, it could be expected to be a centerpiece for critical thinking, as this is one of the central (but not only) features of philosophical thought. Due largely to the efforts of IAPC over the past twenty years, many schools are experimenting with philosophy as a subject in its own right. However, this trend is still quite unusual, and it is likely to remain so for some time. Meanwhile, there is much that can be done now within the already established curricular areas. In the next section I have selected science education for special attention. The benefits of including critical thinking in already established disciplines are no more evident than in the sciences, especially insofar as this might enable science education and moral education to join forces.

SCIENCE EDUCATION AND MORAL EDUCATION

Michael Martin argues that good science education and moral education are mutually supportive.[6] On the one hand, good science education contributes to moral reflection and decision-making by promoting inquiry and discovery skills that enable us to acquire relevant factual information, to test hypotheses, and to weigh the likely consequences of alternative choices. Good science education promotes clarity, thoroughness, perseverance, respect for sound reasoning, impartiality, and open-mindedness—all valuable assets for morality as well.

On the other hand, moral education promotes values essential to good science education. Honesty, fairness, and cooperativeness are all virtues necessary for good scientific practice. Fellow scientists and others depend on the honest reporting of data. It is a matter of fairness (and honesty) to give proper credit to the work of others. Scientists typically work in teams, or at the very least depend on the work of others in furthering their own. Furthermore, questions need to be asked about appropriate or inappropriate scientific research and its resulting technological use. These questions concern biomedical research and treatment, experimentation on humans and animals, military research and the development of weaponry, the use of various forms of energy, environmental quality, and the entire range of scientific activity that can significantly affect public health, safety, and welfare.

These are all matters that concern responsible scientists as well as responsible citizens in general. What better place could there be to begin reflecting on these issues than in classes that could provide the relevant scientific understanding needed to address the moral issues in a well-informed, responsible manner? Michael Martin urges that such reflection begin as early as elementary school, where children may be introduced to possibly problematic ways of conducting scientific inquiry. He worries about the failure to address the underlying moral issues in, for example, animal experimentation:

> Typically, young science students are not made aware by their teachers that there may be moral issues involved in killing or starving members of other species. Indeed, far from science education making young scientists more sensitive to such issues, science courses may kill some children's natural sensitivity to injuring other species because of the callous disregard of the moral issues by the teachers and textbooks.[7]

In Chapter 3 I discussed Harry Stottlemeier's difficulty in answering his teacher's question about Halley's comet. He was daydreaming when his teacher referred to the name of this object with a tail that goes around the sun every seventy-seven years. So he tries to figure out the answer by making an inference from something he knew. Harry comes up with the wrong answer, but he wants to know how his reasoning has misled him, which launches a set of philosophical quests by Harry and his classmates. It is easy to overlook the fact that it is in science class that Harry's philosophical curiosity was aroused; and it is Mr. Spence, the math teacher, who frequently allows his class to explore philosophical ideas. Should such explorations be regarded as digressions from what should be going on in such classes, or might philosophical thinking have something to contribute to the study of science and math? My answer is that although science and math classes typically do not allow much time for such explorations, these subjects can be enriched by encouraging them. Here I will focus on science education.[8]

Science is always "in the making." A fundamental part of science education is learning what has already been discovered in, say, biology, chemistry, or physics. However, science should include more. It should also explore what it is to be a scientist—to make discoveries of one's own, to attempt to confirm or disconfirm current hypotheses, to depend on the findings of others in undertaking one's own work, to share one's results with others, and to be trusted to do good scientific work. These explorations focus on science as an activity undertaken by communities of scientists rather than simply as bodies of knowledge, making it clear that science (or at least good science) has a considerable investment in moral values, most especially honesty and commitment to the pursuit of truth. These values have to do with the ways in which scientists conduct themselves, regardless of what their subject of pursuit might be. But, of course, moral questions can also be raised about appropriate and inappropriate subjects of pursuit. Here the concerns of scientists join with those of nonscientists, those whose lives are affected by the work scientists do.

It is important to bear in mind that science education is not just for those who plan to become scientists. It is for everyone. Furthermore, science education should include more than the empirical study of science; there are important value questions to consider as well. As we become more and more dependent on high technology, there is a growing problem of scientific and technological literacy. Quite apart from concern about whether we are turning out enough scientifically and technologically trained students to keep up competitively at the international level, there are fundamental value questions that need to be addressed. These questions are of two sorts. First, there are questions about the appropriate development and use of technology. For example, is genetic engineering desirable and, if so, in what areas and with what limitations? Is the development of technology for the use of nuclear energy desirable and, if so, in what areas and to what extent? Science and technology can move in many different directions. Which are the most desirable—and for whose (and what) benefit and at whose (and what) risk of harm?

Second, there are questions about the role of citizens in a democratic society who must wrestle with questions of this first sort. How well are we doing at fostering an informed, thoughtful citizenry who can participate meaningfully in addressing issues about the appropriate development and use of technology? Not very well—either in very general terms or in regard to more specific areas of concern such as medical technology or the generation and disposal of waste.

These are not new problems. More than thirty years ago the National Education Association's Educational Policies Commission urged, "What is being advocated here is not the production of more physicists, biologists, or mathematicians, but rather the development of a person whose approach to life as a whole is that of a person who thinks—a rational person."[9] Thus conceived, a rational person could be anyone, not just someone with special expertise. Still, such a person, whether scientist or not, needs to know something about science—and more than most of our students do today. Equally important, science education should include more than what is standardly thought of as science per se. What can this mean?

Michael Martin argues that science education should aim at helping us apply the scientific spirit to all relevant contexts—scientific, practical, moral, and even religious:

An excellent physicist who is mindless and uncritical in buying his son a bike or himself a new car is deficient not just in his consumer education. There is something profoundly lacking in his science education. He would not dream of accepting a new physical theory without careful evaluation of the evidence. Yet he accepts the claims of the manufacturer without a qualm. . . . Similarly, a good chemist who is uncritical of some simple-minded answer to a certain complex moral problem is not just lacking in his moral education, but is also deficient in his scientific education. The well-trained scientific mind would consider the alternatives and the relevant evidence in considering an answer to a problem in chemistry or morality.[10]

Martin suggests that consumer education and some aspects of moral education should be considered parts of science education. He emphasizes the contributions that scientific thinking can make to resolving consumer and moral problems. This is a reasonable suggestion, but only if it is not taken to imply that science always has the last word. Many consumer and moral problems are best viewed as framing a value context within which scientific issues themselves acquire their significance and urgency. For example, it is because we *value* health that the scientific quest for causes and cures of certain diseases is so highly valued. (Even the words "health" and "disease" have connotations that go beyond a value-neutral scientific characterization.)

If education should aim at helping students become rational (or, as I prefer to put it, reasonable) persons, it seems clear enough that the whole person—as scientific-minded, practical, moral, and religious—must be taken into account. In this context, the role of science in education takes on a rather different cast than students usually see. Recall the "common system of 'learning'" that David Benjamin and Jeremy Scott complain about: "listen, take notes, memorize, and regurgitate facts." They found some consolation in studying Thomas Nagel's *What Does It All Mean?*:

We had long been led to believe that science could explain all aspects of the natural world. But having read [Nagel's book], we found that science is not able to answer all of our questions about the world. While looking for viable solutions, we were forced to use careful reasoning and to arrive at conclusions which were consistent with our lives. This type of reasoning carried over into aspects other than philosophy, where it proved to be just as effective. Thus, our introduction to philosophy raised our awareness of the world around us and helped us attain a more thorough method of reasoning.[11]

As already noted, they felt a need for a broader perspective than they had been receiving in school because they "were facing some difficult problems involving ethics and justice." Some of these problems, no doubt, were related to what they were (or, perhaps, should have been) studying in science classes.

Actually, Thomas Nagel's *What Does It All Mean?* was David Benjamin and Jeremy Scott's second introduction to philosophy. They had already read *Harry Stottlemeier's Discovery* as fifth graders. Although *Harry* deals with thinking skills and topics that can contribute to science education, the IAPC materials that are explicitly addressed to science education are designed for third and fourth graders. *Kio and Gus* is the novel for the IAPC program called "Reasoning About Nature," and the accompanying workbook is called *Wondering at the World.*[12] Gus is blind. She and Kio, along with older siblings and Kio's grandparents, share experiences that focus largely on our relationship to the natural environment, with a special emphasis on our relationship to animals. IAPC characterizes its workbook as "helping children think about the world by encouraging them to acquire reasoning and inquiry skills. Through hundreds of exercises and discussion plans, children are shown how these cognitive skills can be applied to the concepts by means of which we understand the world of nature."[13]

Some examples from the workbook nicely illustrate how *Wondering at the World* departs significantly from the kind of science education about which David Benjamin and Jeremy Scott complain. Each of these examples begins with a leading idea that is triggered by a specific passage in *Kio and Gus*. The leading idea is then followed by a series of questions or exercises designed to stimulate class discussion. Here is one about beavers:

> The beaver is a rodent found in Europe and North America. Beavers have thick fur, round heads, small ears, and a scaly, flattened tail. (Their tails are generally about 6 inches wide and 10 inches long. Beavers use their tails as rudders while swimming, as support while gnawing trees, or to slap water in order to warn other beavers of danger.) Beavers weigh from 40 to 50 pounds apiece. American beavers build twig and mud "lodges" with underwater entrances. If the water is too shallow, the beavers construct dams made of tree trunks or mud.[14]

This description of beavers is well suited for the common system of "learning" David Benjamin and Jeremy Scott object to. With the aid of pictures of beavers at work, students might have their curiosity aroused to the point of making the entire exercise painless, if not rather pleasant.

What else, one might ask, could we do with such a passage? The workbook suggests several possibilities. Some thought experiments could be performed: "If you were a beaver, would you gnaw trees?"; "If you were a beaver, would you build dams?"; "If you were a beaver, would you have a flat tail?"; "If beavers could fly, would that make them birds?" What can be gained from such thought experiments? Among other things, students are invited to undertake some conceptual analysis (Are all flying animals birds?); they are encouraged to reflect about what is possible (Could there by a flying beaver?); and they are prodded to engage in imaginative thinking (Imagine you are now a beaver).

Encouraging imaginative thinking can have exciting results. Trying to imagine what it would be like to be a beaver might promote empathic understanding of other species. But it might also help students recognize serious limitations in this regard, as one of the discussions with my group of fifth graders illustrates. I asked the students what they thought it might be like to be a cat. After several students offered standard responses with an anthropomorphic strain, Carlen pondered, "I've always wondered, if I were ever a cat, if other cats speak. When we hear them say 'meow, meow,' they say 'meow, meow' to us. But when they hear us say something, they may say, 'What is that?' " Rick carried this a step further:

It's hard to think if a cat would say, "I wonder what those people sound like." They may not even know what people are. They may just go *buhlalalal*a inside their minds. We don't know it. Like, if you had a wish and you wished you were an animal, you'd probably think like yourself and say, "Oh, *this* is what a cat feels like." But, then if you do that, you don't know what it feels like because you're still feeling part of a human. So you would wish you were just like a cat for one whole day with the natural instincts of a cat and you don't know anything about humans. You'd act like a cat, and you wouldn't really know any human words or anything, unless cats do.

What Carlen and Rick are doing is questioning what the other students seem to take for granted—namely, that we *can* understand what it is like to be a cat. In the process of articulating their worries, they are not only on the edge of the classic philosophical problem of other minds, they are also attempting to work their way out of the egocentric thinking that Jean Piaget claims dominates the thinking of young children and infects our thinking throughout our lives. Resisting egocentric tendencies is, of course, important for successful social relationships and for social understanding generally, but it is also important for understanding and evaluating scientific claims to objectivity.[15]

As Carlen and Rick's comments about what it might be like to be a cat show, even straightforward, descriptive statements, like the passage about beavers, can be used to stimulate serious philosophical discussions which in turn raise important questions about the nature and limits of scientific inquiry. But *Wondering at the World* sometimes directly raises controversial issues. Consider "Chicken Farming," the leading idea in the workbook:

> Chickens are raised for both meat and eggs. In modern poultry farms, chickens spend their entire lives in tiny pens. They lay their eggs, then they are slaughtered for their meat. Opponents of this practice call it "factory farming" and object to it on the ground that it is cruel to these birds to treat them in this fashion.[16]

This passage is followed by a series of factual statements that students are invited to assess in regard to their relevance in sorting out the pros and cons of factory farming. For example:

- Chickens do not seem to be very intelligent.
- Most people like to eat chickens.
- Vegetarians don't eat meat, and that includes chickens.
- Chickens evidently can feel pain.
- Some people say that animals have rights.
- If farmers couldn't raise chickens, they'd lose money.
- Some people say that chickens don't complain.
- Some people say chickens are fed harmful chemicals, so when you eat a chicken, you eat those chemicals.

Students are asked to discuss the relevance or irrelevance of these (or other) factual claims with respect to the issue at hand. What is expected is that they will then attempt to give reasoned support for whatever conclusions they draw, thus developing and exercising critical judgment.

Some might object that such discussions can cause trouble on the home front. What if Amy comes home and declares she will no longer eat meat? One reply is that some children do this without the benefit of such discussions anyway, and it is unlikely that many children will have no acquaintance with the idea of not eating meat. But, objectors might continue, why encourage this behavior? This question deserves several responses. First, it is not obvious that refusal to eat meat will be prompted by such discussions. But let us suppose it will in some cases. If this resulted from an adult discussion of the same issue, would we say that such discussions should not take place? How is it different with children? To say that children are too young to understand and appreciate the nuances of the issues is to adopt a condescending attitude toward their critical thinking abilities. Although there are some sensitive and controversial areas that children may not be ready to discuss, it is not clear why this is one of them. Furthermore, not permitting such a discussion in effect stacks the deck against vegetarianism as children move into adulthood, since by then most will have been spared the need to question how the basic foods for which they now have a long-standing appetite are made so readily available. If, as adults, we acknowledge that factory farming poses ethical problems, we might well ask whether we have the right to deny children opportunities to discuss these problems, while at the same time permitting a vested interest in the form of eating habits to settle in uncritically.

The chicken farming example illustrates that encouraging critical thinking does risk rocking the boat somewhat, which may be why enthusiasm for critical thinking in the schools is not universally shared in our society. However, if these issues are avoided by the schools, how are children to prepare themselves for responsibly coping with the complex, problem-filled world in which we all reside? Voting begins at eighteen. Postponing the development of critical thinking until then is not a promising idea for a democratic society.

Another example from *Wondering at the World* is a leading idea with the heading "Garbage and Sewage." All children know about garbage, and most know something about sewers. But it is unlikely that many (children or adults) know as much about either as they should. Here is an informational passage from the workbook:

> Every community has its "sanitation department," which is responsible for collecting the garbage left for collection by house-holders. (Sanitation workers distinguish between "trash," which is broken or junked materials, paper goods, etc., and "garbage," which contains the remnants of foodstuffs.) The sewage disposal problem is dealt with differently: each community has sewers which collect the sewage from each household and bring it to a central point for treatment. After treatment, it may be disposed of in rivers or streams. But many communities still dump raw, untreated sewage into rivers and oceans, and often the treatment provided is inadequate.
>
> Cities are responsible for about 20 percent of the water pollution problem. The pollution they dump in the water sources reduces the oxygen that is dissolved in the water, and this in turn makes it impossible for fish to live in such water.[17]

The discussion questions accompanying this passage deal primarily with considering alternatives, including what individuals might do if garbage collection ceased or sewers were closed. It is but a short step from these questions to value questions about environmental concerns.

Although a science class can confine itself primarily to descriptions of scientific and technological matters, such descriptions in environmental areas are well-suited for value inquiry as well. For example, several years ago the Michigan Environmental Education Association, with the support of Western Michigan University's Science for Citizens Center, made an effort to integrate the study of chemistry with concern for values. One educational product for high-school chemistry classes is entitled "Hazardous Wastes and the Consumer Connection."[18] This publication begins with something familiar to all consumers: the use of paper and plastic bags. Is the use of one preferable to the other? As long as we raise no questions about how bags are produced or disposed of, it is unlikely that many will have strong preferences for one kind of bag over the other. "Hazardous Wastes and the Consumer Connection" describes the science and technology involved, connecting paper bags with the wood pulp processing industry and plastic bags with the petroleum industry. It also discusses pollution problems associated with the disposal of each kind of bag. Next the publication raises questions about responsible consumer choice and alternatives for minimizing the adverse impact on the environment.

Publications like "Hazardous Wastes and the Consumer Connection" illustrate how the study of science and technology can be naturally linked with value inquiry. They also show the importance of making such links. Although the kind of philosophical reflection encouraged by the IAPC programs is no substitute for scientific and technological education, it can serve a valuable complementary role. Like ecology, philosophy seeks to understand connections and to develop comprehensive perspectives. Philosophy also raises fundamental questions about how we should live our lives, and it attempts to answer these questions in a reflective manner. Philosophical reflection about relationships among science, technology, and values cannot operate in a factual vacuum. But philosophical reflection itself makes this evident. At the same time, this reflection makes clear what is at stake in developing scientific and technological literacy, thereby helping students understand both why they need science education and why that education should not be divorced from value inquiry.

6
Families, Schools,
and Moral Education

The seeds, as it were, of moral discernment are planted in the mind by him that made us. They grow up in their proper season, and are at first tender and delicate and easily warped. Their progress depends very much upon their being duly cultivated and properly exercised.
—*Thomas Reid*, Essays on the Active Powers of the Mind, *1788*

Especially at the elementary-school level, moral education is regarded by many as a matter of "instilling" or "implanting" moral values. Fearing moral indoctrination, some reject the idea that moral education belongs in the public schools. But, as we have seen, moral education in the schools need not be a form of indoctrination. It can be much more like studying morality than having moral values "implanted." But this requires acknowledging, with Thomas Reid, that the "seeds of moral discernment" are present even in the early school years. What is needed are opportunities for children's powers of moral discernment to be "duly cultivated and properly exercised."

Moral discernment is highly valued. We value it in ourselves and others as a mark of reasonableness. But, as Reid says metaphorically, it is only the *seeds* of moral discernment that are "planted in the mind by him that made us."[1] We naturally look to children's caretakers, typically their families, to nourish and protect these seeds while they are so tender, delicate, and easily warped. But this is the language of passivity. To understood fully what Reid means by the seeds of moral discernment "being duly cultivated and properly exercised," we must view children as agents, not merely patients.

In some contexts "cultivated" implies passivity. For example, a field is cultivated by a farmer. It does not cultivate itself. In an educational context teachers might attempt to cultivate appreciation and judgment in their students. However, children can be encouraged to do this for themselves. If moral discernment is a mark of reasonableness, it is clear that at some point children themselves must begin to exercise their powers of judgment—that is, to develop their capacity to think for themselves—and in this they cannot remain passive.[2]

Throughout this book I am trying to sustain the view that moral education belongs within the larger task of helping children develop their capacity for reasonableness. However, this task cannot be done without addressing the concerns families have about the moral development of their children. These include worries about whether it is the business of the schools to enter into the arena of moral education at all. Actually, it is unavoidable that the schools do so to some extent. The real question is how they can do this in a responsible manner.

WHOSE RESPONSIBILITY?

Whose responsibility is it to duly cultivate and properly exercise children's "seeds of moral discernment"? A short answer is: Those who bear primary responsibility for the education of children. A moment's reflection reveals that this short answer requires a rather lengthy explanation. Who does bear primary responsibility for the moral education of children? I will focus on three major candidates. The first is obvious, the second is controversial, and the third is typically underestimated, if not overlooked entirely: they are families, schools, and children themselves.

Families are recognized by law to have a right to morally nurture their children. For example, in the exercise of this right, families may establish rules of behavior for their children, extend or restrict privileges, monitor television viewing, read their children stories with moral messages, and take their children to the church of their choice. Families can also fail to exercise this right responsibly. In cases of child abuse legal intervention may be justified. However, there are more subtle ways in which families can fail responsibly to exercise the right to morally nurture their children. They can simply fail to attend carefully to those aspects of their children's lives that need moral nurturing. Young children may be left too much on their own, they may be unloved even if they are not beaten, and so on. Much of this neglect may go unnoticed by others, and even when noticed, it may be unclear to what extent, if any, legal intervention is permissible. Still, we need not conclude that as long as their behavior is shielded by law, families are fulfilling the moral responsibilities they have to their children.[3] Since a legally recognized right to morally nurture children creates a protected zone for families, it seems reasonable to insist that there is an accompanying moral responsibility to exercise that right responsibly.[4] This is especially so given the obvious dependency and vulnerability of children and the substantial legal power families have to govern the lives of their children.

Of course, nothing said so far implies that *only* families have a legal right to morally nurture children. Families may acknowledge that others, too, have such a right by sending their children to accredited private schools. What about the public schools? In the absence of an approved alternative, the state legally requires children to attend the public schools. Thus, the state accords public schools a right and responsibility to provide a major portion of the education of children. To what extent, if any, should this be understood to include the moral education of children?

Here opinion sharply divides. Oddly, the voices of children are seldom heard or even represented in these disagreements. Yet surely at some point in their formal education, children become moral agents with rights and responsibilities of their own. Full acknowledgement of this strengthens the case for according public schools the right and responsibility to provide an environment within which the "seeds of moral discernment" can be, as Reid puts it, "duly cultivated and properly exercised."

Since national surveys consistently reveal that more than 80 percent of the parents in our society favor some sort of moral education in the schools, we might be tempted to conclude that there already is a virtual mandate for the public schools to place moral education explicitly on their agendas.[5] However, because of the vast differences of opinion about just what is to count as moral education, it is not clear what, if any, mandate there is. For example, many believe morality and religion are inseparable. If they agree with the doctrine of the separation of church and state, they may fear that "secular humanist" teachers will, unwittingly perhaps, undermine the religious foundation of their children's morality. So, if they nevertheless favor moral education in the schools, they will be wary of just how this is to be done (and by whom). Others may simply insist that moral education has no place in state-supported, public schools. Private, sectarian schools, however, are another matter, and that is where they will send their children. Still others might wish to overturn the doctrine of the separation of church and state so that moral education, in full religious dress, may be brought into the public schools.[6]

But even those who believe that morality and religion can and should be separated in a public-school setting may have very different ideas about moral education in the schools. Some believe it is the job of the schools to "indoctrinate" students with certain values. Their detractors object to this as reinforcing a kind of mindless absolutism. Others favor "values clarification," the aim of which is to help students clarify the values they already hold, while at the same time withholding critical evaluation of those values.[7] Their detractors often charge that this approach implicitly reinforces mindless relativism.[8]

Given these controversies, it is no wonder that some families insist that the moral education of their children is their responsibility, and that the public schools should not interfere. However, I argue that they are mistaken in this opinion. In making my case, I suggest a path between the contending parties that at the same time addresses their fears. Three basic points can be made. First, moral education in the public schools should, among other things, strive to help students become reasonable persons. Reasonable people can deeply disagree about many things, including religion. So, aside from any constitutional guarantees, there is good reason for public schools to respect religious differences. Second, helping students become reasonable persons is the most effective way of fighting the twin specters of mindless absolutism and mindless relativism. It would be odd to think of a reasonable person as a *mindless* absolutist or relativist. Whatever attraction such a person might have toward any form of absolutism or relativism would involve some degree of reflection or thoughtfulness. So, the best defense against either form of mindlessness would seem to be to help students develop their capacity to be reasonable. Third, in a pluralist society such as ours, families that attempt to "go it alone" with the moral education of their children are unlikely to succeed—at least not in a way that will serve their children well.

CIVIC EDUCATION: A LINK
BETWEEN SCHOOL AND FAMILY

There is a place where the legitimate concerns of public education and families clearly join. Public education in our society is sustained by a political system committed to certain individual liberties and democratic decision-making.[9] In turn, public education is legitimately expected to help sustain that system by preparing children for citizenship. This is the function of civic education, which aims at helping students acquire the necessary understanding and skills for effective, responsible participation in a constitutional democracy.[10] What, then, are the values civic education should emphasize? Robert Fullinwider suggests the following: the capacity to make independent, rational judgments about civic matters; respect for the rights of others; and the capacity to discuss and defend political views that may differ from one's own.[11]

These civic values form an important part of the social virtue of reasonableness.[12] Civic education's concern for the reasonableness of students joins with the family's concern for the moral development of its children. This is so for several reasons. First, civic values such as respect for the rights of persons are themselves moral values. Thus, no clear separation of civic and moral education is possible. Second, as Fullinwider amply shows, the dispositions that civic education encourages do not, in fact, confine themselves to the civic arena. For example, the ability to discuss and defend political views is not an ability to discuss and defend *only* that. Once encouraged, the critical thinking skills exhibited in the civic arena are likely to show up anywhere. And just as these skills are assets in the political arena, they are assets in other areas of life as well. In any case, if the point of encouraging the critical thinking of children is to help them become more reasonable, then moral education should be seen as an explicit part of the broader educational agenda of the schools. Third, families should want their children to grow up to be well-developed, moral persons.

Finally, we need to consider the perspective of children themselves. They have a *right* to be given opportunities to become well-developed, moral persons.[13] This right is as basic as the right to be given opportunities to develop the ability to read, write, or compute. Families that do not want or do not care whether their children become well-developed, moral persons pose a special problem. The failure of such families to provide adequate opportunities, or their active interference with this, can only strengthen the case for the schools providing such opportunities. And the case for the schools is even stronger if, as seems likely, even the most conscientious families cannot by themselves provide adequate opportunities.

Of course, being a well-developed, moral person involves more than reasonableness, but in our pluralistic society it may be difficult to specify what else is essential. Not all values are specifically moral values, and there is no reason to insist on uniformity across persons. But even within morality there may be many different ways of satisfying plausible criteria for being a well-developed, moral person, and reasonable people might even disagree about some of the criteria. However, broad consensus about some basic features in addition to reasonableness may be attainable. Here are three more candidates:

1. Self-respect.
2. A capacity to resist, if not overcome, egocentricity in circumstances calling for moral sensitivity and judgment.
3. Commitment to other-regarding values (e.g., respect for others, justice, beneficence) with appropriate supportive virtues (e.g., considerateness, compassion, fair-mindedness, benevolence).

Although distinguishable, these features are not independent of one another. In addition, each has a special relationship to reasonableness. For example, someone who is seriously deficient in other-regarding values will not be viewed as a reasonable person. And someone who is excessively egocentric will have distorted other-regarding values and thereby lack reasonableness. Finally, the acknowledgement and appreciation by others that one has the virtue of reasonableness can contribute to one's self-respect.

If reasonableness is one of the virtues families should want their children to acquire, it is indeed a tall order for families to "go it alone." Without the assistance of the kind of civic education Fullinwider describes, how are children to develop the capacity to understand and discuss views different from those they encounter in the smaller circles within which their families may try to enclose them? Nevertheless, families obviously play a crucial role in determining the extent to which children grow up to be well-developed moral persons. On the negative side, various forms of child abuse (physical and psychological) can impede this development, as can parental neglect or absence. Parental modeling of behavior and attitudes can have either a positive or negative effect, as can that of other older family members.[14] If reasonableness is a desired outcome, then inductive modeling is likely to prove most effective.[15] This requires both exhibiting the desired types of attitude or behavior and providing the child with reasons for embracing them. Finally, on the positive side, the unconditional love that parents have for their children is a fundamental source of self-respect and self-esteem.[16]

Thus, en route to becoming well-developed, moral persons, children need from their families good modeling, love and support, and the absence of abuse and neglect. However necessary these might be, they are not sufficient. Taking only these elements into account, the child is portrayed largely as a *patient,* someone to whom something is happening or for whom something is being done. But at some point the child as *agent* must enter the scene. So, we might ask, when does the child "get in on the act"? We need to ask not just what is to be done to and for children, but also what might enable them to do things for themselves.

CHILDREN AS MORAL AGENTS

The four features of a well-developed, moral person outlined above clearly portray the person as an agent, not merely a patient. To encourage the development of these features, it is important to recognize the earliest appearance of those affective and cognitive capacities that are essential to that development.[17] Children's moral learning is well under way before they enter school. They learn about sharing toys, taking turns, distributing dessert fairly, doing household chores, being kind to their pets, helping an elderly neighbor, and so on. This helps prepare them for similar concerns at school—sharing materials, school government, privileges and rights, punishments and rewards, social relationships, and the like. Sorting through and refining one's thinking about such matters is not typically just an intellectual exercise.[18] These are concerns that are of great practical importance to children.

"That's just it," an objector might say. "The problem is that these things do matter to children—too much, in fact. Children aren't ready for reasonable discussion of such issues. Aristotle is right, first they need to be habituated—their passions have to be brought under control by good habits. Give them firm rules and reinforce them. Then, much later, such matters can be discussed." This reasoning underestimates children in two respects. First, it assumes that they do not already have some rather stable moral dispositions by the time they enter school. Second, it assumes that reflection and discussion can contribute little to the refinement of the dispositions that are already somewhat in place. It is again to view children as patients rather than agents.[19]

Fortunately, there is now a great deal of empirical evidence that these assumptions are not warranted. Ask any group of five- to ten-year-old children what they think about lying or fairness, for example, and marvel at the range of thoughtful responses.[20] It is often difficult to see what basic moral distinctions they leave out that adults would put in. For example, favoritism, taking more than one's fair share, not taking turns, listening to only one side of the story, jumping to conclusions, not treating equals equally (and unequals unequally), and the like are readily volunteered as kinds of unfairness.

Still, there is no necessary connection between moral thought and action. A crucial part of the mix is the social environment. Since families constitute only a part of that environment (especially once the child is school-age), it is clear that any adequate account of how children might grow into well-developed, moral persons must focus on much more than the family. The family itself plays a fundamental role, but it is to be hoped that families and schools can work together in encouraging the moral development of children. However, two worries about families should be mentioned—that families contribute either too little or too much to the process.

First, the worry about too little: Families may provide little or no love for and acceptance of their children. They may sustain an environment ranging from indifference to abuse. And they may provide little or no positive modeling. The causes may be various (e.g., poverty, lack of education, family breakdown), but in such circumstances children are bound to be shortchanged. Through a strong natural constitution, strong support outside the family, or good luck, many children in these families will nevertheless grow up to be well-developed moral persons. Many others, however, may not. External support from the schools, social services, or the law may be helpful. In any case, it is unrealistic to expect each family on its own to be able or willing to work things out in the best interests of the child. Government, social services, schools, and family law must work together in trying to provide needed assistance.

Second, the worry about too much: Families can attempt to be too supportive and protective of their children. A family may try to protect its children from an external world perceived to be hostile to what the family's adults most value and want for their children. Or, as already mentioned, the family's adults may be convinced that moral education belongs exclusively in the home. Thus, deliberate attempts by the schools to undertake some of the tasks of moral education are viewed with suspicion and may be vigorously opposed.

EMPOWERING CHILDREN

The cost of trying to keep moral education out of the schools is likely to be high. Deliberately or not, moral values are reinforced (or undermined) in the schools. Cheating is discouraged, respect for students and teachers is encouraged, and so on. In short, educational institutions depend for their viability on the acceptance of basic moral values, values that may or may not match up well with values found in the corridors, the playgrounds, and the streets between home and school—or even in the homes of some children. To expect this situation to work out favorably without moral education being explicitly placed on the educational agenda is quite optimistic.

Thomas Reid notes that our "power of reasoning, which all acknowledge to be one of the most eminent natural faculties of man, . . . appears not in infancy."[21] This capacity, like that of moral discernment, also needs to be duly cultivated and properly exercised. The recent hue and cry that the schools are failing to help students develop critical thinking skills echoes Reid's observation. So there is a nationwide call for getting beyond rote learning. Hardly anyone would oppose critical thinking in the schools—as long as it can stay away from the moral concerns. But schools should not try to prevent critical thinking from entering the moral domain. To deprive students of opportunities in the schools to reflect critically on moral issues is to deprive them of an educational right as basic as any other. No one seriously suggests that students should be legally required to go to school but that math and science education have no place there. Why should it be any different if we substitute "moral education" for "math and science education"? If the answer is that most parents cannot handle the math and science education of their children all by themselves, the same is true of moral education.

Moral education agendas developed exclusively in the home may result in children's overdependency on their families for moral support. The kind of autonomous, critical thinking that children are likely to need once they leave the home to lead their own lives may be blunted by a family that itself exhibits highly egocentric thinking. Although not an inevitable consequence of the morally insular family, the risk of children emerging who are not well equipped to deal with the complexities of a pluralist society is substantial. Finally, we should ask, what about those children whose homes provide little, if any, moral support?

It cannot be the schools' responsibility somehow to make up for everything that the home may fail to provide children. However, the schools can play a major role in contributing to the development of reasonableness in children. For the schools to do well in this endeavor, it is necessary for them to treat children as already capable of some degree of reasonableness even when they first enter school. The aim, then, should be to help them improve this capacity, not to create it for them.

STORIES

We are greatly indebted to Matthew Lipman and Gareth Matthews for their ground-breaking books about the philosophical abilities of children. Equally important, Lipman's novels and workbooks have inspired teachers around the world by modeling what children's philosophical inquiry in the classroom can become, and Matthews's reviews of children's literature remind us of the philosophical riches that can be found in already existing children's literature, if only our eyes are open to them.[22]

Stories have always played an important role in the moral education of children, especially in regard to portraying moral character. Character education is very much on people's minds these days, as evidenced by President Bill Clinton's signing of the Elementary and Secondary Act of 1994.[23] Commenting on bipartisan efforts to bring character education into the schools, the president urged:

We disagree about a lot of things, but we ought to be able to agree that our schools should say people should tell the truth. They should respect themselves and each other. They ought to be good citizens, which means that we should assume responsibility for obeying the law and for helping others to develop themselves and each other. We ought to practice fairness and tolerance and trustworthiness. These things should be taught in our schools, and we shouldn't gag our teachers when they try to do it.[24]

Indeed, honesty, trustworthiness, fairness, self-respect, respect for others, helpfulness, and a sense of responsibility are all welcome virtues that contribute to the virtue I am calling reasonableness. The schools can, and should, play an important role in encouraging them.

Thomas Lickona credits much of the renewed public interest in character education to a perception that society's moral problems are on the increase:

Escalating moral problems in society—ranging from greed and dishonesty to violent crime to self-destructive behaviors such as drug abuse and suicide—are bringing about a new consensus. Now, from all across the country, from private citizens and public organizations, from liberals and conservatives alike, comes a summons to the schools: Take up the role of moral teachers of our children.[25]

There are many ways in which teachers might take up this role, ranging from establishing and enforcing rules of conduct that require honesty, respect, and the like, to serving as role models, to discussing moral values in the classroom. Each of these deserves careful attention. Here, however, my focus is primarily on classroom discussions, especially those stimulated by stories.[26]

Recently William Bennett has published a large collection of children's classics under the title, *The Book of Virtues*.[27] Although a valuable resource for the moral education of children, it has serious shortcomings as well. The purpose of his book, Bennett says, is to assist in the task of teaching moral literacy and the formation of character. This task, he adds, is not political in a partisan sense (although it is political in the sense of preparing children for citizenship in a body politic):

People of good character are not all going to come down on the same side of difficult political and social issues. Good people—people of character and moral literacy—can be conservative, and good people can be liberal. We must not permit our disputes over thorny political questions to obscure the obligation we have to offer instruction to all our young people in the area in which we have, as a society, reached a consensus: namely, on the importance of good character, and on some of its pervasive particulars.[28]

I agree. The real question is whether Bennett's book succeeds in its basic objectives. Has he selected stories, poems, and essays that are "for everybody—all children, of all political and religious backgrounds [that speak to readers] on a more fundamental level than race, sex, and gender"?[29]

Martha Nussbaum finds an uncomfortable tension in Bennett's project.[30] On the one hand, she says, many of the stories and poems Bennett includes encourage nuanced moral reflection and point to the need for moral education that goes well beyond the instillation of simple moral truisms. This characteristic, she says, calls for moral discrimination and invites thoughtful and controversial discussion; it invites liberal, if not radical, thought. On the other hand, Bennett includes what Nussbaum calls "moral treacle," revealing the "Hallmark Card side of Bennett's pedagogy."[31] This aspect, Nussbaum complains, reveals Bennett's conservatism.

Although Bennett is noted for his conservatism, Nussbaum's complaint warrants closer examination. It very nearly suggests that conservative thought, by dwelling in the realm of "literary treacle," is simplistic and does not advance to more reflective levels. The counterpart would be that liberal and radical thought have the opposite qualities. This reading of Bennett's book would be hard to sustain. Nussbaum points out that each chapter focuses on a virtue (e.g., compassion, honesty) and proceeds from the simple to the complex. If conservative thought goes with the simple and more liberal thought with the complex, then Bennett would be unwittingly structuring each chapter to undermine his conservatism, since clearly he wants readers eventually to move onto more complex issues.

In any case, if Bennett's selections in the early portions of each chapter have a politically conservative bias, this would be a mark of failure in his own terms. However, there is another sense in which Bennett's book both is, and should be, conservative. Its avowed intent is to present in their most compelling form those traditional virtues that are necessary elements for moral education. These include self-discipline, compassion, honesty, courage, responsibility, the capacity for friendship, work, perseverance, loyalty, and faith in some sort of goodness.

This conservative strategy seems, in principle at least, the right sort of one to adopt. These are basic virtues desirable for all children to develop. Aristotle's insistence on the importance of virtues in moral education is sound. How the acquisition and development of these virtues should be managed is more controversial. Nussbaum says that Aristotle's view is "that we must begin with good 'habits,' meaning not mindless behavioral conditioning, but patterns of increasingly intelligent choice guided by attachment and love."[32] However, Aristotle is also noted for thinking that children are not ready for moral philosophy. Since he believes children are governed much more by passion than reason, he seems to take a rather dim view of the prospects of reasonableness in children; fear of punishment rather than an appeal to reasonableness is likely to be more effective with children.[33]

Thus, Aristotle seems to share Piaget and Kohlberg's underestimation of the moral capacities of young children. Bennett's arrangement of stories suggests that he may, too. The earliest stories in each chapter are not only simpler than those that come later, but many contain "moral lessons" that emphasize how those who fail to act appropriately will suffer or be punished. For example, the early stories in the first chapter, "Self Discipline," include:

- Robert Louis Stevenson's "Good and Bad Children," with bad children growing up as "geese and gabies"—who will later be hated by their nieces and nephews.[34]
- "Rebecca," who meets an untimely death by slamming doors.[35]
- "Godfrey Gordon Gustavus Gore," whose parents threaten to send him "on a voyage of penance to Singapore."[36]
- "John, Tom, and James," who by virtue of their misdeeds have "all grown up ugly, and nobody cares."[37]
- "Jim," who runs away from home, only to be eaten by a lion.[38]
- "The King and His Hawk," in which the king suffers dearly from his anger and impatience.[39]

Of course, self-discipline is important for our individual well-being; so it is perhaps understandable that a rather large number of stories emphasize how those who lack it sow the seeds of their own misfortune. However, Bennett's first chapter risks setting an unfortunate tone for the book—namely, that virtue pays and vice does not.

Bennett's own commentaries on the stories frequently encourage readers to value virtue for its own sake, and the next several chapters ("Compassion," "Responsibility," and "Friendship") move more quickly into stories of genuine other-regard. Still, early entries in "Honesty" often reinforce "honesty pays" (or "dishonesty punishes") rather than honesty is to be valued either in its own right or for the sake of others, too. The little boy who cried "Wolf" loses his sheep (rather than causing someone else to lose sheep).[40] "Someone sees you from above," says the daughter to the thief, her father.[41] Matilda, who told lies, is burned to death.[42] Pinocchio is shamed by his nose, which grows longer with each lie.[43]

Such stories of honesty make important practical points. But it can be wondered whether they move us far enough in the direction of honesty as a virtue, as distinct from honesty as prudential practice. David Hume's sensible knave helps clarify this distinction:

> A sensible knave, in particular incidents, may think that an act of iniquity or infidelity will make a considerable addition to his fortune, without causing any considerable breach in the social union and confederacy. *That honesty is the best policy,* may be a good general rule, but it is liable to many exceptions: and he, it may perhaps be thought, conducts himself with most wisdom, who observes the general rule, and takes advantage of all the exceptions.[44]

So how is the sensible knave to be answered? Hume says he doubts that anyone who believes this question needs an answer will be convinced by any considerations: "If his heart rebel not against such pernicious maxims, if he feel no reluctance to the thoughts of villainy and baseness, he has indeed lost a considerable motive to virtue."[45] Hume would not consider fear of personal harm or misfortune as the lost motive to virtue. Something more is missing in the sensible knave:

Inward peace of mind, consciousness of integrity, a satisfactory review of our own conduct—these are circumstances very requisite to happiness, and will be cherished and cultivated by every honest man who feels the importance of them.[46]

But all of this is lost on the sensible knave, who, by hypothesis, feels differently about honesty. He is like the grown-up Calvin imagined in Chapter 1. Or he is like the executive at a boardroom meeting in a *New Yorker* cartoon commenting, "Of course, honesty is one of the better policies."

Those already in the grip of honesty as a virtue will not give the sensible knave's conduct a "satisfactory review." The problem, however, is determining how best to help children to become honest persons rather than sensible knaves. Here it seems that stories of integrity are much more promising than "The Little Boy Who Cried Wolf" and "Pinocchio." At the same time, it is important not to make the mistake of going overboard, insisting that one must always tell the truth.[47] Unfortunately, Bennett's very first story in his chapter on honesty is "The Boy Who Never Told a Lie."[48] This little boy "never, never told a lie." He was so loved for always telling the truth

> That every day, as he grew up,
>   'Twas said, "There goes the honest youth."
> And when the people that stood near
>   Would turn to ask the reason why,
> The answer would be always this:
>   "Because he never tells a lie."

It is not until after more than forty pages of stories in praise of unqualified truthfulness that Bennett presents a story that complicates matters. This is an extract from Victor Hugo's *Les Misérables*, which is not a story likely to be shared with younger children. Missing from Bennett's chapter are stories for young children that invite them to reflect more carefully on *why* being truthful matters and why, important as it is, truthfulness is not the only thing that matters. To begin to explore these nuances is to engage in philosophical thought rather than simply to uncritically conform to a rule, "Always be truthful."

Oddly, justice, one of the central Aristotelean virtues, is not one of the special chapter headings in *The Book of Virtues*. Neither are respect (for self or others) or tolerance. The importance of these virtues for reasonableness is apparent. It is also apparent that they require the kind of thoughtfulness to which philosophical reflection can make a significant contribution. These virtues are important in any society but especially in multicultural societies such as ours, which present special moral challenges. How acknowledging both the existence and importance of diversity can avoid collapsing into a form of uncritical relativism is the topic of the next chapter.

7
Moral Diversity

Although national surveys consistently show that an overwhelming majority of adults in the United States would like to see some sort of moral education in the schools, it is not clear how much real agreement this indicates. "*Whose* morality are we talking about?" one might ask. The significance of this question is apparent when we consider the moral diversity among those who ask it. This is not merely a diversity among moral beliefs, which is bound to be present to some degree in any large group of reflective people. Many societies are multicultural, containing within their borders, Amy Gutmann says, "many cultures that interact in some significant way with each other."[1] Thus, a multicultural society will, in part, be characterized by different traditions and practices, some of which may reflect fundamental moral and religious differences.

The United States is such a multicultural society. Constitutional commitment to the separation of church and state, combined with the belief of many that morality is ultimately grounded in religion, poses a serious challenge: How can the public schools place moral education on their agendas without offending fundamental beliefs and practices of at least some significant portions of the public? One response is that, like it or not, moral education cannot be kept out of the schools. As Robert Fullinwider puts it:

> A school that set out deliberately *not* to morally educate its students would simply have to close down altogether. It could not teach children their native language since so much of any natural language is about how to be and not to be. It would have to deprive its students of all stories of human affairs, since those stories are structured by evaluative concepts—by ideas of success and failure, foresight and blindness, heedfulness and heedlessness, care and

negligence, duty and dereliction, pride and shame, hope and despair, wonder and dullness, competition and cooperation, beginning and ending. But without stories of human affairs, a school could not effectively teach non-moral lessons either. It could not teach about inflation, log-rolling, scientific discovery, coalition-building, paranoia, ecological niches, deterrence of crime, price controls, or infectious diseases.[2]

Assuming Fullinwider is right, the question is not *whether* moral education is to have a place in the schools; rather, it is *what* that place should be.

However, when we examine what place moral education should have in the schools, important differences remain even among those who accept Fullinwider's observations. It may be true that simply by enforcing rules, punishing cheating, and evaluating student performance, schools will influence the moral development of children. But those who wish to minimize the role of the public schools in moral education will say that these activities are necessary for a school to operate at all and perform essential functions rather than explicit moral instruction. Thus, one can still hold that although banishing moral education from the schools is futile, and even undesirable, this does not mean that moral education should be made an explicit part of the curriculum. As for teaching nonmoral lessons on inflation, scientific discovery, crime, infectious diseases, and the like, it is true that adults, and even many children, have moral beliefs about these matters. However, this fact alone does not warrant attempting to instruct children about what moral values they should attach to them.

Nevertheless, attempting to minimize the public schools' contribution to the moral education of children poses serious risks. First, it risks impoverishing children's abilities to function as responsible citizens once they become adults, which is something that today's adults may later regret. It is also something about which tomorrow's adults might complain, much as they would if they were not being given the opportunity to develop scientific and mathematical skills. That is, they might complain that they had a right to be assisted in exercising, refining, and developing their moral capacities as they studied subjects that have significant moral dimensions (as history, literature, science, and even mathematics do).

Second, insofar as moral education remains hidden in the shadows of the curriculum, there is a danger that schools will attempt to influence children in ways that cannot pass public scrutiny. Since some form of moral education is bound to take place in the schools, it seems best to have this explicitly acknowledged in the curriculum. Children not only study science, mathematics, history, and literature; they are informed that this is what they are studying. It is presumed that they are capable of engaging in the kinds of thinking these subjects require. But if studying these subjects also contains certain "moral lessons," this fact, too, is something that children can understand. To deny it both underestimates children and increases the risk of indoctrination rather than education.

Still, the challenge of moral diversity, especially in its multicultural forms, remains. The major question this chapter addresses is whether common ground can be found among such diverse perspectives—common ground that is responsive to the various worries one might have about explicitly placing moral education on the agenda of the public schools. Any persuasive account will have to respect different perspectives even as it attempts to articulate common ground.

However, an important point to keep in mind is that in addition to revealing cultural differences, an examination of the multicultural dimensions of a society can reveal similarities. Much depends on how the subject is approached. Fullinwider suggests that in order to sympathetically understand another culture, we need to bear in mind the distinction between *form* and *value*.[3] A simple illustration is rules of the road. In the United States the rule is to drive on the right side of the road; in England it is the left. In the United States there is a heavy reliance on stoplights and stop signs; in England there is greater reliance on roundabouts. However, these rules and practices are designed to serve the same values—safe and efficient travel. In general, Fullinwider observes:

Sensitivity to the form/value distinction is important because it allows us to gauge how, and in what way, another society differs from our own. In some cases, it may well be that another culture differs from ours in the values it serves and promotes. For the most part, however, charitable interpretations of another culture proceed on the assumption that it tries to realize the same deepest values we do, and that its outward differences are simply differences in form.[4]

Fullinwider's examples focus on cultural differences and similarities from society to society, but the same point can be made about many cultural differences and similarities within a single society.

Of course, even if different cultures have common values, it does not follow that their respective forms serve those values equally well. It may not matter whether driving is on the left or right side, but perhaps it can be shown that roundabouts are often superior to stoplights—from either the standpoint of safety or efficiency. This finding would provide some reason for introducing more roundabouts in the United States (something that, in fact, has happened). To appreciate this, however, it is necessary to be open-minded enough to be receptive to new, and possibly strange-sounding, ideas. Such open-mindedness can provide two benefits. First, it makes self-criticism and self-improvement possible. Second, by gaining an understanding of different forms that attempt to realize similar values, one may acquire greater acceptance of and respect for those whose beliefs and practices differ from one's own.

However, there are limits. Drivers accustomed to driving on the right side of the road adapt to driving on the left when they visit England. This change may cause some anxious and awkward moments, but it does not require alteration of basic beliefs in the way that, say, adapting to different religious practices might. Even when two religions share many of the same basic moral values, the forms those values take, along with other beliefs and practices that give religions their distinctive forms, are fundamental for their adherents in ways that driving on one side of the road rather than the other is not. Shifting from one religion to another is not a viable, let alone desirable, option for many. Nor is there any particular reason why this should be otherwise. Unlike driving practices in a particular locale, very different religious practices and beliefs can peaceably coexist.

Insofar as underlying shared values can be discovered among the variety of forms that express those values, respect for different cultural and religious traditions seems a reasonable objective. However, deep differences in values might be discovered—as well as intractability. This, too, has to be carefully factored into moral education. Some of the worries to which this gives rise will be discussed below. Here, however, it is enough to note that the cultural and religious practices associated with morality are seldom as straightforward as rules of the road. Even if their various forms represent efforts to serve the same basic values, discovering that this is so (and how it is so) is not always an easy task. Yet, the rewards of greater understanding and improvement in critical thinking seem clearly to outweigh any frustrations that might result from such efforts. Furthermore, we might say, since multicultural education is concerned with how different cultures interact with each other, moral education cannot responsibly exclude fair consideration of the interests of all who are affected by that interaction. Also, when children in the classroom are themselves associated with different cultures, their sense of identity and self-worth is as much at stake as their ability to engage in critical thought.

Fullinwider points out one of the great dangers of neglecting multicultural education. Particularly in societies that have assumed a dominant economic position in the world, like the United States, there is a tendency to assume cultural superiority. Associated with this tendency is *judgmentalism,* which is marked by gaining satisfaction from boosting one's own sense of moral worth by making negative moral assessments of others.[5] Fullinwider's remedy for judgmentalism is not abstention from judgment; it is the cultivation of open-mindedness. This, he says, is quite teachable:

> We can rehearse students at waiting to make up their minds until they've heard the different sides of a case and we can train them how to follow and evaluate arguments and evidence. We can habituate them to inquire, ask questions, follow leads, seek more information, invite comment, and welcome different perspectives. We can impress upon them cautionary tales of the wrongs that flow from hasty, careless, reckless, and ill-considered judgments.[6]

Thus, Fullinwider advocates deliberately encouraging students to develop good habits of critical thinking. Although this can be done without explicitly including multicultural education, doing it in that context can both enrich students' understanding of other cultures and their critical thinking abilities. But ignoring multicultural concerns is not a real option in most societies today, and certainly not in the United States. Since responsibly addressing those concerns itself requires the exercise of critical thinking skills, multicultural education should go hand in hand with the development of those skills. However, encouraging the exercise of critical thinking skills in the context of multicultural education is bound to raise moral issues in the classroom, thereby placing moral education squarely on the schools' agenda. So, we must next address some common worries about moral education in the public schools.

SOME COMMON WORRIES

Obviously, one fear that many have is that moral education in the schools will be nothing more than the indoctrination of some group's favored "universal" perspective—the inculcation of certain partisan moral beliefs that will be uncritically received by children as if they were universal moral truths. Others fear the absence of indoctrination. They fear that the schools will encourage the permissive and uncritical view that anyone's moral opinions are as credible as anyone else's, thus undermining moral values that should be taken as authoritative. Those who fear indoctrination may ask, "Whose moral values are going to be inculcated and with what authority?" Those who fear its absence may reply, "How can we expect our children to develop sound moral values if none are inculcated?"

In a highly homogeneous, closed society these worries might not arise. In such a society it might seem quite clear both that certain moral beliefs should be inculcated in the young as well as which beliefs these should be. However, for us it is quite evident that at some level there is a great deal of diversity in moral beliefs. We see this not only when we compare different cultures with each other, but also when we look closely *within* any but the most tightknit cultures.

For many, awareness of the diversity of moral beliefs and practices raises the question of whether the validity of moral beliefs can go no further than one's particular cultural identity. This view of morality, commonly referred to as cultural relativism, is typically accompanied by a reluctance to make moral judgments about other cultures and an attitude of tolerance toward those with different moral beliefs. However, should a culture exhibit judgmental and intolerant attitudes, the cultural relativist view implies that this is all right—for that culture. So, there is nothing in the idea of cultural relativism that requires nonjudgmentalism or tolerance, even if most supporters of the cultural relativist view do, in fact, have these attitudes.

However, those who believe there are underlying, universal moral truths can, nevertheless, also share the moral modesty of such relativists. It is one thing to believe there are universal moral truths and quite another to believe one knows what they are, let alone how they should be applied to particular circumstances. In the absence of certainty, a universalist might share some of the relativist's reluctance to judge other cultures. Of course, there are self-assured universalists who have no doubts about the soundness of their own beliefs—only those of others. But even they could concede that however mistaken others may be in their moral beliefs, this does not necessarily mean that those beliefs are less reasonable than their own. Morality, they may say, is not simply a determination of reason. .

Given the broad range of possible responses to moral diversity, what is a teacher to do? Fears of indoctrination are likely to come from relativists and universalists alike. Relativists may fear that the schools will attempt to indoctrinate children with beliefs that are either intolerant of the diversity around them or that undermine children's beliefs which are rooted in local cultural or family traditions. Self-assured universalists may worry that the schools will undermine the beliefs of their children by attempting to accommodate the diversity around them—the schools will either explicitly or implicitly inculcate a relativistic attitude. Or, they may fear, the schools might attempt to inculcate what they take to be universal values but mistaken ones. In short, self-assured universalists fear the schools will be relativistic. Relativists (and even some universalists) fear the schools will be universalistic. Finally, there are those who reject both self-assured universalism and relativism but fear what the adherents of either view might do in the schools.

These worries should be taken seriously. Many (but not all) universalist views are intimately bound up with religious views. Constitutionally in the United States, public schools are not to deliberately promote or denigrate the religious beliefs of students. As James Herndon puts it, children have the same fundamental, constitutional rights as adults "not to have religious or other orthodoxy imposed upon them and the rights to respect for their beliefs, religious or otherwise."[7] So, from a constitutional point of view, teachers need to avoid both moral/religious indoctrination and the subversion of moral/religious beliefs. From a moral point of view this approach should be avoided, too. As Herndon points out, respect for the dignity and reasoning powers of students requires it.[8]

Respect for the dignity and reasoning powers of students also requires teachers to resist pronouncing for the students that certain answers to morally challenging issues are right or wrong. This resistance is sometimes confused with another view: students, as well as their teachers, often say that what they really like about classroom discussion of moral issues is that there are no right or wrong answers. A teacher might well say that for purposes of classroom discussion, students will not be judged or graded in terms of whether their views are right or wrong. But this means only that other evaluative criteria will be used, such as how carefully one articulates and supports one's views or how well one takes other views into account. This approach is quite compatible with there actually being right or wrong views, even if teachers never pronounce that such and such is right or wrong. Students can be expected to come up with the most supportable views they can discover. If it is assumed (rather than argued) that no views are more supportable than any others, this task would lose its point.

One possible way to avoid the confusion between not making pronouncements about what is right or wrong and there not being any right or wrong views is to keep insisting on the distinction whenever students or parents fail to grasp it. However, there is a better way to deal with the problem: make it clear that the task of students is to clarify and critically examine their own views and listen carefully to and respond critically, but respectfully, to the views of others. If this is made clear, it is unlikely that students will conclude that all answers are equal, even if everyone is respected as an equal in the inquiry. Some answers will be regarded by students as more adequate than others, even when it is not clear what the very best answer is, or even whether there is a "best" answer. For there surely are answers that are less adequate than others. For example, students may not know the best way for teachers to evaluate students, but they know that failing students simply because they wear glasses, have blond hair, or have freckles is unacceptable—and they can explain why. On such matters, no authoritative figure is needed to confirm their judgment.

What this example illustrates is that important as it is to acknowledge and respect the multicultural aspects of our society, this should not obscure the common moral ground that often cuts through our differences. It can be agreed that all schools should oppose arbitrary and capricious treatment of students. Students should be treated respectfully rather than disparagingly, kindly rather than cruelly, fairly rather than unfairly, and so on. Although the concepts of respect, kindness, and fairness are anything but precise, there are central, uncontroversial instances of each—as well as of their contraries.

This point is not restricted to the allegedly simpler world of children but can be extended to the adult world as well. Amy Gutmann points out, "No culture or political community with which we are familiar gives its members good reasons for rejecting principles or practices that protect innocent people from being enslaved, tortured, murdered, malnourished, imprisoned, rendered homeless, or subject to abnormal physical pain and sickness."[9] She is not saying, of course, that innocent people are never treated in these ways, but rather that members of all cultures or political communities with which we are familiar have good reason to condemn such practices. This still leaves a vast area of morality open for critical discussion. Although Gutmann accepts the notion that there are universal moral principles that cannot be reasonably rejected, these principles underdetermine particular moral practices, leaving considerable room for rich and creative variations in local customs and practices. Further, space is also left for fundamentally unresolved, yet reasonable, moral disagreement. A more detailed consideration of the example of rules of the road nicely illustrates these points.

As already noted, in the United States (and most of the world) people drive on the right-hand side of the road, using the left for passing. In England it is the opposite. Both practices are instances of a more general rule that driving should be regularly on only one side of the road rather than, say, randomly on either. Of course, there are more than two ways to avoid complete randomness. Driving on the right side on Monday through Thursday and the left side on Friday through Sunday is a regular pattern. Or the pattern could change monthly, and so on. None of these other possible alternatives is taken seriously because of the confusion and danger that would result from their adoption. Efficient, safe travel, we might say, is valued in both the United States and England. In regard to these ends, which rule is better—drive on the left or drive on the right? There is no obvious reason to insist that either is superior to the other (although some might nevertheless wish to argue the case). Still, both are superior to an indefinite number of other possibilities.

There are many other driving rules and practices—traffic signals, stop signs, yield signs, roundabouts, as well as common courtesies. Are roundabouts preferable to traffic signals? Informed, reasonable people might disagree. Even if no one would say that one is always preferable to the other, there might well be disagreement about the preferability of one to the other in particular kinds of conditions (e.g., urban vs. rural settings).

However, it should be noted that these disagreements pivot around more than one value. Presumably, safety is valued by all reasonable people. So is efficient travel. And people may have other values (for example, driving for pleasure, driving in a relaxed manner). Taking all these values into account is difficult, and it requires modification of some ends in light of others. The values of safety and efficiency alone make this clear. Absolute safety is unattainable as long as we have moving automobiles. So, we must ask, "How safe is safe enough?" Obviously, at some point efficiency and safety compete with each other. Even though it is known that a speed limit of 55 mph reduces accidents and fatalities, expressways permit 65 mph. Although no one seriously argues that the limit should be lowered to 40 mph or raised to 100 mph, many might argue for a return to 55 mph, while others might argue for 75 mph (closer to the actual speed of a rather high proportion of drivers). Just what the range of reasonable disagreement is can be left unspecified without affecting the main point. Whatever that range is likely to be, at some point reasonable people may strongly disagree about the values of safety and efficiency in relation to one another. But this does not mean there are no large areas of agreement about the importance of both safety and efficiency. (No one will argue seriously, for example, that a 65 mph limit should be set in school zones.)

There are two other aspects of this rules of the road analogy that should be mentioned. First, any rule of the road is bound to have exceptions: one should stop at a stop sign—unless a runaway truck will ram into the back of your car. These exceptions cannot all be stated in the rule because that would make the rule too complex even if (contrary to fact) we could list all the possibilities. The exceptions depend very much on particular circumstances, something relativists are fond of emphasizing. However, the justification of exceptions itself appeals to more general considerations (such as safety), which means that good judgment must accompany whatever rules there are. Furthermore, much as we might wish for a rule about rules, there is no algorithm for when a rule is no substitute for good judgment.

Second, when in England one ought to drive on the left-hand side and conform to the local rules. When in the United States one ought to drive on the right-hand side and conform to the (often different) local rules. Is this not, then, a relative matter? It is. But, again, the justification for conforming to local rules appeals to more general considerations of efficiency and safety. It is just that when these considerations are applied to different locales (including their different practices), they warrant driving differently. This conformity does not preclude criticizing the local rules with which one ought to comply. There is no contradiction in believing that one ought to comply with rules that themselves ought to be improved or even eliminated, within limits. (If some people were shipwrecked on the coast of a society that had a practice of enslaving shipwreck victims, they would not be obligated to comply with this practice.)

But from what perspective might local rules and practices be criticized? Amy Gutmann poses the challenge: "Where can anyone find an Archimedean point outside any culture or political community from which to justify the overriding of local understandings?"[10] It might be thought that without such an Archimedean point, valid criticism is not possible and universal moral aspirations are illusory. Gutmann rejects both conclusions, but with important reservations. A closer look at what she has in mind will prove useful.

DELIBERATIVE UNIVERSALISM

Amy Gutmann's specific concern is political ethics rather than ethics or morality in general, and she focuses on adults rather than children. Nevertheless, what she says has important implications for the moral education of children. As already mentioned, Gutmann characterizes a multicultural society as one that includes many cultures that significantly interact with each other.

A culture, says Gutmann, is a human community "associated with ongoing ways of seeing, doing, and thinking about things."[11] If we are to speak of distinctive cultures within a given society, there must be some striking differences among these ways of seeing, doing, and thinking about things. However, not all such differences will be moral differences. Distinctive features of language, social environment, and even family structure need not reflect moral differences at all. But even when they do, the differences need not reflect fundamental disagreements with other cultures. As rules of the road illustrate, striking differences in practices are compatible with shared fundamental values.

Although larger than a few families, a culture can be, and often is, smaller than an entire society. This explains why a country such as the United States can be referred to as a multicultural society. Furthermore, since a culture need not be defined by geographical boundaries, even a small community can have multicultural features. Even individuals can, and often do, have multicultural features, particularly when their parents and other relatives have strong associations with more than one culture.[12]

One might think that once those from different cultures mix together so that geographical distinctiveness is lost, cultural distinctiveness will be lost, too. However, this has not happened in the United States, and the disappearance of richly diverse cultures into a larger, more uniform culture would be a regrettable loss. Nevertheless, the viability of a multicultural society depends on social compatibility at some level. That is, some shared values are necessary, even if the particular forms they take may sometimes differ.

However, even if the mixing of different cultures in one society need not undermine cultural distinctiveness, the perceived need for shared societal values poses another danger. More likely than cultural differences disappearing is the emergence of some forms of cultural dominance, especially in the political arena. When not all cultural voices are given a serious hearing, injustices result. At the same time, when different voices are given a serious hearing, fundamental moral disagreements on some matters can be expected to surface. Gutmann's main concern is what to make of the fact that reasonable people may find themselves in such disagreements, especially when this seems to reflect cultural differences. Gutmann offers four theoretical perspectives on these multicultural concerns: cultural relativism, political relativism, comprehensive universalism, and deliberative universalism. She favors deliberative universalism; the following explains why.

Cultural relativism resolves ethical questions in terms of whatever dominant norms prevail in a given culture. These norms have no validity beyond the culture that adopts them. Gutmann notes two problems with this view. First, it is difficult to find enough homogeneity within a given culture to determine a set of norms comprehensive enough to address the basic moral concerns of its members. Gutmann cites the disagreement among Mormons about the practice of polygamy as an example. Second, even when dominant norms can be found, cultural relativism cannot provide a standard to evaluate the justice of dominant views. Dominance settles questions of justice by virtue of assertion and power, not moral justification. But, to take an especially egregious case, social consensus within a dominant group that slavery is acceptable does not justify it.[13] Unfortunately, cultural relativism offers neither a means for resolving disagreements when social consensus breaks down nor a meaningful way of protesting against injustices the majority may inflict on the minority. These difficulties often arise within a given culture (e.g., the Mormons). They are even worse when they arise in a multicultural setting.

Political relativism makes no effort to resolve substantive disagreements by determining which of the conflicting views is actually right. Instead, it calls for procedural resolutions. Internal disagreements call for just procedures to resolve them. Impartial judicial hearings and trials by jury are attempts to provide just procedures. Gutmann agrees that just procedures are necessary for human well-being, but they are hardly sufficient. Who gets to decide, judge or jurors? How are judges and jurors selected? Even if judges and jurors agree that there should be freedom from enslavement, torture, and poverty, these are basic human goods, says Gutmann. They are not merely procedural goods. In fact, just political procedures cannot guarantee that people will not be unjustly denied such basic goods.

Political relativism, says Gutmann, "rightly endorses argument, negotiation, and adjudication among people with diverse cultural identities and conflicting moral positions," but this presupposes that those who disagree have substantive positions from which they are arguing.[14] Even though accepting procedural means for resolving disagreements is compatible with retaining these commitments, she says, this is no substitute for them.[15] So, political relativism still leaves us with the problem of grounding our basic moral values.

For Gutmann, the shared defect of cultural and political relativism is that they allow "too little room for recognizing the distinctively human capacity for creative and morally reflective identity, which cannot be reduced to a reflection or entailment of any given communal identity."[16] But both also issue the fundamental challenge of all forms of relativism to find an Archimedean point from which local understandings might be criticized.

Gutmann's response is to reject the assumption from which it proceeds. That assumption is that no particular culture, or any combination of cultures that interact, is internally resourceful enough to provide us with opportunities for critical self-reflection. Gutmann suggests an alternative view, a kind of practical reasonableness, "exercised by people who assess the moral understandings of the cultures and political communities with which they identify rather than accept them as morally binding or an unalterable aspect of their identity."[17] Critical assessment can be triggered by an awareness of conflicts among existing understandings. Nevertheless, the criteria for assessing these conflicts can come from within shared social understandings. Further, wrestling with these conflicts can give rise to new social understandings.

As already noted, Gutmann points out that some moral principles and practices do have universal features. In response to the claim that all widely accepted moral concepts and principles are of local origin, Gutmann says that the cultural relativist "must claim that the universality of these principles is a cosmic coincidence or else concede that some ethical considerations either transcend particular cultures or are immanent in every culture because of certain basic features of human nature that are, strictly speaking, intercultural."[18]

These universal, moral features of different cultures suggest to Gutmann that there are limits to what can count as a "morality" at all. Anything that might count as a morality must make room for talk about the injustices of murder, deceit, and torture, and it must be responsive to others' pain and oppression. To this she adds three requirements of reasonableness about social justice: one, a merely prudential or self-regarding view is insufficient; two, inferences and empirical claims must be challengeable by reliable methods of inquiry; and three, premises that are not empirically or logically supportable should, nevertheless, not be radically implausible.[19]

Finally, Gutmann points out that even if we cannot stand outside all cultures when we make moral judgments, we need not be judging from inside one and only one culture. Martin Luther King, Jr., spoke to all cultures on behalf of the weak, voiceless, and exploited. How could he succeed in doing this? Gutmann's answer is that doing so "depends on the possibility of justifying actions to people who do not share the same communal attachments."[20] King found such a possibility in basic human goods that "span the considerable diversity of modern cultures and support a set of ethical standards that are universal at least for the world as we know it and human beings as we know them."[21]

Gutmann appeals to a kind of moral universalism. However, she is quite careful to restrict its scope. The third and fourth perspectives on multicultural concerns are comprehensive universalism and deliberative universalism. Comprehensive universalism, Gutmann insists, has an unattainable aspiration by insisting that there are moral principles that are sufficient to resolve all fundamental moral conflicts. It is not entirely clear whether Gutmann is committed to the view that there cannot be such a set of principles, or that as matters stand right now there are moral issues about which people reasonably disagree. However, in practical terms, it may not matter which view she has in mind. The basic point is that we are not now in possession of a comprehensive set of universal principles that both command the assent of all reasonable people and yield univocal resolutions of issues about which there seems to be fundamental disagreement—and we have little reason to believe this will ever change.

In any case, Gutmann's view implies that at least for all practical purposes it is best to exchange comprehensive universalism for a less ambitious view. She offers deliberative universalism, a view that is committed to basic, universal moral principles that can be employed to settle many moral issues (such as murdering the innocent, arbitrary arrests, or systematic deception on the part of government) but which leaves room for reasonable disagreement about some fundamental moral concerns (such as abortion).

Even if Gutmann were to concede that the ambitions of comprehensive universalism cannot be shown to be unattainable in principle, her practical point would not be undermined. A fair-minded assessment of moral discourse today seems to support her notion that there are some fundamental moral issues about which reasonable people disagree—and that these disagreements are not merely factual but more deeply moral. Acting as if this were not so invites settling such disagreements by force, indoctrination, or suppression rather than by education.

What educational implications might the adoption of Gutmann's deliberative universalism have? It encourages forums for public deliberation. Even where there are fundamental differences, these can be discussed openly, critically, and respectfully. As Gutmann puts it, conflicts that involve fundamental moral disagreements "are best addressed and provisionally resolved by actual deliberation, the give and take of argument that is respectful of reasonable differences."[22] Of course, this approach need not be restricted to areas of fundamental disagreement. It can characterize moral discussion of less divisive issues as well.

Gutmann has in mind adult, public forums for discussion of political justice issues. But her notion of deliberative universalism has considerable promise for the classroom as well. The benefits she describes for deliberative discussion of political justice apply equally well to classrooms designed for moral discussion:

1. Forums that are well designed for deliberation are more fair than those that use coercive or indoctrinative measures.
2. Respect is shown for all reasonable opinions.
3. Mutually respectful people are more open to changing their minds when they hear good objections to their views.
4. There is a greater chance of discovering better resolutions of differences.
5. "Deliberation encourages people with conflicting perspectives to understand each other's point of view, to minimize their moral disagreements, and to search for common ground."[23]

These all seem to be desirable aims of moral education in the schools. The classroom is not "value-free." At the same time that it is receptive to the fundamental commitments students already have, such a classroom encourages critical reflection and reinforces open-mindedness, listening to and understanding others, respecting others, and respecting oneself. These are essential attributes for citizens in any viable, culturally diverse society, and what better place to foster them than in classrooms of students who are beginning to learn their way as members of such societies.

8
Moral Confidence

The previous chapter may alleviate some worries about whether moral education belongs in the public schools—but not completely. Admittedly, moral differences are to be respected, and indoctrination is to be shunned. Yet, it might be objected, this situation introduces another danger, a kind of implicit skepticism that lends itself to moral instability. The desire for some moral certainty is understandable. We want to be able to engage in moral reflection with some confidence, and we may wonder how this is possible without moral certainty about at least some things. If children lack this confidence, how can they help but flounder, especially in a classroom that encourages open inquiry? Furthermore, certainty and the confidence that goes with it are not enough. Children, the objection goes, need to be certain about the right sorts of things; that is, their confidence needs to be well placed.

Some may conclude that imparting moral certainty, or at least not undermining it, is an essential part of moral education. How, they ask, can this be done in a classroom that shies away from final, authoritative pronouncements? This question assumes that making authoritative pronouncements will have the desired effect. But there are at least two reasons for thinking they will not. First, children may see these pronouncements only as external admonitions, proscriptions to be heeded when adults are present but otherwise ignored. Second, what if the authoritative pronouncements are themselves misguided or otherwise inappropriate?

We could try to reduce these two worries to one. It may be thought that if the pronouncements are good ones, children will see this and internalize them, so the only problem is to make sure that the right moral values are selected. However, if children will internalize values they see to be desirable, it would seem that authoritative pronouncements are not necessary. In fact, there is a risk that children's ability to see that the values are desirable will be impeded by the authoritarian tone of the teacher. However, worries that in the absence of authoritative pronouncements children will not internalize desirable values may be based on something else. This is the supposition that they are not ready to internalize such values in any other way. It may be thought that their moral character and associated cognitive abilities are not sufficiently developed.

This view seems to be an implication of the influential cognitive-developmental theories of Jean Piaget and Lawrence Kohlberg.[1] Piaget's view is that well into their early school years, children's moral orientation pivots around fear of punishment and respect for authority. Kohlberg's more complex developmental account agrees that even into their early school years, children respond primarily to the fear of punishment; but he distinguishes fear of authority from respect for authority. For Kohlberg, positive respect for authority usually does not come into play until children are at least ten or eleven years old. Furthermore, it is Kohlberg's view that most adults do not move beyond this "law and order" orientation. If these theories are basically true and teachers grasp their import, the implications for moral education in the schools are significant but, as I now try to show, somewhat troubling.

MORALITY IN STAGES?

Piaget and Kohlberg offer encouragement to parents who worry that their children's basic moral development is completed before they even enter school. They reject this Freudian view in favor of the idea that moral development depends on cognitive development. Thus, basic moral changes can be expected to occur well into the school years and even into adulthood. Of course, this may be unwelcome news to parents who would like to minimize the influence of the schools and peer groups on their children's moral development. But for many it is a relief to know that their first, often fumbling efforts at parenting may not have sealed their children's moral fate. However, Piaget and Kohlberg do accept Freud's view that even well into the early school years children are basically self-centered. Morality for young children is first grounded in the fear of punishment or loss of love and then in an "instrumental egoism" of reciprocal exchange.[2] Even Carol Gilligan's critique of Kohlberg's neglect of the affective side of moral development accepts the view that early childhood is basically self-centered in these ways.[3]

Unfortunately, this view of the self-centeredness of young children conflates egocentric and egoistic behavior. What is overlooked is the possibility that much apparently egoistic behavior is only egocentric. Egoistic behavior is self-centered in the sense that one is seeking something for oneself. Egocentric behavior is self-centered in the sense that one does not fully understand or take into account the different perspectives of others. Although someone's behavior on a particular occasion can be both egoistic and egocentric, it need not be. For example, a younger brother may buy a present for his older brother that is no longer of any interest to the older brother. The older brother may then permit the younger brother to use it. If we surmise that the younger brother bought the present with precisely this in mind, his behavior will be construed as egoistic. But it should be noted that this interpretation assumes that the younger brother *does* understand the perspective of his older brother. So if he behaved egoistically, he was not entirely egocentric. However, if the younger brother's thinking was basically egocentric, he might not have behaved egoistically at all. Suppose the younger brother failed to realize that his older brother no longer shared the same interests. He might then have bought a present he mistakenly thought would please his older brother, which would be egocentric but not egoistic behavior.

The extent to which young children are self-centered—and how this is to be understood—is a central concern for child rearing. If parents believe that their children will respond only to threats of punishment or the withdrawal of love, what is reinforced is a morality of threats. The longer this is reinforced, the more firmly entrenched it is likely to become (and the greater the danger of its becoming abusive). If, as Kohlberg suggests, children are responsive only to such threats well into their early school years, how is it, we might wonder, that they *ever* acquire genuinely other-regarding concerns? Kohlberg's apparent answer is that at roughly age seven or eight children's social understanding is transformed through further cognitive development. At this point they are able to understand perspectives other than their own, thus enabling them to empathize with others. However, seven or eight years of parental reinforcement of a morality of threats, plus another two or three years in an authoritarian school environment, is likely to make such a transformation quite difficult.

Psychologist Martin Hoffman points out a fundamental problem with Kohlberg's account:

It is . . . conceivable that a person could understand the social order and see its functional rationality quite well, discuss moral dilemmas of others intelligently and take the role of most anyone—and still act immorally himself and experience little or no guilt over doing so. Indeed, these social insights might just as readily serve Machiavellian as moral purposes.[4]

Not only is this conceivable, but it is precisely how sociopaths are typically characterized by psychiatrists.[5] Since Kohlberg supposes that young children do experience guilt, it is clear that he is not thinking of young children as sociopaths. However, he apparently is not thinking of their experience of guilt as reflecting genuine concern about the well-being of others. Instead, guilt is strictly tied to real or imagined threats of power or punishment. So Hoffman still has a point. If children are egoistic from the outset and remain so until age seven or eight, perhaps as they acquire greater social understanding they will simply incorporate this within their egoistic perspective. Thus, moral development could be seen as a gradual development of enlightened self-interest—that is, a more sophisticated form of egoism.[6]

Finding this implausible, Hoffman offers us a different view of young children. He provides convincing evidence that very young children are capable of genuinely empathic responses to the distress of others.[7] These responses manifest some awareness of the very different perspectives of others and also seem to manifest a genuine concern for the distress of others. William Damon's *The Moral Child* presents further evidence of this responsiveness from recent research on the moral development of children.[8] So there is good reason to suppose that nonegocentric and nonegoistic behavior is possible much earlier than Kohlberg allows. Since both are essential to later moral development, it is important for parents to be attentive and responsive to early manifestations.

Recall Thomas Reid's observation about the "seeds of moral discernment," whose "progress depends very much upon their being duly cultivated and properly exercised."[9] If parents believe their children are not ready to accept nonegoistic reasons for behaving or not behaving in certain ways, they will not cultivate the "seeds of moral discernment" in that direction. In fact, by substituting egoistic reasons in their stead, parents may actually contribute to the warping of those "seeds." If children are capable of nonegocentric thinking at a very early age, parents would do well to reinforce and provide opportunities for their children to develop this capacity. By assuming that their children are not capable of nonegocentric thinking until well into their school years, parents may actually reinforce and prolong the "tunnel vision" that so often impedes the development of moral sensitivity.

Piaget and Kohlberg's cognitive-developmental approach depicts moral development as proceeding in stages, with each successive stage bearing distinctive cognitive features. Children cannot proceed from one stage to the next until their cognitive abilities are sufficiently developed to appreciate the greater cognitive complexity of the next stage. For example, very young children can sort out three objects according to their size, determining which is largest, smallest, and middle-sized, but only when they can see all three at once. Older children can infer that if the red ball is larger than the blue one, and the blue one is larger than the yellow one, then the red ball is larger than the yellow one—even when the balls are out of view.

Later, children will be able to reason even more abstractly: If A is greater than B, and B greater than C, then A is greater than C, no matter what is being compared. But it is the ability to engage in reciprocal thinking that is crucial to moral development. For example, greater than and smaller than are reciprocally related, as in: If A is greater than B, and C is smaller than B, then A is greater than C. For Piaget and Kohlberg, reciprocal thinking is crucial to moral development because it enables one to understand and appreciate the perspectives of others, and it is a necessary feature of reasoning with universal principles.

Golden Rule reasoning, for example, requires us imaginatively to put ourselves in others' shoes. I am to do unto others as I would have them do unto me. How would I feel if others treated me in the way I am contemplating treating them? First I have to imagine what it would be like to be in their position, not with my wants and desires but theirs. Then I have to imagine how I, in their shoes, would evaluate being treated in the way I am thinking of treating them. Sissela Bok puts it this way:

We need to learn to shift back and forth between the two perspectives, and even to focus on both at once, as in straining to see both aspects of an optical illusion. In ethics, such a double focus leads to applying the Golden Rule: to strain to experience one's acts not only as subject and agent but as recipient, and sometimes victim.[10]

Precisely how this shifting back and forth should be characterized, and what we might expect it to yield, is problematic.[11] But, in any case, it is clear that rather sophisticated reciprocal thinking is required.

Piaget and Kohlberg hold that the ability to engage in reciprocal thinking is essential to transcending the egocentricity that they believe characterizes children well into their early school years. Egocentric thinking is marked by either an inability or failure to understand how others' perspectives may differ from one's own. In other words, insofar as we are egocentric, we assume others see things as we do. In addition to characterizing young children as highly egocentric, Piaget and Kohlberg also see them as primarily concerned with short-term personal gain and the avoidance of punishment. From a moral perspective, then, they are both egocentric and egoist.

The educational implications of this view are striking. As Gareth Matthews suggests, for Piaget and Kohlberg the early stages of moral development seem actually to be premoral stages.[12] Whatever conception of obligation young children have, it does not seem to be one of *moral* obligation. This is because their conception focuses only on what is likely to happen to them (personal loss or punishment) if they are caught. Lying, being careless, cruel, or unfair is wrong because of what will happen to me, not because of what might befall others. So, it seems, implicit threats or enticements need to be used on young children in order to get them to do as they ought. But young children do not share the same conception of "ought" as their elders. The implication is that young children are not ready to begin to think for themselves—at least not without powerful and obvious external incentives. The morality of young children is, as Piaget and Kohlberg would say, entirely *heteronomous:* what counts as moral is determined (and dictated) by others.

What Piaget and Kohlberg favor is the development of *autonomous* morality, and heteronomous stages are seen as necessary steps toward that end. What counts as moral at the autonomous level need not differ significantly from heteronomous morality in regard to content. The key difference is that moral maturity requires thinking for oneself. The acceptance of a norm, standard, or principle is done so autonomously when one sees why it is desirable and accepts it for that reason. Therefore, the important contrast concerns *why* we accept certain oughts, rather than *what* those oughts direct us to do. This why affects what we mean by ought. Thus, for Piaget and Kohlberg, heteronomous imposition of moral content on young children seems necessary, even into the early elementary-school years. Eventually, children (or young adults) need to free themselves from this heteronomous tether, but in such a way that they retain whatever desirable content can be extracted from the heteronomous domain.

Kohlberg believes that most adults never do leave this heteronomous domain, which seems to imply that moral education programs in the schools should have rather conservative expectations. Although autonomous morality is the ultimate goal for Kohlbergians, no stages can be skipped, so a good deal of time will first have to be spent refining and reinforcing stages that fall far short of the ideal endpoint. Most adults, Kohlberg claims, operate primarily in the conventional stages of seeking the approval of others or adopting a "law and order" perspective. But it seems implausible to suppose that the problem is basically a lack of cognitive development. We have already noted Martin Hoffman's point that it seems possible that someone might give an egoistic slant to each of Kohlberg's six stages. Increasing cognitive sophistication could, he says, be turned to Machiavellian advantage rather than put into the service of Kohlberg's favored Kantian principle of universal respect for human dignity. Manipulating others (treating them merely as means to your ends) can be done more or less well. Those with very well-developed cognitive abilities can, it seems, use them for good or ill (as many sociopaths do).

Hoffman's response to this problem is to urge us to notice signs of children's concerns for the well-being of others much earlier and to employ "inductive" (or reason-giving) methods of moral education as soon as this is feasible. He offers examples of sophisticated helping behavior in children well before they enter school. Here is one:

> Michael and Paul were struggling over a toy, resulting in Paul's crying. Michael appeared concerned and let go of the toy so that Paul would have it, but Paul kept crying. Michael paused, then gave his teddy bear to Paul, but the crying continued. Michael paused again, then ran to the next room, returned with Paul's security blanket, and offered it to Paul, who then stopped crying.[13]

Hoffman offers that the most plausible explanation of what occurred is that "Michael, as young as he was, could somehow reason by analogy that Paul would be comforted by something that he loved in the same way that Michael loved his own teddy."[14] Matthews amends this explanation by suggesting that Hoffman requires us to assume that Michael thought he *ought* to comfort Paul.[15] This would mean that Michael responded in a moral, not merely a premoral, way. Whether or not this is the best explanation of Michael's behavior in this particular instance, Matthews believes that explanations like this clearly fit some preschool children's behavior.[16] He concludes: "That means, they act with some kind of understanding that what they are doing is a good thing to do because, say, it will help someone out, or comfort someone, and not just that it might be a way to avoid being punished or a way to get rewarded."[17]

If Hoffman and Matthews are right, induction (or reason-giving) offers a much richer range of possibilities than Piaget and Kohlberg suggest. For Piaget and Kohlberg, the range of reasons children can be expected to respond to is quite limited in their early school years. In Kohlberg's case, for example, only those reasons operative in his first two stages would come into play, which means that the message to early elementary-school teachers who wish to promote the moral development of their students is to try to enhance the most sophisticated self-interested reasoning children of that age can acquire. Admittedly, these two stages are only preparatory for the more other-regarding, later stages of development, but the fact that those stages come, if at all, only later should be worrisome. What if reinforcing self-interested reasoning actually impedes, or even blocks, the development of more other-regarding attitudes? By overlooking children's nonegoistic capacities, teachers would unwittingly seem to increase the likelihood of Hoffman's Machiavellian worry becoming a reality for at least some children.

Of course, Piaget and Kohlberg would agree that teachers should reinforce and encourage generosity, kindness, fair play, honesty, and mutual respect among young children in the classroom and the playground. However, they seem to underestimate the contribution this reinforcement can make to the moral development of children, especially insofar as classroom discussion is concerned. As mentioned in Chapter 1, William Damon cites five basic social and emotional sources of young children's sharing: (1) children approaching each other through their common interest in toys and other objects; (2) their deriving pleasure "through the symmetrical rhythm of turn-taking with toys and other objects"; (3) urgings of parents and peers to share when possible; (4) children's natural empathic responses to other children who want to share or take a turn, especially when adults help them understand that excluded children will be unhappy; and (5) wanting playmates to reciprocate.[18] If the fourth source is ignored or underplayed, the remaining sources may seem congenial to the idea that young children are predominantly self-interestedly egocentric. However, once the fourth source is emphasized, the other sources take on richer possibilities. This is because the fourth source refers to not only empathy but also supporting, other-regarding reasons.

Therefore, it seems that the method of induction (reason-giving) can be employed in ways that encourage nonegocentric, caring behavior much earlier than Piaget and Kohlberg's theories suggest. Furthermore, the research of Richard A. Schweder, Elliot Turiel, and Nancy C. Much indicates that children as young as four years old are capable of distinguishing among conventional, prudential, and moral rules much as adults do (using obligatoriness, importance, and generalizability as criteria for moral rules).[19] For example, like adults they are capable of distinguishing throwing paint in another child's face as morally wrong from the unconventionality of wearing the same clothes to school every day.

Thus, the conceptual repertoire of even preschoolers is often quite sophisticated morally. If this is so, then it seems that at the very least, some revision of cognitive-developmental stage theory is needed. One way of revising it might be to retain the stages but revise the expected ages of children occupying them, thereby acknowledging that on occasion even preschoolers sometimes employ Kohlberg's stage three or four reasoning rather than only stage one or two.

However, this sort of adjustment is more radical than it might seem at first. Kohlberg's theory insists that moral development proceeds in stage-like, incremental steps. We operate mainly in one stage but partly in the immediately adjacent stages. No stages are skipped, and there are no "regressions" to earlier stages. Once one enters them, more advanced stages are seen to be preferable, both cognitively and morally. Finally, advancement to the next stage is facilitated by being confronted with dilemmas that cannot be dealt with effectively in one's current stage of development. Thus, advancement is accomplished by cognitive readiness for advancement and conflict. Cognitive readiness for operating in several stages at once seems present in very young children, while older children seem cognitively ready for all stages.[20] Finally, as adults we may recognize each of the stages as representing familiar reasoning, but we may wonder whether these are best characterized as stages or as different ways of reasoning available to us, depending on the context of judgment.[21]

Aside from the fact that we may find each of the stages represents reasoning that in certain contexts seems perfectly reasonable, there is a basic feature of Kohlberg's stage theory that should give us pause. The stages bear striking resemblance to familiar philosophical theories of morality. Stages one and two are variations on egoism. Stages three and four are variations on cultural relativism. Stages five and six pit utilitarianism and social contract theories against Kantian morality. Although Kohlberg sometimes speaks of children as young moral philosophers,[22] he seems to characterize their philosophizing about morality in a very special way: children in search of a unifying theory. The sequence of stages can be viewed as a succession of replacing flawed theories with better ones.

What may go unnoticed is that Kohlberg's (as well as Piaget's) account is philosophically skewed from the outset. All development is assessed in relation to the favored Kantian outcome. However, the assumption that this favored outcome is best is philosophically contentious. This does not mean that a Kantian view is not best, but from the standpoint of adults undertaking philosophical quests, it must seem presumptuous to assess all progress in relation to an already established outcome. It is no less presumptuous in regard to the philosophical quests of children. If we were to ask not which outcome is best but which might be accepted by reasonable inquirers, the number of candidates immediately swells. Furthermore, not all candidates will bear the marks of comprehensive, unifying theories such as the utilitarian and Kantian ones familiar to philosophers. The most salient mark of those theories is that each is organized around one fundamental moral principle, which provides the underlying rationale for all more specific moral determinations. Thus, for utilitarians, all of morality is grounded in some rendering of the "the greatest good for the greatest number."[23] Kantians rely on renderings of the Categorical Imperative, which requires willing one's judgments to be universalized so that anyone could justifiably act similarly, and in such a way that respect for human dignity is preserved.

Comprehensive, unifying theories such as these model what Thomas Reid characterizes as a *geometric* system of morality, "where the subsequent parts derive their evidence from the preceding, and one chain of reasoning is carried on from the beginning; so that, if the arrangement is changed, the chain is broken, and the evidence is lost."[24] This "top-down" approach can be contrasted with what he calls a *botanical* system, "where the subsequent parts depend not for their evidence upon the preceding, and the arrangement is made to facilitate apprehension and memory, and not to give evidence."[25]

It is evident that Reid himself favors the botanical model. But if our aim is to encourage the moral reflection of children, it is not necessary to decide which of these two models is actually the better fit for morality. For purposes of guiding initial moral inquiry, the botanical model seems best both pedagogically and morally. It seeks organizational structure and refinement of concepts without presuming a final form that must be satisfied. Some children may be inclined toward a more geometric quest, but many will not.[26] Eventually those who become philosophers will ally themselves with pluralists like Reid or monists like John Stuart Mill or Immanuel Kant. First, however, there is much unknown terrain to explore.

THEORETICAL UNCERTAINTY

It may seem that acknowledging that there is much unknown territory to explore leads back to the worries about moral uncertainty discussed at the outset of this chapter. The apparent promise of developmental theories like Piaget and Kohlberg's is that although children may initially see things with uncertain eyes, their teachers can have a solid framework within which to lead them. If well led, children eventually may begin to see that framework for themselves (thus becoming, for example, utilitarians or Kantians). However, teachers who themselves have geometric leanings may find their confidence shaken when they realize that reasonable people may differ about what the best moral system is. If moral certainty at any level of thought can be no greater than our moral certainty at the top level, then doubts about, say, utilitarian or Kantian principles should infect the entire chain. So it is only by ignoring the philosophically controversial aspects of Piaget and Kohlberg's developmental theories that a moral geometer's certainty can be sustained. However, this seems to be a false certainty. Furthermore, this security comes at a stiff price, for it presumes that if warranted certainty is obtainable at all, it can be so only for an elite group of "moral experts." The rest of us—and most especially, children—must either remain uncertain or commit ourselves to a set of beliefs that we can only hope is on the moral mark.

Philosopher R. M. Hare poses the problem rather starkly.[27] He says that morally we operate at an intuitive level in ordinary, everyday life. If we are well brought up, we will have appropriate moral dispositions (for example, to be fair, honest, trustworthy, considerate). Although we operate daily on an intuitive level that reflects these dispositions, we cannot *justify* our moral judgments at this intuitive level. We need to move to the critical level of moral thinking. Our intuitions, Hare says, have no "probative value." For all we know, prior to moving to the critical level, our intuitions may be no more than prejudices.

If this challenge to our intuitions were made not by a philosopher but some sort of provocateur, we might well be upset. It is not merely that the provocateur is suggesting that some of our basic moral judgments may be arbitrary or groundless. These judgments are, by Hare's own account, expressions of rather stable moral dispositions that we have—dispositions to be fair, honest, trustworthy, considerate, and so on. What seems to be challenged is our conception of who we take ourselves to be, what we stand for, and what our basic commitments are. I say, "I can't tell a *lie like that*" (one so blatant, so harmful, so betraying, so self-indulgent, so manipulative, and so on). *Intuitively*, I say, this seems so wrong. "Ah, what are 'intuitions'?" asks the provocateur. "For all you know, just the opposite may be right, or at least not wrong." I reflect for a moment on how I would feel if I were on the receiving end of such a lie, and imagined feelings of anger, betrayal, and distrust arise. These imagined feelings restore my confidence that my objection to the lie is not groundless or arbitrary.

But Hare is a philosopher, not a provocateur. He insists that we must move our thinking to a critical level to provide an underlying justification for our intuitions. Thinking at the critical level requires impartial reflection of two sorts. First, we must examine our preferences without first ranking them morally. Second, we must employ the logical concept of universalizability: whatever we judge to be right or wrong in one case must be judged right or wrong in all relevantly similar circumstances. Hare is confident that following this procedure will support utilitarianism.

However, Hare's position is quite controversial.[28] Many doubt that his utilitarian conclusion follows from his premises about preferences and universalizability. Others have doubts about his premises. In moving to the level of critical thinking, Hare seems to require us somehow to detach ourselves from our intuitions and, presumably, their underlying moral dispositions. Otherwise our reflections will be tainted by the very matters under critical examination. But how am I to do this? I seem to lose my center. How am I to proceed if I cannot employ any of my intuitions or their underlying dispositions? Stripped of these, it seems that *I* am under attack, not just my intuitive judgments.

Once again it seems that we are in search of an Archimedean point from which a critical assessment can be made—this time of ourselves, not just cultural norms and practices. Just as Amy Gutmann argues that we do not need (and cannot obtain) such an Archimedean point in order to engage in critical reflection on cultural norms and practices, this is not necessary (or possible) in evaluating our intuitions. As moral agents we cannot escape them, even as we attempt to assess them. Or, if we could, we would in effect suspend our moral agency, thus throwing into doubt our competency to make appropriate assessments at that time.

In any case, there is little assurance that if Hare's critical frame of mind were obtainable, his utilitarian perspective would prevail. Disagreement at this level is at least as likely as at the intuitive level, but it is not necessary to resolve these disagreements here. It is sufficient to point out that regardless of who, if anyone, might have the most defensible view, there is enough reasonable disagreement to warrant something less than certainty at this level of inquiry. Hare's view seems to imply that warranted moral certainty at the everyday level depends on certainty at the more theoretical level, and it is just this conclusion that Thomas Reid counsels us to avoid. He reminds us that morality is everyone's business, not just moral philosophers', and that "knowledge of it ought to be within the reach of all."[29] He urges us to avoid the "gross mistake" of supposing that "in order to understand his duty a man must needs be a philosopher and a metaphysician."[30] It should be noted that Reid does not say philosophical reflection is unnecessary in order to understand our duty. Instead he denies that this understanding requires one to be a philosopher or metaphysician, or to keep company with grand systematic thinkers such as Plato, Kant, or Mill. Just as we can distinguish thinking scientifically from being a scientist, we can distinguish thinking philosophically from being a philosopher.

How much, if any, philosophical thinking is necessary for understanding our duty is another matter. Although Reid believes that much of everyday morality is uncontroversial, he acknowledges that "there are intricate and perplexed cases even in Morals wherein it is no easy matter to form a determinate judgment."[31] Philosophical reflection certainly has a role to play in such cases. But learning the contours of even the more clearly demarcated areas of morality can call for philosophical reflection on the meanings of basic moral concepts, standards, and principles; their relationships to one another; and their applications in actual circumstances. However, the inquiry should proceed from the "bottom up" (botanically) rather than the "top down" (geometrically). Reid's main concern is that we guard against the grand systems of philosophy thwarting the reflective inquiry of ordinary people. Thus, wherever the higher reaches of philosophy might ultimately land us, we need not attain them in order to be able competently to negotiate questions of right, wrong, duty, and so on.

Reid's optimism should not be confused with naivete about what "everyone knows." However "plain" much of morality is, this is so only insofar as we are clearheaded and careful in our thinking; and, he points out, there are reasons why this often is not the case:

> There is . . . no branch of Science wherein Men would be more harmonious in their opinions than in Morals were they free from all biass and Prejudice. But this is hardly the case with any Man. Mens private Interests, their Passions, and vicious inclinations & habits, do often blind their understandings, and biass their judgments.[32]

Given this situation, it seems there is much for children to discuss, regardless of whether they end up as utilitarians or Kantians. In fact, in a typical classroom discussion children might well begin to articulate utilitarian or Kantian ideas. But more commonly there will be vigorous discussions of fairness/unfairness, honesty/dishonesty, respect/disrespect, kindness/unkindness, helping/harming, loyalty/disloyalty, responsibility/irresponsibility, and other notions that are already playing an important role in their lives. These notions will be explored through their application both to rather straightforward examples (such as taking turns) and to more complex examples (such as the relative importance of effort, ability, and opportunity in determining what one deserves).

It may be thought that without an overarching general theory serving as a beacon, neither teachers nor students will be able competently to find their way about. However, it is the burden of the next section to show that this is not so.

MORAL CERTAINTY

As adults, there are many things about which we are morally certain. Our lists may differ significantly but they overlap significantly, too. The greatest agreement is likely to congregate around specific examples. Judith Lichtenberg suggests the following: "A man has sexual intercourse with his three-year-old niece. Teenagers standing beside a highway throw large rocks through the windshields of passing cars. A woman intentionally drives her car into a child on a bicycle. Cabdrivers cut off ambulances rushing to hospitals."[33] Lichtenberg is morally certain that each of these is a clear and uncontrovertible instance of wrongdoing. I agree. What is it that warrants such confidence? Although each example she offers is an example of a *kind* of wrongdoing, the kinds in question are quite specific. More inclusive ways of characterizing wrongdoing are hazardous and likely to result in generalizations to which we can imagine possible exceptions.

For example, is it *always* wrong, under any imaginable circumstance, for a cabdriver to cut off an ambulance rushing to a hospital? A moral mischief-maker might quip, "What if the cab itself is rushing to the hospital—with a severely injured person (after it was noticed that the ambulance driver inadvertently took off with someone already dead)?" "But," Lichtenberg might retort, "*that's* not the example I had in mind." "Of course not," the mischief-maker replies, "but just how *would* you describe your case in order to disallow exceptions like this?"

However difficult it might be to specify exactly what we have in mind, it does not seem that our confidence in Lichtenberg's examples should be undermined. We can recognize clear instances of such wrongdoings.

But this is not because we have confidence in more general moral considerations from which these are deducible. Rather, it seems to go the other way around. Whatever more general, or inclusive, considerations we find owe their certainty, in part, to our confidence about these more specific sorts. Further, although we may turn to philosophers or theologians for help, we need not wait for their endorsement. Nor is it clear that the most fundamental grounding of our moral certainty about such matters comes mainly from the efforts of parents and teachers to imprint values in us. This is not to deny the importance of adult reinforcement nor the possibility that they can discourage a child's acceptance and appreciation of such certainties. But, it seems, children themselves have capacities that naturally move them in this direction—unless the harshness of their surroundings discourages the exercise of those capacities. One indication that the kinds of moral certainties Lichtenberg brings to our attention are linked to such capacities is our response to those who apparently do not share her reaction to the examples she presents. As Lichtenberg says, this is a sign of pathology, not merely difference.

However, Lichtenberg also points out the limitations of what she is saying. Warranted moral certainty cannot take us far. Nevertheless, it does give us something from which to proceed, and this is what must be acknowledged when children arrive in school. They are not (morally) blank slates. Indeed, there are nuances, difficulties, and uncertainties, but there are certainties, too, and the schools should not be expected to shy away from them. How they are best presented and how they should be understood by teachers is another matter, and about these matters there can be uncertainty.

The kinds of moral certainties Lichtenberg discusses seem to be more closely linked to general dispositions to react to certain kinds of wrongdoing than to exceptionless principles. Thus, we are disposed to react negatively to what we take to be unfairness, reckless regard for human life, and so on. Although we may find it difficult, if not impossible, to frame exceptionless principles that ground our more particular judgments, we can readily provide lists of criteria we rely on in making those judgments. The criteria that appear on our lists represent what we care about morally: fairness, respect, consideration, helpfulness, honesty, and so on. That we care about them is evidenced by our reactions to what we take to be examples either of these concerns or their opposites.

AN ILLUSTRATION: HELPFULNESS

Motivation to help others occurs remarkably early in the lives of children. We have already mentioned Martin Hoffman's example of fifteen-month-old Michael comforting Paul after struggling over a toy. Although it would be implausible to suppose that Michael is already operating from specifically moral concepts, his response to Paul's discomfort is a precursor of what later will be a part of his moral character.

Let us imagine another child, say, Barbara at age four. She is shopping in a grocery store with her father. When her father receives change from the clerk, he asks Barbara if she would like to put some coins in a container marked with a picture of a poor, underfed child. Barbara asks about the child and with obvious satisfaction drops the coins in the container. At some point, if not now, it is clear that Barbara's willingness to help those in need will be fully moral. It will be as much a part of her moral makeup as, say, being honest or fair is for her.

But what does this mean? To say that she is honest, for example, is not to say that she never engages in deceptive behavior or even that she never lies.[34] She will not tell the local bully where her best friend is hiding, even if she has to lie. And, like most, there are times when she is tempted to lie or deceive even when she thinks it would be wrong to do so. Yet she believes she should be honest and usually she is. So, while basically honest, Barbara is no absolutist about truthfulness.

Barbara also wants to help those in need, an admirable trait. We might compare Barbara with Forrest Carter's Little Tree, a somewhat older American Indian child.[35] Little Tree notices a little girl with no shoes and seemingly little else by way of possessions. He tells his grandmother, who makes some moccasins for her. Little Tree presents the moccasins to the girl, much to her obvious delight. So far, so good. But the story now takes a surprising turn. The little girl's father asks her where she got the moccasins. She points to Little Tree. Then the father whips her hard on the legs and back with a switch, makes her take off the moccasins, and returns them to Little Tree, saying: "We'uns don't take no charity . . . from nobody . . . and especial heathen savages."[36] Later Little Tree's grandfather comments on the episode:

> On the trail, Granpa said he didn't bear the sharecropper no ill. Granpa said he reckined that pride was all he had . . . howsoever

misplaced. He said the feller figgered he couldn't let the little girl, ner any of his young'uns, come to love pretty things for they couldn't have them. So he whipped them when they showed a liking for things they couldn't have . . . and he whipped them until they learned; so that in a little while, they knowed they was not to expect them things.[37]

What has Little Tree learned? That giving to others is wrong? Hardly. What he has learned is that one must pay careful attention to the larger context in which giving takes place because in some instances it may do more harm than good. This concept may never have occurred to Little Tree before. It was beyond his small world and likely beyond his imagination. However, the lesson he learned put together several things for him: scarcity of goods, giving, kindness, the infliction of pain, coping, and pride. He had some understanding of each of these but not in these relationships to one another.

Little Tree also learned something else, with broader implications. Little Tree recounts, "Granpa said he didn't fault me fer not catching on right off." His grandfather told him that he had the advantage over Little Tree of having seen something similar a few years earlier. He saw a father whip two of his daughters when he saw them looking at a Sears Roebuck catalog:

Granpa said that feller took a switch and whipped them young'uns 'till the blood run out of their legs. He said he watched, and the feller took the Sears Roebuck catalog and he went out behind the barn. He burned up the catalog, tore it all up first, like he hated that catalog. Granpa said then the feller set down against the barn, where nobody could see him, and he cried. Granpa said he seen that and so he knowed. Granpa said ye had to understand. But most people didn't want to—it was too much trouble—so they used words to cover their own laziness and called other folks "shiftless."[38]

So Little Tree learned several things—that things are not always what they seem; that one might, nevertheless, be able to understand (which is not necessarily to approve); and that we have a tendency not to take the effort to understand. Thus, initially assuming others are (or should be) like us, we may exaggerate the differences between ourselves and them that we first notice. Little Tree has also learned that while helpfulness is important, one may have to work hard at getting that right.

It looks as though Little Tree has made some moral progress. However, if we try to cast this progress in terms of an absolutist perspective, we will find that Little Tree's understanding is far from adequate. He has just learned that although giving is sometimes good, it may misfire in quite serious and unfortunate ways. It is not clear how general Little Tree's understanding is at this point. If anything, he is now more cautious—less likely to generalize too quickly, more likely to want to examine the particular circumstances more thoroughly. Yet he does not necessarily have a more general perspective from which to evaluate his progress. Giving to others in need is still good, but not unqualifiedly.

Cultural relativism fares no better here. Should Little Tree say to himself, "Giving to the poor is good or bad—depending on the culture or community in question"? Little Tree might conclude that it was wrong for him to give the moccasins to the little girl because she lives in a community that does not approve of such an act (at least not if done by a "heathen savage"). No doubt there is something relative here. Little Tree has learned that he must pay attention to the circumstances in which giving takes place. But he does not necessarily look disapprovingly at what he did and approvingly at what the father did, nor does his grandfather. Little Tree's grandfather does not condemn the father, and he tries to help Little Tree become more understanding; but his grandfather hardly thinks that what the father did is right either.

Therefore, it might be better to say that Little Tree has gained a lesson in critical thinking. His eyes have been opened to new possibilities, and he now sees his moral world somewhat differently. Normally commendable behavior (giving to one in need) has proven to be problematic. Normally unacceptable behavior (whipping a child for accepting a gift) is seen as understandable, however flawed. Is Little Tree now hopelessly confused? Has he lost his footing because of this unexpected turn of events? There is little reason to suppose either. As narrator, Little Tree conveys the sense that he has increased his understanding. It is not that giving to others in need is not good; it is simply not an unqualified good because it can bring harm with it.

However, as other possible scenarios illustrate, not just any harm counters the good that comes from giving. Imagine Little Tree giving the moccasins to the little girl, who then trips and falls while dancing merrily in celebration of her good fortune. Without the gift the accident would not have happened. Or, as she is dancing in the street wearing her new moccasins, a father (not her own) grabs her, throws her on the ground, and takes the moccasins home for *his* shoeless child. Would these unfortunate consequences convince Little Tree that he should not have presented the little girl with the moccasins? Should they? Notice the reaction to Little Tree's act of giving. Perceived as charity from an unworthy, the gift is refused and the original recipient of the moccasins, the little girl, is punished. So matters are quite complex, whether or not Little Tree sees this yet.

We see Little Tree learning moral lessons the hard way—by being immersed in a situation calling for a response that has real consequences. Although classroom discussions themselves have moral dimensions, the classroom affords children space in which to develop and exercise their moral imagination from a safer distance. In the next chapter I examine some of the educational gains such discussions might provide.

9

Case by Case Reasoning

Robert Fullinwider suggests that we see moral education as something like learning a vocabulary, learning how to use words and concepts. This is what children do in their daily affairs as they sort out what it means to share, take turns, treat others fairly or unfairly, tease, make friends, and so on. Much of this activity takes place outside the classroom, and it is well under way before children enter school for the first time. Fullinwider adds, "A moral education supplies tools of evaluation (a vocabulary) rather than a doctrine for adhesion (dogma)."[1]

The implication for moral education is that students need to be encouraged to use these tools in the classroom. That is, they need to be encouraged to engage in evaluative thought—with each other. Much of this involves classifying cases as similar or different from one another in relevant respects, a task that requires analogical reasoning. As Fullinwider says:

> Moral argument arises over appropriate classifications and re-classifications and it proceeds by analogy. "This case is like that one," I claim. "No it isn't," you counter. And as in the example about Susie being stuck-up, we end up contesting about the relevant features of the present case, so that we can finally come to agreement, if we can, on which paradigm case determines the issue.[2]

This process resembles the notion of *casuistry* that Albert Jonsen and Stephen Toulmin have done much to revitalize.[3] This chapter explores the potential of casuistic methods of reasoning for the moral education of children.

CASUISTRY: USE AND ABUSE

Jonson and Toulmin attempt to extract casuistic methods of reasoning from Jesuit and rabbinical traditions and apply them to contemporary medical ethics. Their work was inspired by seeing these methods in action when the Belmont Report emerged from the deliberations of the National Commission for the Protection of Human Subjects of Biomedical and Behavioral Research.[4] What enabled the commission to complete its task, they say, was its turning to cases and looking for points of agreement from which a policy statement might be developed. Eventually shared principles were formulated (concerning, for example, respect for persons, beneficence, and just treatment of subjects). Prior to that, principles were only provisionally offered; much more secure was agreement about the specific cases that had prompted the establishment of the commission in the first place (a broad range of inappropriately conducted experiments on human beings).

Jonsen and Toulmin are well aware of Blaise Pascal's scathing critique of seventeenth-century Jesuit casuistry. Pascal catalogued many abuses of casuistry. The "mental reservation" is a good illustration. If asked by a parent whether he has finished his homework, John may say, "Yes," but silently add, "last week's." Thus, by clever manipulation of words, John succeeds in getting permission to watch a favorite television program. Popular definitions of casuistry today depict it as "sophistical, equivocal, or specious reasoning"[5] or "subtle but misleading or false application of ethical principles."[6]

Training children in such cleverness is hardly what is needed, but this is not what Jonsen and Toulmin have in mind in attempting to revitalize casuistry. They emphasize the constructive side of casuistry that sorts out relevantly similar and different kinds of cases and that provisionally formulates principles that can provide guidance in future cases, all the while being open to the possible need for revision in light of new and unexpected cases. Although vulnerable to abuse, casuistic reasoning can also guard against the indiscriminate use of principles by making careful note of relevant, often complex, nuances that warrant "taking exception to the rule." This requires good character as well as good reasoning. Open discussion of cases also can check abuses; thus John's disingenousness will be transparent if he explains his tactics to others.

David Boeyink compares casuistry with common law:

Paradigm cases establish a precedent to be tested, revised, expanded or contrasted based on similar, but not identical, cases. Like common law, ethical principles are developed and given content only through their operation in cases; not deductively established and then applied.[7]

Boeyink applies casuistic analysis to the construction of a code of ethics for the newsroom. Similarly, this is the recommended method for developing a better understanding of research ethics in a recent book, *Research Ethics: Cases and Materials,* edited by Robin Levin Penslar.[8] Paradigms of appropriate and inappropriate research procedures are presented first. These are then followed by more complex cases that can be compared and contrasted with the more clear-cut cases.

Successful use of casuistic methods depends on both good character and familiarity with the context under consideration. In Boeyink's case, it was thoughtful, experienced journalists. In the research area, cases were prepared with the assistance of biologists, psychologists, and historians familiar with research ethics problems in their respective fields.

Casuistic methods seem to have been employed in the early 1920s by the ethics committee of the American Association of Engineers.[9] Case by case the committee, composed of respected engineers, examined representative ethical problems that engineers face. Then they formulated a set of principles and guidelines they found most relevant to how they had resolved the more particular cases. As a glance at the history of engineering codes of ethics reveals, from time to time professional engineering societies introduce changes. Occasionally these changes are striking (such as in the early 1970s when protecting public health and safety replaced loyalty to employers or clients as the engineer's paramount duty. Yet, given the nature of engineering practice, many of the basic provisions have remained stable over time.

All of the above instances of casuistic reasoning seem to function in contexts where at least some shared values can be presumed. Is this possible with children? The playground and the institutional setting of the school both provide fertile ground. So do materials that might be presented in the classroom, particularly in the form of examples and stories. In fact, Fullinwider says that moral education is largely *case-based*:

"It is from a background of richly described exemplary cases, situations, and characters that we structure our moral reactions and the criticisms and revisions we make of them."[10]

Gareth Matthews nicely outlines how we might expect conceptual change to occur in children as their experience broadens and deepens through the consideration of such cases:

> A young child is able to latch onto the moral kind, bravery, or lying, by grasping central paradigms of that kind, paradigms that even the most mature and sophisticated moral agents still count as paradigmatic. Moral development is . . . enlarging the stock of paradigms for each moral kind; developing better and better definitions of whatever it is these paradigms exemplify; appreciating better the relation between straightforward instances of the kind and close relatives; and learning to adjudicate competing claims from different moral kinds (classically the sometimes competing claims of justice and compassion, but many other conflicts are possible).[11]

Matthews's approach to moral development has at least three advantages over the cognitive-developmental approach of Piaget and Kohlberg. First, it is descriptively accurate without depending on a unifying, but controversial, moral theory. At the same time, it is compatible with some such theory eventually resulting from moral inquiry. Thus, initial moral inquiry fits Reid's botanical model rather than a geometric model. As Matthews puts it, children develop a working understanding of basic moral concepts at a very early age; what follows is enlargement and refinement of these concepts rather than their displacement. Second, it credits young children with being moral rather than premoral agents. Thus, it reduces the gap between children and adults by placing them in a world of shared moral understanding and resists adult condescension toward children. Third, paradigms retained from childhood provide the desired certainty from which both children and adults can proceed in their exploration of less clear and more controversial areas of morality. Thus, while adults have the advantage of experience and a greater grasp of conceptual nuances, even very young children can have considerable moral sophistication.

Matthews identifies five dimensions across which moral development takes place. The first is the acquisition of paradigms, clear-cut instances of, say, lying, dishonesty, cruelty, kindness, and the like. The second dimension relates to one's relative success in offering defining characteristics of concepts (for example, seeing that lying typically involves the intent to deceive rather than simply saying something false). Matthews is careful to point out that fully satisfactory definitions are hard to come by and admits that he has been unable to come up with one for lying.[12] Yet, he adds, we can have a good working grasp of moral concepts even if we lack fully satisfactory definitions. Understanding a central paradigm is a start. Coming up with defining characteristics refines our understanding and enables us to work with more subtle cases.

Matthews's notion of having a working grasp of a concept stands in striking contrast to Socrates' insistence that Euthyphro should be able to explain what all just or righteous acts have in common if he is to explain why prosecuting a murderer is just or righteous.[13] Socrates expresses surprise that Euthyphro is so confident that it is just to prosecute one's own father for murder. He presses Euthyphro to tell him first what all just acts have in common that makes them just. Since Euthyphro is unable to do this, readers are encouraged to conclude that he has little, if any, understanding of what is just. So, they are led to think, Euthyphro could not really justify what he is setting out to do. Very possibly he could not. But this is not because he has little, if any, understanding of what is just but because he lacks sufficient understanding of what justice requires *in cases like this*. Unfortunately, Socrates' insistence that only a complete definition will suffice discourages Euthyphro from proceeding in the more modest fashion suggested by Matthews. Thus, we cannot really tell how much understanding of justice Euthyphro has.

Matthews's third dimension of moral development involves determining the range of cases falling under a concept as well as dealing with borderline cases (such as whether knowingly writing a check that will bounce is lying). The fourth dimension, the one to which Kohlberg gives greatest attention, is the ability to adjudicate conflicting moral claims. Normally we should not lie, but what if being truthful will cause someone serious harm? What if being fair to one person will result in being cruel or unkind to someone else? What if the only apparent way to save a life is to steal something (Kohlberg's classic Heinz dilemma)?

Matthews's final dimension is moral imagination. This involves, first of all, being able to understand what needs to be taken into consideration, including the perspectives of others. But it also involves being able to resolve, or at least reduce, conflicts by thinking creatively of alternative ways of dealing with these conflicts. Sometimes this may be accomplished by thinking of a novel solution that satisfies everyone concerned. Sometimes it is necessary to come up with compromises that although less than fully satisfactory to everyone, one can nevertheless "live with"—what Martin Benjamin calls "integrity preserving compromises."[14]

An important implication of both Fullinwider and Matthews's understanding of moral development is that the moral experiences of children and adults overlap significantly. The complexity of adult moral life may be much greater. But, as Matthews puts it, the differences are much more a matter of enlarging our basic understandings than totally replacing them:

> As Susan grows and develops we hope she will enlarge her stock of paradigms from handing out cookies fairly to distributing work assignments fairly among workers of varied abilities to, perhaps, refusing to change the rules in the middle of a game. And we hope Susan will grow along other dimensions of moral development as well. But the simple paradigms of distributive justice will stay with her permanently. And no contrast between the virtuosity of her later reasoning and the naivete of her early appeal to simple paradigms can establish that those early actions were not really performed from a sense of fairness.[15]

Whatever reach one's moral outlook ultimately attains, moral learning is initially quite local, with particular examples playing a crucial role. It is within these local circumstances that our earliest paradigms emerge. Although local in their origins, these paradigms enable us to undertake with some confidence moral inquiry into less familiar territory. Sometimes we proceed without due caution, and as we have seen in the case of Little Tree, this experience may provide us with important moral lessons. One of these lessons is that while our paradigms may enable us to engage fruitfully in moral inquiry, even our most basic moral concepts remain somewhat open-ended. For example, although each of us may be able to provide a paradigm example of fairness, it is rather easy to come up with examples that leave us unsure about what fairness requires. Definitions of moral concepts in terms of necessary and sufficient conditions are rare. Surprises are much more common, as we shall see in the case of lying.

LYING

Children engage in deceptive behavior before they tell outright lies. They also have rather well-developed linguistic skills before they tell deliberate lies. Currently the best evidence is that a crucial transition takes place typically between ages three and four. Four-year-olds are capable of telling deliberate lies, whereas three-year-olds typically are not.[16]

What is the key difference between three- and four-year-olds that accounts for the former's inability to tell deliberate lies? In order to tell a deliberate lie, one must understand that another person can hold false beliefs, and that this can be brought about by telling someone something that one believes to be false. Typically, one acts on the intention to deceive by claiming that something is true, while all along believing it is not true. Apparently children under four have great difficulty in false belief tasks because they have not yet caught on to the idea that others can be mistaken in what they believe.

Just how the world of three-year-olds should be understood is not entirely clear. They can engage in behavior that is deceptive, even by using words; but they cannot yet deliberately lie.[17] Janet Wilde Astington attributes this to younger children still operating only within first-order intentional systems.[18] Although first-order intentional systems, she says, do not involve thinking about what others believe, they do include thinking about what others will do. Second-order intentional systems include both. Children under four seem inclined to say aloud what they believe is true, yet they do not do this because they attach any particular value to truthfulness. They are in the habit of saying what they take to be true but not because they perceive anything wrong with saying what they take not to be true.

However, once children can lie matters change. They can now deliberately depart from that to which they have become accustomed—saying what they take to be true. Thus, children are not born liars, and they are not born truthful. But by the time they can deliberately lie, somehow they have already developed techniques of deception. Around age four they develop a new weapon: They learn that getting someone to believe something false is sometimes effective (at least in the short run) in avoiding difficulties, getting what one wants, and so on.

The suggestion that most children cannot deliberately lie until about four years of age raises an interesting question. The word "lie" becomes part of children's vocabulary long before they are four. What do they understand lie to mean? Curiously, recent research by Wimmer, Gruber, and Perner supports Piaget's observation that children as old as six and even seven often think of lying simply as "saying what is false."[19] Astington suggests that this may be because typically no more explicit characterization is offered by parents or other influential adults.

This has important implications for how lying is evaluated by children. Adult injunctions never to lie cannot be expected to be taken seriously, since it is obvious to children long before they are six years old that people sometimes say false things simply because they do not know what is true. This observation is part of the insight they gain at age four. Astington notes that although children as old as six or seven do use "lie" as roughly equivalent to "saying what is false," they nevertheless distinguish between culpable and nonculpable lies. They base this distinction on intentions they attribute to speakers. Therefore, it is likely that by the time children enter school, they have already questioned the absolute prohibition of lying, at least in the broad sense of saying what is false. However, sorting out acceptable from unacceptable false utterances is not easy, even for adults. Some assistance could be useful.

How might children be assisted? One way is through stories. All of us have heard the story of George Washington and his father's cherry tree. William Bennett includes this story in his *Book of Virtues* as one of the first stories in the chapter entitled "Honesty."[20] This is precisely where most of us would expect it to be placed in a book of stories about various virtues. After all, young George says to his father, "I cannot tell a lie, father. I did it with my hatchet." But how are we to understand young George's statement? Is he saying that he can *never* tell a lie—that not lying is, for him at least, an *absolute*? This is one way of reading the story, and I suspect that this is how many of us have read it. As adults, we realize this is overstatement, for we can all think of at least some exceptions to the rule. Yet we might appreciate the story for children precisely because it does not hedge. It confirms the importance of being truthful and avoids watering this down at the risk of washing away truthfulness in a torrent of rationalization. Here is something firm and certain from which a child can proceed. Qualifications can (and will) come later.

Yet it takes just a little imagination to raise problems with this story. Suppose we change it a bit. Young George sees his father run into the house and hide in the basement. Minutes later a would-be assailant, armed with knives and guns, appears at the door and asks young George if his father is home. George says, "I cannot tell a lie. He is hiding in the basement." Would George's father praise him for his honesty? Would we? Would a young child?

It seems that the inspiration children get from the actual story very much depends on the context described. It is interesting to note that the story ends like this:

> Mr. Washington put his hand on the boy's shoulder. "Look at me," he said. "I am sorry to have lost my cherry tree, but I am glad that you were brave enough to tell me the truth. I would rather have you truthful and brave than to have a whole orchard full of the finest cherry trees. Never forget that, my son."
>
> George Washington never did forget. To the end of his life he was just as brave and honorable as he was that day as a little boy.[21]

The closing paragraph notably shifts the reader's attention to something more than truthfulness. Young George has been *brave* (in telling the truth when he feared what would happen to him). He was *honorable* in acknowledging he made a mistake (i.e., in telling the truth in this kind of circumstance). It is never asked whether a brave person might sometimes lie, or whether an honorable person might sometimes lie. This question presumably is left for the young reader to answer—if not now, then sometime later.[22]

It might be cautioned that it is best not to complicate a young child's mind with variations like the one I presented. They are not ready for such subtleties, and much can be undone if young children are invited to reflect in this way. However, young children sometimes do have to reflect in this way, as life outside the school sometimes puts them or their loved ones in jeopardy ("Are your parents home?" asks the voice at the other end of the telephone). There is also the extreme case of the children of Le Chambon in World War II. Philip Hallie notes that Magda Trocme worried that the children would have to unlearn lying after lying to the Nazis about whether the little village was harboring any Jews.[23] However, her daughter, one of those children, said they never had to unlearn lying. These extraordinary circumstances called for their assistance. The fact that they lied did not incline them to think that lying, in general, is all right. In other words, the children understood what was at stake. It was, Hallie says, a situation of "life-and-death ethics," which has to do with hurting and helping people. Betrayal, torture, humiliation, and killing all loom large in such circumstances. So the suspension of ordinary constraints against lying is not surprising and this requires no weakening of those constraints in other, more ordinary circumstances.

What about deliberately introducing young children to some of the complications of speaking truthfully? Here is one such story that, incidentally, presents a version of the George Washington story that does urge us never to lie, Gloria Skurzynski's *Honest Andrew*.[24]

Andrew Otter hates crayfish, but he does not want to hurt his mother's feelings. So, when his father asks, "Isn't this good, Andrew?" Andrew replies, "Uh huh." His father puts more crayfish on Andrew's plate. Instead of eating the crayfish, Andrew keeps pushing it into his cheeks. Unable to swallow the fish, his mouth is completely full when his mother puts dessert on the table.

Andrew mumbles, "Excuse me," and gets up to leave the table, trying to say that he wants to go out and smell petunias. Thinking he is out of sight of his parents, he spits out the crayfish. Alas, his father sees him do this. Andrew quickly says that he was just baiting the fish traps. The story continues:

> "You're not telling the truth, Andrew. I followed you. You had your whole dinner in your mouth, and you spit it into the river. Why did you do that?"
>
> "Because *I hate crayfish!*" Andrew cried.
>
> "Why didn't you say so?"
>
> "I didn't want to hurt Mama's feelings. And you would have made me eat it anyway, wouldn't you?"

"I suppose so," Papa Otter said, "but I wouldn't have given you more. What you did wasn't honest, Andrew. And then you lied about it." He took Andrew by the ear. "You and I are going to have a talk about honesty."[25]

What does Papa Otter say to young Andrew? He shows him a sign ("the otter motto") that says, "AN OTTER OUGHT TO BE HONEST." He then illustrates this motto with two examples. The first example is an otter walking four miles to return a fish that another otter had dropped. The second is a young otter confessing that he ruined his father's mud slide ("I did it, Father. I cannot tell a lie."). Insisting that otters value honesty "above all else," Andrew's father smiles when Andrew responds, "From now on I'll always tell the truth."[26]

The rest of the story recounts Andrew's problems in trying to live up to his word—as well as the difficulties this causes his parents. Mama Otter introduces Andrew to Professor Beaver, who asks, "How are you, young man?" Andrew gives the professor a very detailed answer about his cuts and bruises. As he begins to tell about his problems with crayfish, the Professor grows weary and excuses himself.

Mama Otter tells Andrew that he should not go on and on; he should just say, "Fine, thank you." But, sticking to his commitment to being truthful, Andrew corrects his Aunt Prissy when she remarks, "Why, you're quite a big otter, Andrew."[27] After Mama Otter tells Mrs. Woodchuck that she has a darling baby, Andrew comments, "Darling? She's ugly." He adds, "Her face is all wrinkled. She looks like she slid face-down on a mud slide."[28]

Embarrassed and angered, Mama Otter takes Andrew home and makes him face the wall for the rest of the day. Andrew's defense was that he was only being honest. Papa Otter explains that it is wrong to be rude:

"Then I shouldn't be honest and truthful?"
"Of course you should. But you mustn't hurt people's feelings."[29]

Andrew replies that this is why he said he liked crayfish:

"That was dif . . . ," his papa sputtered. "That was . . . um . . . humph. . . . That was . . . Oh, my!" Papa Otter's shoulders drooped.

His mustache drooped. He looked so bewildered that Andrew felt sorry for him.[30]

Now it is Andrew's turn to offer a suggestion. "Should I always tell the truth, but be as nice and polite about it as I can?"[31] Papa Otter agrees that this is *exactly* what he should do. Andrew has an early opportunity to try out this new understanding when Mama Otter announces they are having salamander stew for dinner. The story concludes:

Andrew slumped down on his chair. "Mama," he said, "you are the sweetest, nicest mama in the whole world. Your eyes are big and bright. Your fur is warm and soft. You wear pretty earrings, and I HATE SALAMANDER STEW!"[32]

What should the young (or older) reader conclude? Most will realize that Andrew (and his parents) still has much more thinking to do. Where might our reflections go from here? A first observation might be that no one in the story seems to recognize a distinction between honesty and candor. Andrew seems to believe that if he is does not completely reveal what he is thinking, then he is not being honest. But this approach seems rather severe. How could friends maintain secrets that are no one's business but theirs? We might also note that Andrew is not asked if he likes salamander stew. So why assume he is not honest if he does not volunteer his hatred of salamander stew?

Does the introduction of these problems undermine the value of being truthful? There is little reason to think so. Readers can still admire Abe Lincoln Otter and George Washington Otter. What they have discovered in the story (if not already in their lives) is that being truthful is not the *only* value—and in some circumstances, perhaps not the most important value. This is something that most children learn rather early. What *Honest Andrew* does is encourage this early realization without at the same time inviting general skepticism about the importance of truthfulness. Instead, truthfulness is placed alongside other common values, such as consideration and politeness. But even so, much is left unresolved. The discussion must go on—thoughtfully and reflectively—and based on one's experience to that point.

RECIPROCITY: A DIALOGUE
AMONG TEN-YEAR-OLDS

Honest Andrew models, in an amusing way, an adult-child exchange that may be as instructive for Andrew's father as for Andrew himself. Of course, this is a fictional account. How might a good discussion of moral problems go among real children? Some years ago, I had the good fortune of participating in a videotaped discussion of a challenging set of circumstances with a group of ten-year-olds. I published the transcript of this discussion in chapter 9 ("Reciprocity") of *Philosophical Adventures with Children*. Lawrence Kohlberg read this transcript and shared with me his written, but unpublished, analysis of the transcript.[33]

Kohlberg comments that my discussion of reciprocity and the Golden Rule with children is just what his theory of moral development predicts will occur in good developmental moral discussions. He concludes that while "ignoring psychological moral stages and focusing on a moral philosophic understanding of Socratic inquiry," my way of leading the discussion "is much the same sort of teaching which we advocate, with much the same results." At a very general level this statement is probably true. However, I believe there are important differences when we look at more specific features of Kohlberg's commentary.

At the outset of my chapter "Reciprocity," I noted that Kohlberg's account of moral development holds that moral reasoning is advanced by being thrown into "disequilibrium." Children find that their customary modes of reasoning are not adequate for handling certain problems, and successful resolution requires advancing to the next stage of moral reasoning. Stages form a hierarchy involving progressively greater cognitive complexity and advancement toward a universal moral perspective in which rights and duties stand in a fully reciprocal relation to one another. Since moral development depends on conflict, Kohlberg recommends the use of hypothetical moral dilemmas at strategic times as a teaching device in moral education.

Observing that much of moral life calls for moral discernment even though no dilemmas may be involved, I suggested an alternative approach. The model, adapted from IAPC's Philosophy for Children programs, encourages children to sort out subtle and complex features of situations calling for moral reflection. Like Kohlberg's, this approach emphasizes reason-giving rather than simply conclusions. However, dilemmas receive no special emphasis, nor is there any need to sort out the reasoning into different cognitive-developmental stages, although cognitive abilities, affective dispositions, and experiential background need to be taken into account.

Of course, Kohlberg could object that ignoring his theory of development does not invalidate it. However, it was not my objective in "Reciprocity" to invalidate his six-stage theory. Rather it was to show that an exclusive focus on moral dilemmas is likely to leave out much of the depth and richness in the moral thinking of children. "Reciprocity" contains a transcription of the responses of a group of ten-year-olds to a story that raises questions about when it is appropriate to "return in kind." The story is from Matthew Lipman's novel *Lisa*, the sequel to *Harry Stottlemeier's Discovery*.[34] In the passage I read to stimulate discussion Harry and Timmy go to a stamp club, where Timmy trades stamps. Then they go to an ice cream parlor, but Timmy discovers he has no money. Harry offers to buy Timmy a cone. Timmy accepts, but adds that he will buy next time. As they are leaving the store, one of his classmates trips Timmy. Timmy retaliates by knocking the tripper's books off the table. Then Harry and Timmy run out of the store and down the street:

> "I couldn't let them get away with it," Timmy remarked when they saw that they weren't being pursued and could slow down to a walk. "He didn't have to stick his foot out." Then he added, "Of course, I didn't have to do what I did either. But, like I said before, turnabout is fair play."
>
> "Somehow," Harry thought, "it isn't quite the same thing." But he couldn't figure out why. "I don't know," he said finally to Timmy. "The purpose of your stamp club is to exchange stamps. So when you give someone stamps, you're supposed to give something back. Just like if someone lends me money, I'm supposed to give it back. But if someone pulls a dirty trick on you, should you do the same thing to him? I'm not so sure."
>
> "But I had to get even," Timmy protested. "I couldn't let him get away with it, tripping me like that for no reason."
>
> A bit later they met Lisa and Laura. Harry told the girls what had happened and why he was puzzled. "It reminds me," remarked Lisa, "of last year when we were learning about how some sen-

tences could be turned around and would stay true, while others, when you turned them around, would become false."

"Yeah," Harry agreed, "but there we found a rule. What's the rule here?" Lisa tossed her long hair so that it hung over her right shoulder. "It looks like there are times when it is right to give back what we got and other times when it is wrong. But how do we tell which is which?"[35]

This passage seems ripe for casuistic analysis. It presents a couple of paradigmatic examples (trading stamps, taking turns buying ice cream cones). It presents a more problematic case (striking back). It invites readers to explore whether the more straightforward cases can help clarify the more puzzling cases. Finally, it suggests that we might learn something from Harry and Lisa's earlier attempt to form rules about sentences beginning with "all" and "no." There Harry's initial boldness in generalizing from a few cases was replaced by a more cautious, provisional approach. Rules could be proposed, but one must remain open to finding exceptions that require restricting their scope, adding qualifications, or even reframing them more radically. At the same time, there is no suggestion that one understands so little that one hardly knows where to begin the inquiry.

How does discussing a passage like this differ from discussing a moral dilemma? When we face a moral dilemma, we are pulled in conflicting directions. We think we have *reasons* for going either way—or for avoiding both ways. None of the choices seems to be without moral cost, and we are very likely perplexed about what the right choice is or even whether there is a right choice. However, this uncertainty does not mean that all is in doubt. Experiencing a situation as a moral dilemma involves seeing that some things definitely do matter. If the choice is, say, between fairness and preventing harm, what makes the choice difficult is that both fairness and the prevention of harm are recognized to be morally important. After all, perhaps one could both be unfair and fail to prevent harm.

This suggests that even in the absence of dilemmas, there may be much to discuss. To appreciate the possible conflicts among recognized moral values, we need to have some grasp of what those values are, and as the passage from *Lisa* illustrates, this calls for careful reflection. But, puzzled as they are, Harry and his friends do not see themselves as struggling with moral dilemmas. Timmy, at least initially, has no doubt that retaliation is called for. Even if Harry succeeds in casting seeds of doubt Timmy's way, it is not clear that this will create a dilemma for Timmy. He might wonder if he really did *have* to get even. Or he might wonder if knocking the tripper's books off his desk succeeded in making things even. Or he might wonder, as my group of ten-year-olds did, what it means to "get even," whether it is possible to get even, and whether it is desirable to try.

Harry, on the other hand, has little doubt that Timmy's act of retaliation was inappropriate. He also has no doubt that trading stamps is appropriate and that one ought to repay borrowed money. What puzzles him is how to *explain* the similarities and differences among these and other instances of "returning in kind." Lisa shares his puzzlement. Making progress in resolving puzzlements like these is a fundamental part of moral development. Perhaps dilemmas will arise at some point in discussing these matters, but as Matthews points out, this is only one of several dimensions of moral development. Equally important are dealing with paradigms, defining characteristics of concepts, determining the range of cases, and engaging the moral imagination. As I attempt to show, these are the most prominent features of my group's discussion of "returning in kind."

For more than thirty minutes the group raised and attempted to answer questions such as the following:

- What are likely consequences of retaliating? Will this simply set off a chain of events that no one (other than the attention-seeking initiator, who may use this as an excuse to become even more aggressive) wants?
- Does retaliation really "get things even"? Does this notion even make sense?
- Is it important to distinguish between *wanting* to do something and *having* to do it?
- Is it right to respond to an acknowledged wrong by returning in kind? (Do two wrongs make a right?)
- What alternative courses of action are possible, and with what likely consequences?
- Is self-defense a reasonable first response, or only if one's first course of action fails?

- What should the person who is tripped or hit be trying to accomplish in responding one way rather than another? Preventing things from getting worse (for whom?)? Getting even? Teaching a lesson? (Are these last two different? If so, how?)
- How is hitting back different from (a) making an exchange of goods; (b) paying back a debt; (c) returning a favor; (d) extending a favor; (e) responding to someone who does not return a favor or who never extends a favor?
- Keeping these examples in mind, what does the Golden Rule *mean*? Is it a good rule?

Once I shared the *Lisa* passage with the group, my role was to facilitate discussion. Occasionally I asked a question, but the students themselves largely took charge of the course of the discussion. Looking back at what transpired, I continue to be fascinated with the thoroughness of their treatment of the issues. What, I often wonder, would adults want to add that they overlooked? We might make comparisons with other kinds of situations that ten-year-olds will understand and have to wrestle with only later, but this does not detract from their understanding of the moral nuances of situations within their range of experience.

Without reaching consensus about how each of the situations described should be handled, there was an underlying recognition that reciprocal relations in human affairs tend to generate chains of "returning in kind": attacks invite counterattacks; counterattacks encourage counter-counterattacks; favors encourage favors in return; extending trust encourages trust in return. But, as children are well aware, reciprocity does not always occur. Counterattacks do sometimes work. Favors are sometimes not returned. Trust sometimes simply renders us vulnerable. How to stop an undesired chain (e.g., hitting) from getting started, or how to stop it once it has started, is a challenge at any age. Thus, as the students again realized, ideals have to be related to realities. Chip suggested a two-stage strategy: First ignore the instigator, but defend yourself if that does not work. In response to those who were reluctant to extend favors without evidence that they would be reciprocated, Rick replied that it was worth the risk: If everyone did favors without worrying about receiving favors in return, everyone would benefit—from someone, even if not from those to whom one extends favors. These were thoughtful responses, made in full awareness of the uncertainties present in the situations being discussed.

Kohlbergians might accept much of what I have said so far but reply: "Of course moral thinking is not confined to moral dilemmas. Dilemmas are useful in helping children advance to the next stage. But children within given stages think in characteristic ways. In fact, the children in your group nicely illustrate this. Their responses waver primarily between stages 2 and 3, with Rick's final remark about favors bordering on stage 4."[36] Such a reply would satisfy me, but only partly. It would concede the main point made at the outset of "Reciprocity"—namely, that moral educators should engage children in thinking about much more than dilemmas. However, as the Kohlbergian reply suggests, this concession can be made without in any way challenging the general developmental framework Kohlberg advocates. This is a framework that insists not only that moral development takes place in a stage-like, invariably sequential manner, but also that each stage is morally more adequate than its predecessors.

I agree with Kohlberg that the kinds of comments the children in my group made are just the kinds of comments Piagetians and Kohlbergians would predict from a group of ten-year-olds. Our differences are not so much over *what* children are likely to say (i.e., the words, phrases, and sentences they utter) as over the *meaning* of what they say and how this should be morally evaluated.

Consider Kohlberg's analysis of Penny's opening remark about the Golden Rule. I had just asked whether the students thought that it was right for Timmy to retaliate. Penny replied, "I think that when somebody does something to you, you should be expecting something from them, because like the old saying, 'Do unto others as they do unto you.'" Kohlberg takes this to be a stage two Golden Rule response to the question, "What does the Golden Rule say if somebody walks up to you on the street and hits you?" Citing a study he conducted, he comments, "Stage 1 and 2 children almost always said, 'Hit him back, do unto others as they do unto you.'" In contrast, a stage three response involves thinking like ten-year-old Paul: "Well, it's like your brain has to leave your head and go into the other guy's head and then come back into your head; but you still see it like it was in the other guy's head and then you decide that way."

However, a sympathetic reading of Penny's reply would not place it in stage one or two. She was not saying that Timmy should hit back. In fact, it is only somewhat later that we can see what she was saying. Immediately after her opening remark, the other children began talking about what the person who tripped Timmy was trying to accomplish. That is, they first tried to get clear about the perspective of the *aggressor*—which is just what stage three Paul says one should do ("it's like your brain has to leave your head and go into the other guy's head").

Here is Penny's second comment, made just a few minutes later:

> I agree with Emily. It would be better to walk away, because if you push off his books, well, he was probably expecting it, because he knew that bothered you. So, if he knew you'd try to every time he saw you, he'd probably try to trip you. So if you just walked away, then he wouldn't think it bothered you.

Notice how this comment focuses on what the aggressor expects. Looking back at her first comment, it now seems clear that Penny was not advocating that Timmy retaliate. She was actually pointing out that we should give some thought to what the aggressor was expecting, which would provide some basis for predicting what the consequences of retaliating might be. So a plausible reading of her opening remark is that it is the aggressor who will use Timmy's retaliation as a reason to do even more.

Rather than suggest that Penny was explaining what the Golden Rule means to her, it is more plausible to suppose that she was explaining how the aggressor would use it. As the surrounding discussion reveals, ten-year-olds are fully aware of the tactics some use to "justify" their aggressive, bullying behavior. Arnie "accidentally" trips Timmy. Timmy knocks Arnie's books off the table. Arnie now says, "I'll get you for that!"—or at least this is what Timmy fears as he runs down the street with Harry. So it is Arnie who is expecting something when he trips Timmy. It is *his* expectation Penny is referring to when she cites the "old rule." This does not necessarily mean that she agrees with this interpretation of the "old rule," but she has strong suspicions about how Arnie understands it.

A Kohlbergian might now reply, "Okay, let's put Arnie and Timmy in stages one and two, and put Penny in stage three along with Carlen, Kurt,

Chip, and Emily." This interpretation is better only in regard to attributing greater insight to Penny. But it does not concede enough. Consider what Kohlberg says about stage three. We have already seen what he says about Paul. He continues:

> Stage 3 interpretations of Golden Rule reversibility, however, do not yield fair decisions nor are they completely reversible. As a result, they lead to no determinate moral resolution of a situation. In the "Heinz steals the drug" dilemma, the husband reaches one solution if he puts himself in his wife's shoes, another in the druggist's [from whom the drug would be stolen]. Or again, in the Talmudic dilemma of a man with a water bottle encountering another man equally in danger of dying of thirst, a stage 3 interpretation of the Golden Rule logically leads to their passing the water bottle back and forth like Alphonse and Gaston.

But this indecisive flipping back and forth does not characterize *any* of the children discussing the *Lisa* passage. Indeed, they did try to understand the perspective of the aggressor. But they did not first side with Timmy, then the aggressor, then Timmy, and so on. They had no doubts about the inappropriateness of what the aggressor did. The question they were asking was what should Timmy do? Understanding the aggressor's perspective (what he "expected") was seen by them as essential for giving appropriate advice to Timmy (and to one another).

What I conclude is that Kohlberg's attempt to characterize the thinking of these children as stage three is a bad fit. A better fit might be stage five, which Kohlberg describes this way: "Reversibility at stage 5 means reciprocity of rights. In the stage 5 subject's words: 'Morality means recognizing the rights of other individuals to do as they please as long as it doesn't interfere with somebody else's rights.' " I wish I had presented such a statement to my group of students. They might have said something like this:

Penny. Yes, I agree. Arnie had no right to trip Timmy.
Kurt. Yeah, what did Timmy ever do to Arnie?
Carlen. I think everybody has the right to walk without being tripped—as long as they're not hurting anybody else.

Emily. Sure. It'd be different if Timmy had been kicking people as he walked by them.

Rick. But what if everyone went around tripping and kicking people?

Carlen. And it wouldn't stop with tripping and kicking. Who knows where it would stop.

Chip. I agree with all that. But it doesn't answer the question. What should *Timmy* do now? Arnie didn't have any right to trip Timmy, but does that give Timmy the right to do something back?

Rick. Two wrongs don't make a right.

Penny. Besides, if Timmy tries to get him back, that's just what Arnie expects.

Larry. Yeah. Then Arnie will get back at Timmy, and Timmy will need to get even again. Well, actually there's no such thing as "even" here.

Emily. Well, maybe there's another way. I bet Arnie will just get bored tripping Timmy and stuff like that if people just ignore him when he acts that way.

Kurt. But what if he doesn't stop? What if he keeps on hitting?

Carlen. Then you have to defend yourself. But first ignore him.

Kurt. But what if he doesn't really *hit* you? What if he just keeps poking at you and standing in your way? What do you do then?

Kurt's last comment invites further refinement, and it is a safe bet that virtually every ten-year-old knows just what he is talking about and is as anxious as he is to know where to "draw the line." Children facing such circumstances have difficult choices to make. In some instances they face very unpleasant dilemmas. However, as the extended discussion by Penny, Chip, Carlen, and the others makes clear, quite apart from such dilemmas there is much more to be clarified.

Furthermore, it is even possible that by implementing some of their suggestions, children will be able to anticipate and avoid having to face some of these dilemmas, at least in their more extreme forms. The Hastings Center group of educators mentioned in Chapter 2 cited the importance of helping young professionals avoid being caught by surprise (and without adequate preparation) as a major reason for studying ethics as a part of their career preparation. There seems to be no need for the introduction of "preventive ethics" to be delayed until college years.[37]

CONVENTIONAL AND CRITICAL MORALITY

I continue to resist Kohlberg's attempt to diagnose the comments of the *Lisa* discussion group in terms of his stages of moral development. Most of the comments are classified as stages two or three, with one by Rick being credited as nearly stage four. So am I saying that their comments deserve to be placed in stage five or even stage six? No, my main point is that Kohlberg's stages seem not to capture the nuances of children's reflections about moral issues. Furthermore, he seems to vastly underestimate the moral reasoning not only of children but also of adults. According to Kohlberg, stages one through four involve heteronomous rather than autonomous reasoning. What he means is that prior to stage five, moral reasoning is, at best, conventional and uncritical. Standards are uncritically accepted from one's parents, peers, community, authoritative institutions, and the like. Kohlberg estimates that 80 percent of American *adults* never get beyond the conventional thinking of stages three and four. But this estimation seems highly implausible. The *Lisa* group, as well as countless other groups of children who are encouraged to discuss moral issues in the classroom, amply displays critical thinking abilities. This does not mean that they accept the moral principles encased in Kohlberg's stages five and six (although some might, at least on some occasions), and it does not mean that their critical thinking abilities are as well developed or usefully employed as they could be. But their thinking cannot be fairly characterized as merely conventional either—unless conventional and critical thinking are not distinct as Kohlberg supposes.

In fact, Robert Fullinwider challenges the dichotomy between conventional and critical thinking that Kohlberg attempts to draw.[38] For example, Fullinwider says:

> Stage 4 cannot be characterized as the uncritical and unimaginative use of rules with specific social content; otherwise there would be a stage—involving critical and imaginative use of rules with specific social content—intermediate between it and stages 5 and 6, whose own principles lack content.[39]

Children's literature itself seems to support Fullinwider's criticism. For example, Marie Winn's *Shiver, Gobble, and Snore*, a fictional story for young children, contrasts a kingdom ruled by a king who has arbitrary rules about virtually everything (rules to which he is the exception) with Shiver, Gobble, and Snore's attempt to live without any rules at all.[40] The threesome fares no better on their own than in the kingdom until they realize that they need rules after all—good rules. So young readers are invited to reflect on what makes a rule a good one, how such a rule might be fairly established and applied, and why there seems to be a need for rules in the first place.[41]

Fullinwider's view is that learning moral conventions is itself, in part, acquiring critical tools for evaluating conventions and practices:

> *Criticism and convention go together.* The power and force of social criticism generally resides precisely in its imaginative application and extension of well-known precepts or paradigm cases or familiar critical practices.[42]

Honest Andrew seems to nicely model what Fullinwider has in mind. Such stories seem to presume that children are capable of engaging in critical thought about practices and institutions that make up a significant part of their daily lives.

As already noted, for Fullinwider learning about morality is learning to apply moral concepts and make distinctions among a variety of cases. He adds that "this acquired capacity is intuitive rather than technical. Learning morality is like learning how to write, not like learning geography or mathematics."[43] Thus, he says, we learn by doing, much like we learn how to write—through practice and "with the advice, recommendations, and corrections of those who already do it well." Children begin with a few basic concepts and rules (such as "take turns" and "don't hit people"). Apparently agreeing with Thomas Reid that moral reasoning is for the most part taxonomic, Fullinwider says children become better reasoners as they are prompted to apply and refine their understanding of these concepts and rules. Thus, they can be encouraged to classify cases under the appropriate moral descriptions: courage or foolhardiness, candor or insensitivity, and so on. But this classification process involves more than cognitive mastery. It also includes feelings of guilt, shame, and regret at wrongdoing, appreciation for being treated well, resentment at being wronged by others, and the like.

Finally, Fullinwider points out that the moral education of children can be greatly assisted by reading literature, which stimulates the moral imagination by allowing us indirectly to experience the lives of others. History, drama, and art can play a similar role. Like Reid, Fullinwider is skeptical about the relevance of abstract moral theories for the moral education of children. "Moral knowledge," he says, "is knowledge of practice, not knowledge of theory."[44] This is why his final criticism of Kohlberg's theory of moral development is that it is really a theory about stages of theoretical sophistication—an approximation of the comprehensive Kantian theoretical framework he favors.[45] Even if one obtained such theoretical sophistication, it would be at such an abstract level that applying the theory still underdetermines practical judgment in particular cases; and it is judgment that children need, says Fullinwider, not theory.

This is essentially Reid's point that one need not be a philosopher or metaphysician in order to know one's way about morality. But it does not mean that there is no need to be reflective in philosophical ways.[46] Building grand theories can be a result of thinking philosophically, but it is not a defining feature. Careful questioning and conceptual analysis are characteristically philosophical wherever they ultimately might lead. If Reid is right in saying that morality is more like botany than geometry, then there may be no need to scale the heights. In any case, even if one eventually does, that is not where reflection begins, at least not in morality.

10
Concluding Thoughts

Families, religious institutions, schools, neighborhoods, playgrounds, peers, the entertainment world, and the social environment in general all contribute to the moral education of children—for good or ill, deliberately or not. Whatever else a good moral education should involve, it should cultivate the reasonableness of children. Here I have argued that the schools can and should play a major role. By respecting even young children as active moral agents, there is no need to fear that absent indoctrination, children will lack a starting point from which to reason. Of course, since reasonableness is a social virtue it is not morally neutral. So it places some contraints on what is morally acceptable. But it does this by appealing to one's moral sensitivities and understanding rather than by attempting to implant uncritically held values.

Throughout this book I have appealed to the considerable philosophical curiosity and abilities of children. But even if parents and teachers are convinced that children are capable of significant philosophical thinking, some may not want it. The open-endedness of philosophical thinking is bound to hit sensitive nerves from time to time. Some may worry about children prematurely raising questions about adults "molding" them into becoming the sorts of persons they want them to be.

However, children must learn to cope with many voices, not only those of parents, religious leaders, and teachers, but also those of peers, the entertainment world, and the rest of our diverse and challenging world. At some point children need to be well equipped to critically evaluate the welter of messages bombarding them. As R. M. Hare says:

> For as long as it is possible to foreseee, there will be no chance, even if it were a good thing, of seeing to it that only one set of values is available to the children in our society. We have got to try to fit

them to make, *for themselves,* the choices with which they will inevitably be faced. And these will be choices, not just of hair-styles, but of some of the most fundamental elements in their ways of life. The choices may be made explicitly and with an understanding of what is happening, or they may be made by going with the crowd, which nowadays means the crowd of their own age group; but they will be made.[1]

It would be naive for parents to think that they alone can enable their children successfully to negotiate their way through all the confusing, sometimes perilous, options facing them daily.

Furthermore, whatever the schools do or do not include in their curricula, children obviously will be exposed somewhere to ideas that threaten to "rock the boat." Given this inevitability, encouraging philosophical reflection in children might be better regarded as ally than foe—both by children themselves and those who want them to become responsible and reasonable adults. Hare adds, "In a pluralist society like our own, in which nobody has the power to indoctrinate everybody, the only solution is to teach as many people as possible to think as well as possible."[2]

In making the case for including philosophy in the schools, I have relied heavily on programs prepared by the Institute for the Advancement of Philosophy for Children. However, there is a virtually unlimited supply of children's literature that can be used, and teachers can develop imaginative exercises to supplement already existing curricular materials. Many of the IAPC exercises could themselves be used in this way. For example, consider this exercise from *Philosophical Inquiry,* the manual for *Harry Stottlemeier's Discovery.*

A teacher comes into her classroom one day with a large bag of candy. She explains that the candy is a gift to the class, and she's been told that she must distribute it *fairly.*

Now, she says, "What is fair? Would the fairest thing be for me to give the most to those who deserve the most? Who deserves the most? Surely it must be the biggest and strongest ones in the class who deserve the most, for they probably do most things best."

But the teacher is greeted by a large outcry from the class. "What you propose is most unfair," they tell her. "Just because this one is better at arithmetic or that one at baseball, or still another at danc-ing, you still shouldn't treat us all differently. It wouldn't be fair to give some members of the class, say, five pieces of candy where others might get one piece or none at all. Each of us is a person, and in this respect we're all equal. So, treat us as equals and give us each the same amount of candy."

"Ah," the teacher answered, "I'm glad you've explained to me how you feel about this. So, although people are very different from each other in many respects, fairness consists of treating them all equally."

"That's right," the pupils answer. "Fairness is equal treatment!"

But before the teacher has a chance to distribute the candy, the phone rings, and she's called down to the office. When she gets back some minutes later, she finds that the children have all been fighting over the candy. Now each of the biggest and strongest chil-dren has a big handful of candy, while the remainder have varying amounts, and the smallest children have only one each.

The teacher demands order, and the class becomes very quiet. Obviously she is very disturbed about what the children have just done. But she's determined to be fair, and fairness, they've all agreed, is equal treatment. So, she tells the children, "You've taught me what fairness is. Each of you must give back one piece of candy."[3]

As might be expected, most children who hear this story immediately object that this is not fair. Adults might think that young children are likely to dwell on various ways of more fairly handling the distribution of the candy. And they would be correct. However, this point is not all that children discuss, at least not a group to whom I once read this story.[4]

Adults realize that this story is about more than the fair distribution of candy. It is about fairness generally, and especially about the ideas of dessert and treating people equally. But young children realize this, too. In the space of fifteen minutes the group with whom I met dis-cussed the fairness of grading: Should those who are less able get higher grades because they try harder? Should grades be awarded for group accomplishments rather than just on an individual basis (e.g., 90 percent of the class performing at a certain level)? They discussed the importance of having special opportunities for students with disabilities to receive awards, as in the Special Olympics. At the same time, many insisted that the most able should also have special opportunities. They discussed group punishment as an alternative to individually differentiated punishment (both of which they had undoubtedly experienced). In short, in just a few moments, they displayed an understanding of different, and often competing, bases for awards and punishments. While appreciating the importance of equality, they realized that this is complicated by differences in opportunities, experiences, abilities, efforts, and actual accomplishments. They shunned simplistic solutions and seemed to gain satisfaction from articulating complicating factors. They wanted to leave nothing out that might affect a reasonable determination of fairness.

Admittedly, they did not discuss the fairness or unfairness of various taxation schemes (for example, flat vs. graduated rates). Such concerns will come in due time. IAPC uses this same story with its high-school materials as a stimulus for discussing taxation.[5] Meanwhile, young children have a wealth of examples that they can usefully discuss—not only to prepare them for difficult issues they will have to face later, but also to help them cope with difficult issues they face now. It seems clear that children of various ages are capable of engaging in constructive discussion of the sorts of questions this little story stimulates. This is so whether they are participants in a full-scale Philosophy for Children program or simply invited to respond to this story taken by itself. The issues raised are important for children as well as adults. And they are difficult.

One difficult issue facing children is how to treat friends and enemies, an issue that raises important questions about justice. Taking the bull by the horns, David A. White and Sheila Schlaggar report challenging Plato and Aristotle's view that moral philosophy is not appropriate for children by having their sixth graders read selections from Plato and Aristotle.[6] Here is the opening paragraph of an essay on justice by one of their students:

> I do not think justice is doing good to your friends and bad to your enemies. If you harm an enemy when they have done nothing, you are being unjust. If you are good to your friends, no matter what, you would not be just in doing so. Justice is not, then, being good *at all times* to your friends and bad *at all times* to your

enemy. Justice should not be defined as such. Your friend is not always inherently good. An enemy is not always scheming against you if he is in his right mind. So treatment as such would not be right or just.

Admittedly, this essay is an exceptional statement by a sixth grader in a program for gifted and talented students. However, as I hope the various illustrations in this book show, the thoughts expressed are not beyond the understanding of ordinary sixth graders or even younger children. Such thoughts cannot plausibly be regarded as simply the result of indoctrination. It is much more likely that the belief that one should always do good to one's friends and harm to one's enemies is the result of indoctrination. It is also much more likely to result in serious harm than this sixth grader's more critically held beliefs.

R. M. Hare contrasts educators and indoctrinators in the following way:

> The educator is waiting and hoping all the time for those whom he is educating to start *thinking*; and none of the thoughts that may occur to them are labelled "dangerous" a priori. . . . At the end of it all, the educator will insensibly stop being an educator, and find that he is talking to an equal, to an educated person like himself— a person who may disagree with everything he has ever said; and, unlike the indoctrinator, he will be pleased. So, when this happens, you can tell from the expression on his face which he is.[7]

Nevertheless, some may be distrustful of philosophical approaches to ethics. Surveys consistently indicate that the vast majority of adults say they favor moral education in the schools, but that does not mean they have the same kind of thing in mind. How many, for example, would agree with this letter to the editor of a major newspaper?

> Ideally, moral training should be given to children in the home by precept and by example. But at this point we have to face the fact that in too many cases this is not happening. Millions of children are not being sent to Sunday School. The only hope for developing a morally responsible society is to have "moral behavior" taught in the school. Whose morals should be taught? What's wrong with the Commandments of God for openers?

This viewpoint seems to be a call for moral indoctrination (with a particular religious slant) rather than for reflective discussion of moral concerns. As such, its place in the public schools is very problematic from a constitutional point of view. This objection may encourage some religious groups to confuse philosophy with "secular humanism." They may protest what they fear is the undermining of the religious commitments they wish their children to have. But philosophical inquiry is committed to the open examination of ideas, not to the unseating (or support) of religion. Furthermore, at least in the public schools, it is not the proper role of philosophy—or any other subject—to aim at either undermining or bolstering religion.

There is no denying that the introduction of philosophy invites some problems, and I in no way wish to minimize the difficulty of resolving them in a satisfactory way. Here I only wish to point out that these problems are not the special province of philosophy. Even science invites problems, as the creationism controversy in biology so amply illustrates. Those who advocate the strengthening of critical thinking skills need to be fully aware of what this process entails. Although critical thinking to some extent takes on special forms in particular disciplines, there are no disciplines within which critical thinking cannot raise people's hackles. Furthermore, the critical spirit is unlikely to be confined to only one discipline and only to "safe" topics. No doubt there are some who quite candidly assert that they do not want children to become critical thinkers. At some point, however, we must ask not what some fearful adults want for children, but what kind of education is needed for children to become thoughtful, responsible citizens in a democratic society. The answer includes determining both what kinds of educational institutions our society needs and what educational rights children themselves have.

The real fear, however, is that too many may take Samuel Butler's satirical words as serious advice:

> To parents who wish to lead a quiet life I would say: Tell your children that they are very naughty—much naughtier than most children; point to the young people of some acquaintance as models of perfection, and impress your own children with a deep sense of their own inferiority. You carry so many more guns than they do that they cannot fight you. This is called moral influence and it will

enable you to bounce them as much as you please; they think you know, and they will not have yet caught you lying often enough to suspect that you are not the unworldly and scrupulously truthful person which you represent yourself to be; nor yet will they know how great a coward you are, nor how soon you will run away, if they fight you with persistency and judgment. You keep the dice, and throw them, then, for you can easily manage to stop your children from examining them. . . . True, your children will probably find out all about it some day, but not until too late to be of much service to them or inconvenience to yourself.[8]

It is my hope that this book helps mitigate some of the understandable worries about moral education in the schools, thereby further reducing the temptation to opt for the method Butler so forcefully satirizes. A much better alternative is to promote the reasonableness of children, thus empowering them to think for themselves, both now as children and later as the responsible adults we hope they will become.

Notes

CHAPTER 1. REASONABLE CHILDREN

1. Thomas Reid, *Essays on the Active Powers of the Mind*, in *Philosophical Works*, vol. 2, with notes by Sir William Hamilton (Hildesheim: Gekorg Olms Verlagsbuchandlung, 1895). Originally published in 1788, all references to Reid are to this edition.

2. Ibid., p. 595.

3. Ibid., p. 649.

4. Ibid., p. 595.

5. Ibid.

6. Laurance J. Splitter and Ann M. Sharp, *Teaching Better Thinking: The Classroom Community of Inquiry* (Melbourne: Australian Center for Educational Research, 1995), p. 6.

7. The notion of a community of inquiry is central to Philosophy for Children's understanding of philosophy in the classroom, as Splitter and Sharp's book emphasizes throughout. I will discuss this idea in more detail in later chapters. See also Ann M. Sharp, "The Community of Inquiry: Education for Democracy," *Thinking* 9:2 (1991): 31–37, and John C. Thomas, "The Development of Reasoning in Children Through Community of Inquiry," in Ronald Reed and Ann M. Sharp, eds., *Studies in Philosophy for Children: Harry Stottlemeier's Discovery* (Philadelphia: Temple University Press, 1992), pp. 96–104.

8. Splitter and Sharp, p. 7.

9. *Kalamazoo Gazette*, September 13, 1989.

10. *Kalamazoo Gazette*, July 9, 1992.

11. *Kalamazoo Gazette*, November 27, 1991.

12. *Kalamazoo Gazette*, July 7, 1993.

13. W. H. Sibley, "The Rational and the Reasonable," *Philosophical Review* 62 (1953): 557.

14. See, e.g., Jean Piaget, *The Child's Conception of the World* (London: Kegan Paul, 1929) and *The Moral Judgment of the Child* (New York: Free Press, 1965).

15. For a summary of recent research challenging Piaget's assessment of children's egocentricity, see Janet Wilde Astington, *The Child's Discovery of the Mind* (Cambridge, Mass.: Harvard University Press, 1993), esp. pp. 6–14 and 167–68.

16. Ronald Dworkin, *Taking Rights Seriously* (Oxford: Oxford University Press, 1977), p. 133.

17. John Rawls, *Political Liberalism* (New York: Columbia University Press, 1993), p. 56.

18. Ibid., p. 58.

19. Max Black, "Reasonableness," in R. F. Dearden, P. H. Hirst, and R. S. Peters, eds., *Education and the Development of Reason* (London: Routledge and Kegan Paul, 1972), pp. 194–207.

20. Ibid., p. 202.

21. Ibid.

22. R. S. Peters, "The Development of Reason," in *Psychology and Ethical Development* (London: George Allen and Unwin, 1974), p. 122.

23. Albert Jonsen and Stephen Toulmin, *The Abuse of Casuistry: A History of Moral Reasoning* (Berkeley: University of California Press, 1988), p. 17.

24. *The Belmont Report: Ethical Principles and Guidelines for Protection of Human Subjects of Biomedical and Behavioral Research*, Publication no. OS 78-0012 (Washington, D.C.: DHEW, 1978).

25. Ibid., pp. 1–2.

26. See Martin Benjamin, *Splitting the Difference: Compromise and Integrity in Ethics and Politics* (Lawrence: University Press of Kansas, 1990), for an excellent discussion on the importance of compromise.

27. Roughly speaking, affective capacities are capacities for emotion and feeling and cognitive capacities are capacities for rational and logical thought. Just what relationships these capacities have to one another in the moral domain is subject to much debate. I address many of these issues in *On Becoming Responsible* (Lawrence: University Press of Kansas, 1991). See especially chaps. 4–8.

28. *Kalamazoo Gazette*, April 9, 1993.

29. A good summary of research in this area is chap. 2 in William Damon, *The Moral Child* (New York: Free Press, 1988).

30. Ibid., chap. 3.

31. Ibid., p. 49.

32. Ibid., p. 35.

33. Ibid.

34. Ibid.

CHAPTER 2. AIMS AND GOALS
OF MORAL EDUCATION

1. For example, see Daniel Callahan, "Goals in the Teaching of Ethics," in Daniel Callahan and Sissela Bok, eds., *Ethics Teaching in Higher Education* (New York: Plenum, 1980), pp. 61–74. There the emphasis clearly is on students as active learners rather than passive recipients of moral instruction. In higher education "ethics" is considered a subject that studies morality. "Ethics'" may

also be construed more narrowly as applying to professions and businesses, often in relation to a code of ethics. Thus, there are more specialized courses on business and professional ethics as well as more general courses that study morality as a whole.

2. The Hastings Center group discussed goals and objectives in teaching ethics in higher education, but "ethics" in this context typically means "the study of morality." So, at the level of higher education, teaching ethics is thought of as helping students study morality, which I suggest, is a good way of approaching moral education in the schools as well.

3. Ibid.

4. This worry is precisely what prompted Matthew Lipman to undertake the project of presenting logic to elementary school students. The resulting success of Philosophy for Children no doubt exceeded his initial expectations, but it confirms his insight that logic cannot wait.

5. Arnold Lobel, *Frog and Toad Together*, an I CAN READ Book (Harper and Row: New York, 1971). Page references are listed in parenthesis in the text. I am indebted to Gareth Matthews for first suggesting to me the philosophical importance of Frog and Toad stories. See Matthews, *The Philosophy of Childhood* (Cambridge, Mass.: Harvard University Press, 1994), for some of his reflections on these stories.

6. Lobel's Frog and Toad are both male. My Turtle and Mouse are also male. It might be interesting to tell these stories with a mix of male and female characters or with only female characters.

7. Judy Varga, *The Dragon Who Liked to Spit Fire* (William Morrow: New York, 1961). I wish to thank Diane Worden for bringing Judy Varga's story to my attention—and for suggesting that it is a story about bravery, both physical and moral.

8. See Jean Piaget, *The Moral Judgment of the Child* (New York: Free Press, 1965); Lawrence Kohlberg, *The Psychology of Moral Development: Essays on Moral Development*, vol. 2 (San Francisco: Harper and Row, 1984).

9. Piaget and Kohlberg claim that children do not get beyond predominantly egocentric thinking until well into their school years.

10. This example was brought to my attention by Ann Diller, "On a Conception of Moral Teaching," in Matthew Lipman, Ann M. Sharp, and Frederick Oscanyan, eds., *Growing Up with Philosophy* (Philadelphia: Temple University Press, 1978), pp. 326–38. Diller's discussion of this passage is very illuminating.

11. *Lisa* is one of several children's novels written by Matthew Lipman. It is published by the Institute for the Advancement of Philosophy for Children (IAPC) at Montclair State University, Upper Montclair, New Jersey. The IAPC programs will be discussed in greater detail in Chapter 3.

12. Clyde Evans, "The Feasibility of Moral Education," in Lipman, Sharp, and Oscanyan, *Growing Up with Philosophy*, pp. 157–73.

13. Ibid., p. 168.

14. In fact, Clyde Evans is reporting on a session that was videotaped. In the videotape, "No Clearcut Answers," one of the children uses the very words,

"What if everyone did that?" Another comments that the carnival might have to go out of business.

15. Gareth Matthews, *Philosophy and the Young Child* (Cambridge, Mass.: Harvard University Press, 1980), p. 28.

16. Gareth Matthews, *Dialogues with Children* (Cambridge, Mass.: Harvard University Press, 1984), pp. 92–93.

17. Ibid., p. 95.

18. This program was held in the Ransom Public Library in Plainwell, Michigan. Library Director Jan Park secured a grant from the Michigan Council for the Humanities for the program.

19. Sadly, when I met with them in their final year of high school, they vigorously complained about the absence of philosophical discussions in their schooling during the intervening years.

20. What follows is adapted from chap. 5 of my *Philosophical Adventures with Children* (Lanham, Md.: University Press of America, 1985), now out of print.

21. *Harry Stottlemeier's Discovery* is one of several children's novels written by Matthew Lipman to stimulate philosophical discussion. The main characters are children who are approximately the same age as the children discussing the stories. These novels are available through the Institute for the Advancement of Philosophy for Children, Montclair State University, Upper Montclair, New Jersey. The following passage is from p. 11.

22. Another aspect of unfairness that emerges in the passage is Fran's sense that she was singled out because she is a girl and is black. Larry and the others did not bring up this, perhaps because they were only recalling the episode rather than rereading it.

23. Sissela Bok, *Lying: Moral Choice in Public and Private Life* (New York: Pantheon, 1978).

CHAPTER 3. PHILOSOPHY FOR CHILDREN

1. Matthew Lipman, *Harry Stottlemeier's Discovery* (Upper Montclair, N.J.: Institute for the Advancement of Philosophy for Children, 1974).

2. See, for example, any of the issues of *Thinking* and *Analytic Teaching*, two journals devoted to the philosophical thinking of children. They regularly feature examples of philosophical discussions in the classroom.

3. Lipman, *Harry*, pp. 16–17.

4. Ibid., p. 95.

5. For further discussion of this dialogue, see my *Philosophical Adventures with Children* (Lanham, Md.: University Press of America, 1985). I have observed children as young as second graders posing similar questions in classroom discussion—and with equal enthusiasm.

6. For the full transcript of the session I am about to discuss, see chap. 4, "If All Animals Were Cats . . . ," in my *Philosophical Adventures with Children*.

7. David Benjamin and Jeremy Scott, "Review of Nagel's *What Does It All Mean?" Thinking* 7:4 (1989): 29.

8. Ibid.

9. Ibid.

10. Ibid.

11. What follows are highlights of a thirty-minute discussion in John Foster's class at Kalamazoo's Lincoln School. Foster was one of several Kalamazoo public-school teachers introducing students to *Harry Stottlemeier's Discovery* in the early 1980s. A fuller discussion of this session is in chap. 11, "Self-Knowledge," in my *Philosophical Adventures with Children*.

12. Matthew Lipman, *Pixie* (Upper Montclair, N.J.: Institute for the Advancement of Philosophy for Children, 1981). This children's novel is accompanied by the workbook, *Looking for Meaning*, also published by IAPC.

13. For a good summary of the empirical evidence of this capacity (and its relevance for moral development), see William Damon, *The Moral Child* (New York: Free Press, 1988).

14. The first *Pixie* episode identified in the manual as involving empathy begins on page 4, line 23: "Walking down the hall, Isabel and I held hands, like we always do. We didn't talk, because each of us was thinking. I was thinking how lucky I was to have a friend who wouldn't try to get my secret out of me. Maybe she was thinking the same thing, because all of a sudden she stopped and hugged me, and I hugged her back—right at the top of the stairs." There is a striking difference between this example and the accompanying teacher's manual exercise on empathy (*Looking for Meaning*, p. 21). The empathy in *Pixie* seems to be a *shared* understanding, which is itself an act of (silent) communication. The examples in the exercise all describe a situation and conclude by asking the reader, "How do you think so-and-so felt?" Important as such imaginative exercises are, none involve anything like the "meeting of minds" illustrated by Pixie and Isabel. The moral significance of the latter needs exploration, too.

15. On the other hand, by discussing different senses of words such as "right," for example, a rough demarcation of "moral" can be expected to emerge. Compare: "Turn to the right at the corner." "The right answer is 37." "That's the right way to do it." "It wouldn't be right to take that without paying for it." "It wouldn't be right to lie about it." "Don't I have a right to talk too?" That *Pixie* readers are ready to explore such conceptual nuances is evidenced by the fact that children as young as four years old intuitively grasp differences among prudential, conventional, and moral rules. See Richard A. Shweder, Elliot Turiel, and Nancy C. Much, "The Moral Intuitions of the Child," in John H. Flavell and Lee Ross, eds., *Social Cognitive Development: Frontiers and Possible Futures* (Cambridge: Cambridge University Press, 1981), pp. 288–305.

16. These pairings are intended only to illustrate contrasting terms rather than rigid "either/or" thinking. For example, between clear-cut cases of fairness or unfairness are many shadings (somewhat unfair; fair with respect to . . . , but).

17. *Looking for Meaning*, p. ii; emphasis added.

CHAPTER 4. WHAT IS CRITICAL THINKING?

1. This section draws from my "STS, Critical Thinking, and Philosophy for Children," in Paul T. Durbin, ed., *Europe, America, and Technology: Philosophical Perspectives* (Netherlands: Kluwer Academic Publishers, 1991).

2. Robert Ennis, "A Conception of Critical Thinking—With Some Curriculum Suggestions," American Philosophical Association, *Newsletter on Teaching Philosophy* (summer 1987): 1. Ennis and Stephen P. Norris offer the same definition in *Evaluating Critical Thinking* (Pacific Grove, Calif: Midwest Publications, 1989), p. 3, where they claim that their definition is a close approximation of what educators generally mean by "critical thinking."

3. Ennis, "A Conception of Critical Thinking," p. 1.

4. Of course, if one already knows that Mickey Mouse is not a rabbit but a rodent, this should lead one to the conclusion that it is a mistake to believe that all rodents are rabbits. But someone receptive to this reasoning should already know that this first premise is a mistake.

5. E. D. Hirsh, *Cultural Literacy: What Every American Needs to Know* (New York: Houghton Mifflin, 1987).

6. Of course, there is a trivial sense in which belief must be involved. Beliefs will be formed about what the various sentences mean, what does or does not follow from them, and so on. But the focus is on *meaning*, not on what beliefs one should have or on what one should do.

7. Matthew Lipman, *Thinking in Education* (New York: Cambridge University Press, 1991), p. 115.

8. Ibid., p. 17.

9. Ibid., p. 119.

10. Ibid., p. 19.

11. Ibid., p. 116.

12. Ibid., p. 237.

13. Immanuel Kant, *Logic*, trans. Robert S. Hartman and Wolfgang Schwartz (Indianapolis, Ind.: Bobbs-Merrill, 1974), p. 74. This passage is cited in Lipman, *Thinking in Education*, p. 237.

14. Ibid.

15. Ibid.

16. Peter Facione, ed., "Report on Critical Thinking," American Philosophical Association Subcommittee on Pre-College Philosophy, University of Delaware, 1989.

17. Roughly half of the panelists were from philosophy, 20 percent were from education, and 20 percent from the social sciences; the remainder were from the physical sciences. Peter Facione describes the Delphi Method in the following way: "In Delphi research experts participate in several rounds of questions which call for thoughtful and detailed responses. Achieving a consensus of expert opinion using the Delphi Method is not a matter of voting or tabulating quantitative data. Rather the expert panelists work toward consensus by shar-

ing their reasoned opinions and being willing to reconsider them in light of the comments, objections and arguments offered by other experts" ("Report on Critical Thinking," pp. 4–5). Thus, critical thinking is built into the method used to arrive at a consensus about critical thinking.

18. Ibid., p. 3. It is interesting to note that both Ennis and Norris were panelists, as was Matthew Lipman, whose work in Philosophy for Children will be discussed below. Notably absent from the list, however, is John McPeck, who will be discussed in the next section.

19. For discussions of available tests, see Robert Ennis, "Problems in Testing Informal Logic Critical Thinking Ability," *Informal Logic* (January 1984), and Ennis and Norris, *Evaluating Critical Thinking*.

20. Discussion of this problem is taken from my "Critical Thinking vs. Creative Thinking: Problem-Solving or Problem-Creating?" in Ronald Reed and Ann M. Sharp, eds., *Studies in Philosophy for Children: Harry Stottlemeier's Discovery* (Philadelphia: Temple University Press, 1992), pp. 87–95. This problem was inspired by problem 5 of the WASI test in Arthur Whimbey and Jack Lockhead, *Problem Solving and Comprehension*, 3d ed. (Philadelphia: Franklin Institute Press, 1982), p. 4. The WASI problem does not provide 20 as a possible answer, thus making it more likely that 15 will be selected. However, as the discussion above shows, 5 and 10 could be selected, and they are among the WASI choices.

21. Ennis, "Problems in Testing," p. 4.

22. Ibid.

23. John McPeck, *Critical Thinking and Education* (New York: St. Martin's Press, 1981), p. 149.

24. Ennis, "Problems in Testing," p. 4.

25. Personal letter. Mr. Christoph indicated he taught an accelerated math class for seventh graders.

26. In Plato, *Five Dialogues*, trans. G. M. A. Grube (Indianapolis, Ind.: Hackett Publishers, 1981), pp. 70ff. Connecting *The Meno* with this problem was first suggested to me by my colleague Joseph Ellin.

27. The significance of this "digression" is discussed in the next chapter.

28. Floyd Dell, "Idle Curiosity," reprinted in *Thinking* 1:3/4: 7.

CHAPTER 5. CRITICAL
THINKING IN THE SCHOOLS

1. John McPeck, "Critical Thinking and the 'Trivial Pursuit' Theory of Knowledge," *Teaching Philosophy* 8:4 (October 1985): 295.

2. Ibid., p. 296.

3. Ibid.

4. Ibid.

5. Students' difficulty in making sense of their educational experience as a

whole is discussed at length in Matthew Lipman, *Philosophy in the Classroom* (Philadelphia: Temple University Press, 1980).

6. Michael Martin, "Science Education and Moral Education," *Journal of Moral Education* 15:2 (1986): 99–108.

7. Martin, "Science Education and Moral Education," p. 105. A decade has passed since Martin wrote these words, and we might wonder if much has changed. Certainly much has on college and university campuses where there are animal welfare committees that examine research protocols. And, no doubt, there have been significant changes in school labs, too. However, it does not follow that there is much *discussion* of these or other moral issues in science classes. In fact, there are remarkably few educational materials explicitly devoted to raising moral issues in the context of science education at even the high-school level. Not surprisingly there is even less at the elementary- and middle-school levels. However, this may be changing, at least at the high-school level. For example, Theodore Goldfarb (State University of New York at Stony Brook) has recently directed a three-year National Science Foundation project for high-school science teachers. This project, "Ethics and Values in the Science Classroom," consisted of summer workshops in which teachers prepared detailed lesson plans that integrate the discussion of relevant moral issues into the regular science curriculum. Similar projects need to be undertaken throughout the K–12 curriculum, with published results made available for all science teachers.

8. Michael Matthews has recently argued at length that science education would benefit immensely if its teachers were well versed in the history and philosophy of science; see *Science Teaching: The Role of History and Philosophy of Science* (New York: Routledge, 1994). However, he only briefly discusses connections between science and morality, and he fails to note possible links between logical skills and moral reflection in science (or elsewhere). I concentrate here on connections between science and morality.

9. Educational Policies Commission, *Education and the Spirit of Science* (Washington, D.C.: National Education Association, 1964), p. 16; cited in Michael Martin, "The Goals of Science Education," *Thinking* 4:2 (1985): 20.

10. Martin, "Goals," p. 20.

11. David Benjamin and Jeremy Scott, "Review of Nagel's *What Does It All Mean?*" *Thinking* 7:4 (1989): 29.

12. These materials can be obtained from IAPC at Montclair State University, Upper Montclair, New Jersey. In "Science Education and Moral Education," Michael Martin complains: "In *Kio and Gus* no ethical issues connected with scientific inquiry are seriously considered and no strong connections are made with ethical investigation. Yet there is abundant opportunity to do so" (p. 107). Indeed, there are abundant opportunities, and I will explore some of them below. As I also said of the *Pixie* program, there is a great deal of material in the *Kio and Gus* program that is designed with moral education in mind even though the words "moral" or "ethical" may not be used. What can be conceded is that

many more connections can be made, which is just what reflective students and teachers will do once they catch on to the philosophical spirit of *Kio and Gus*.

13. This is taken from IAPC's Philosophy for Children catalogue of materials.

14. *Wondering at the World*, p. 353.

15. Ironically, when I showed a videotape of the discussion within which Carlen and Rick's comments occurred, the first question from the audience was, "Do you often permit digressions like this?" The next comment, followed by many nods of agreement, was that there seldom would be time for such digressions in the already crowded school day. The audience consisted of fifty teachers in a gifted and talented program, none of whom demurred!

16. *Wondering at the World*, p. 227.

17. Ibid., p. 391.

18. Edith Assaff, David W. Chapman, and Augusto Q. Medina, "Hazardous Wastes and the Consumer Connection," Hazardous Chemicals Education Project of the Michigan Environmental Education Association, published by Western Michigan University's Science for Citizens Center, Kalamazoo, 1984.

CHAPTER 6. FAMILIES, SCHOOLS, AND MORAL EDUCATION

1. Thomas Reid, *Essays on the Active Powers of the Mind*, in *Philosophical Works*, vol. 2, with notes by Sir William Hamilton (Hildesheim: Gekorg Olms Verlagsbuchhandlung, 1895), a reprinting of the original 1788 publication. Some may balk at the theistic tone of Reid's remark. God does play a part in Reid's account of morality, but nothing I say in this chapter requires his theistic assumptions. The essential point here is simply that moral development begins at a very early age and that its "seeds," as it were, will grow only in a suitable environment.

2. This does not mean that children are to be regarded as adults. Moral discernment requires experience as well as judgment. And there is much that young children are not experientially or emotionally ready to confront. However, as will be shown later, many have already developed a surprisingly sophisticated understanding of morality by the time they enter school.

3. This point follows from the broader notion that moral and legal responsibility are distinguishable. For example, if I agree to meet a struggling student in my office at 3:00 P.M. but cavalierly decide to play golf instead, this is a failure in moral, not legal, responsibility.

4. Whether there is a legal responsibility as well is a more difficult matter, one best settled by legal experts. In any case, whatever legal responsibility may exist now or through future changes in law, it is unlikely to reach as far as moral responsibility does.

5. Thomas Lickona, *Educating for Character* (New York: Bantam, 1991), p. 21, observes: "For more than a decade, every Gallup poll that has asked parents whether schools should teach morals has come up with an unequivocal yes. Typ-

ical is the finding that 84 percent of parents with school-age children say they want the public schools to provide 'instruction that would deal with morals and moral behavior.' " Lickona's earliest citation is a 1976 Gallup poll (reported in *New York Times*, April 18, 1976).

6. For a very constructive attempt to show how morality and religion can be distinguished without detracting from either, see Larry P. Nucci, "Doing Justice to Morality in Contemporary Values Education," in Jacques S. Benninga, ed., *Morality, Character, and Civic Education in the Elementary School* (New York: Teachers College Press, 1991), pp. 27–33 especially.

7. See, for example, Louis E. Raths, Merrill Harmin, and Sidney Simon, *Values and Teaching* (Columbus, Ohio: Charles E. Merrill, 1966).

8. "Mindless absolutism" and "mindless relativism" should not be construed as representing anything clear or precise. Those who use these expressions are speaking pejoratively of positions they (fairly or unfairly) attribute to their opponents. "Mindless," as applied to both "absolutism" and "relativism," implies uncritical acceptance and application. So, it may be alleged, "mindless absolutism" favors "implanting" universal, and possibly exceptionless, moral principles in children. Children are not invited to critically evaluate these principles. Instead, children are to be indoctrinated to accept and apply them, thus circumventing their critical intelligence. Similarly, "mindless relativism" allegedly encourages uncritical acceptance of the view that "any moral opinion is as good as any other."

9. The civic education argument that follows is based on Robert Fullinwider, "Science and Technology Education as Civic Education," in Paul T. Durbin, ed., *Europe, America, and Technology: Philosophical Perspectives* (Netherlands: Kluwer Academic Publishers, 1991), pp. 197–215.

10. For a detailed discussion of where civic education might best fit in the curriculum, see Alita Zurav Letwin, "Promoting Civic Understanding and Civic Skills Through Conceptually Based Curricula," pp. 197–211, in Benninga, *Morality, Character, and Civic Education*. Clearly, classes in government, history, and the social sciences are natural homes for civic education. But there are other places as well, such as literature and the languages. Letwin discusses educational materials developed by the Center for Civic Education, a California nonprofit corporation that develops programs for both private and public schools. Another good discussion of civic education is Carolyn Perieira, "Educating for Citizenship in the Early Grades," pp. 212–26, in Benninga, *Morality, Character, and Civic Education*. She discusses the elementary-school curriculum *Educating for Citizenship*, field-tested in more than fifty urban and rural Maryland schools.

11. Fullinwider cites Amy Gutmann, *Democratic Education* (Princeton, N.J.: Princeton University Press, 1987); Brian Crittenden, *Parents, the State and the Right to Educate* (Melbourne: University of Melbourne Press, 1988); and William Galston, "Civic Education in the Liberal State," in Nancy L. Rosenblum, ed., *Liberalism and the Moral Life* (Cambridge, Mass.: Harvard University Press, 1989).

12. The social features of reasonableness are discussed in some detail in Chapter 1.

13. This is at least a moral right. Whether it can plausibly be construed as a legal right as well is a question best left for legal experts. I would think that there *should* be such a legal right, even if presently there is none. What respect for such a right would entail for families, schools, and others would still be subject to much debate. However, the importance of acknowledging such a right is the recognition that children themselves have a *claim* in the matter.

14. For convenience I will refer to parents as the significant adults in family life, but I make no special assumptions about what constitutes a standard family. There may be one or two natural parents present or none at all. There will be at least one adult, however related to the children. Beyond this, nothing I say is intended to support one particular family arrangement over another. How families might best be structured is an interesting and important topic, but it is not the topic of this book.

15. Inductive modeling has two important features. First, adults model attitudes and behavior not by didactic instruction but simply by exemplifying them. Children, in turn, actively participate by observing adults and inductively "catching on" to the *kinds* of attitudes and behavior that are exemplified. Children themselves then begin to exemplify such attitudes and behavior. For more on inductive modeling, see Martin Hoffman, "Empathy, Role-Taking, Guilt, and the Development of Altruistic Motives," in Thomas Lickona, ed., *Moral Development and Behavior* (New York: Rinehart and Winston, 1976), pp. 124–43.

16. "Unconditional'" may seem too strong, since parental love can be withdrawn under some circumstances. However, what is meant by unconditional is that the child does not have to do anything or have any special qualities in order to be loved by his or her parents. Such love is not conditioned by one's accomplishments or special characteristics. For a good discussion of unconditional love and its importance for developing self-respect and self-esteem see Laurence Thomas, *Living Morally: A Psychology of Moral Character* (Philadelphia: Temple University Press, 1989).

17. Roughly speaking, affective capacities are capacities for emotion and feeling, whereas cognitive capacities are capacities for rational and logical thought. Just what relationships these capacities have to one another in the moral domain is subject to much debate. I address many of these issues in *On Becoming Responsible* (Lawrence: University Press of Kansas, 1991); see especially chaps. 4–8.

18. For a more detailed discussion of the affective aspects of moral understanding, see ibid., especially chap. 3, "Accountability, Understanding, and Sentiments."

19. For a good discussion of how philosophical reflection can contribute to the refinement of emotional dispositions, see Matthew Lipman, "Using Philosophy to Educate Emotions," *Analytic Teaching* 15:2 (1995): 3–10.

20. For detailed examples, see Matthew Lipman, Ann M. Sharp, and Frederick Oscanyan, eds., *Growing Up with Philosophy* (Philadelphia: Temple Univer-

sity Press, 1978), especially the selections by Martin Benjamin, Ann Diller, Clyde Evans, and R. M. Hare in chap. 11, "The Possibilities of Ethical Inquiry in the Schools"; Gareth Matthews, *Dialogues with Children* (Cambridge, Mass.: Harvard University Press, 1984); Michael S. Pritchard, *Philosophical Adventures with Children* (Lanham, Md.: University Press of America, 1985); and any of the publications of the Institute for the Advancement of Philosophy for Children at Montclair State University, Upper Montclair, New Jersey.

21. Reid, *Essays*, p. 595.

22. Matthews regularly contributes reviews of philosophical children's literature in IAPC's journal *Thinking*. Others in recent years have begun writing about philosophically useful children's stories. For example, a number of Australian writers have recently published materials: Phil Cam, *Thinking Stories*, 1, 2, and 3 (Sydney: Hale and Iremonger, 1994) and *Thinking Together* (Sydney: Hale and Iremonger, 1995); Tim Sprod, *Books into Ideas: A Community of Inquiry* (Australia: Hawker Brownlow Education, 1993); and Chris de Haan, Lucy McCutcheon, and San MacColl, *Philosophy with Kids*, 1, 2, and 3, and *More Ideas and Activities* (Melbourne: Longman House, 1995).

23. Reported in *CEP Character Educator* (winter 1995): 3.

24. Ibid.

25. Lickona, *Educating for Character*, pp. 3–4.

26. Lickona's *Educating for Character*, in addition to making a significant contribution in its own right, provides a comprehensive summary account of many innovative character education projects now under way across the country.

27. William Bennett, ed., *The Book of Virtues* (New York: Simon and Schuster, 1993).

28. Ibid., p. 13.

29. Ibid.

30. Martha Nussbaum, "Divided We Stand," *New Republic*, January 10/17, 1994, pp. 38–42.

31. Ibid., p. 39.

32. Ibid, p. 38.

33. I discuss Aristotle's views of moral development more fully in chap. 2, "On Becoming a Moral Agent," in *On Becoming Responsible*. See especially pp. 12–13 and 17–21.

34. Bennett, *The Book of Virtues*, p. 23.

35. Ibid., p. 26.

36. Ibid., p. 27.

37. Ibid., p. 29.

38. Ibid., pp. 35–37.

39. Ibid., pp. 37–39.

40. Ibid., p. 602.

41. Ibid., p. 604.

42. Ibid., pp. 607–8.

43. Ibid., pp. 609–13.

44. David Hume, *Enquiries Concerning Human Understanding and the Principles of Morals,* 3d ed., ed. P. H. Nidditch (Oxford: Clarendon Press, 1975), sec. 9, pt. 2, pp. 282–83. This is reprinted from Hume's 1777 edition.

45. Ibid.

46. Ibid.

47. In Chapter 9 I present a more detailed consideration of the nuances of honesty and lying in children.

48. Bennett, *The Book of Virtues,* p. 601.

CHAPTER 7. MORAL DIVERSITY

1. Amy Gutmann, "The Challenge of Multiculturalism in Political Ethics," *Philosophy and Public Affairs* 22:3 (summer 1993): 171.

2. Robert Fullinwider, "Science and Technology Education as Civic Education," in Paul T. Durbin, ed., *Europe, America, and Technology: Philosophical Perspectives* (Netherlands: Kluwer Academic Publishers, 1991), pp. 206–7.

3. Robert Fullinwider, "Ethnocentrism and Education in Judgment," *Report from the Institute for Philosophy and Public Policy* 14:1/2 (winter/spring 1994): 7. Similarly, Robert V. Hannaford makes a distinction between codes and standards in order to explain how diversity and shared values that cut across differences are compatible with each other; see chap. 9, "Universal Moral Principle: Critically Relativised Judgments," in his *Moral Anatomy and Moral Reasoning* (Lawrence: University Press of Kansas, 1993), pp. 148–75.

4. Fullinwider, "Ethnocentrism and Education," pp. 7–8.

5. Fullinwider bases much of his analysis of judgmentalism on Caroline Simon's "Judgmentalism," *Faith and Philosophy* 6:3 (July 1989): 275–87.

6. Fullinwider, "Ethnocentrism and Education," p. 11.

7. James Herndon, "Ethics Instruction and the Constitution," *Thinking* 7:1: 9.

8. Ibid.

9. Gutmann, "The Challenge of Multiculturalism," p. 189.

10. Ibid., p. 188.

11. Ibid., p. 171.

12. Ibid., p. 183.

13. Ibid., p. 178.

14. Ibid., p. 187.

15. Ibid.

16. Ibid., p. 188.

17. Ibid.

18. Ibid., p. 190.

19. Ibid., p. 191.

20. Ibid., p. 192.

21. Ibid., p. 193.

22. Ibid., p. 197.
23. Ibid., p. 199.

CHAPTER 8. MORAL CONFIDENCE

1. Piaget's views on moral development are best represented in *The Moral Judgment of the Child* (New York: Free Press, 1965). Kohlberg's basic writings are found in *The Philosophy of Moral Development: Essays on Moral Development*, vol. 1 (San Francisco: Harper and Row, 1981) and *The Psychology of Moral Development: Essays on Moral Development*, vol. 2 (San Francisco: Harper and Row, 1984).

2. "Instrumental egoism" for Kohlberg is understood as "back scratching"— "You scratch my back and I'll scratch yours." This is self-serving in the following sense: I will do things that will benefit others but only in the actual or expected return of benefits from them. Thus, there is an expectation of fully reciprocal exchange of benefits and, therefore, no unilateral sacrifice.

3. Carol Gilligan, *In a Different Voice: Psychological Theory and Women's Development* (Cambridge, Mass.: Harvard University Press, 1982). Gilligan criticizes Kohlberg for overemphasizing justice, rights, duties, and abstract universal principles. Equally important for morality, she argues, are compassion, caring, and responding to the needs of others, regardless of whether there is a strict duty or obligation to do so. So Gilligan contrasts what she calls a "morality of care" with Kohlberg's "morality of justice."

4. M. L. Hoffman, "Moral Development," in P. A. Mussen, ed., *Carmichael's Manual of Child Psychology*, vol. 2 (New York: Wiley, 1970).

5. See, for example, William McCord and Joan McCord, *Psychopathy and Delinquency* (New York: Grune and Stratton, 1965). I discuss the question of whether sociopaths are morally responsible for what they do in chap. 3 of *On Becoming Responsible* (Lawrence: University Press of Kansas, 1991).

6. For a fuller discussion of this and related problems, see my *On Becoming Responsible*, chap. 7.

7. According to Hoffman, even infants give evidence of empathic responses to the crying of other infants. However, at this stage infants apparently have no clear sense of the distinction between themselves and others, so Hoffman refers to this as "global empathy." Still, as young children develop their understanding of the perspectives of others, empathy becomes differentiated. This is not an escape from egoism, for it is only at this point that ego itself clearly emerges, but now there can be concern both for others and self. Equally important, nonegocentric understanding begins to develop much earlier than Kohlberg suggests. Hoffman's earliest example is an eighteen-month-old child comforting another toddler. There is little reason to suppose that very young children cannot respond to overt expressions of adult distress as well. However, the understanding of more subtle and complex forms of suffering no doubt must await appropriate cognitive development.

8. William Damon, *The Moral Child* (New York: Free Press, 1988), chap. 2, "Empathy, Shame and Guilt: The Early Moral Emotions." See also Lawrence A. Blum, *Moral Perception and Particularity* (New York: Cambridge University Press, 1994), especially chap. 9, "Moral Development and Conceptions of Morality"; Laurence Thomas, *Living Morally: A Psychology of Moral Character* (Philadelphia: Temple University Press, 1989), chap. 3, "Parental Love: A Social Basis for Morality"; and Robert V. Hannaford, *Moral Anatomy and Moral Reasoning* (Lawrence: University Press of Kansas, 1993), chap. 4, ""Moral Reasoning and Action in Young Children."

9. Thomas Reid, *Essays on the Active Powers of the Mind*, in *Philosophical Works*, vol. 2, with notes by Sir William Hamilton (Hildesheim: Gekorg Olms Verlagsbuchhandling, 1895), a reprinting of the original 1788 publication, p. 595.

10. Sissela Bok, *Lying: Moral Choice in Public and Private Life* (New York: Pantheon, 1978), p. 28.

11. For valuable discussions of the complexities, see the essays on the Golden Rule in Marcus G. Singer, ed., *Morals and Values* (New York: Scribners, 1977). Singer's own writings, both there and elsewhere, are particularly illuminating. See, for example, his entry on the Golden Rule in Lawrence C. Becker and Charlotte B. Becker, eds., *Encyclopedia of Ethics*, vol. 1 (New York: Garland, 1992), pp. 405–8.

12. Gareth Matthews, *The Philosophy of Childhood* (Cambridge, Mass.: Harvard University Press, 1994), p. 55.

13. Martin Hoffman, "Empathy, Role Taking, Guilt, and Development of Altruistic Motives," in Thomas Lickona, ed., *Moral Development and Behavior* (New York: Holt, Rinehart, and Winston, 1976), p. 129.

14. Ibid.

15. Matthews, *The Philosophy of Childhood*, p. 57.

16. For further support of Hoffman and Matthews's conclusions, see Damon, *The Moral Child*, especially chap. 2, "Empathy, Shame, and Guilt."

17. Ibid., p. 58.

18. Ibid., p. 49.

19. Richard A. Shweder, Elliot Turiel, and Nancy C. Much, "The Moral Intuitions of the Child," in John H. Flavell and Lee Ross, eds., *Social Cognitive Development: Frontiers and Possible Futures* (Cambridge: Cambridge University Press, 1981), p. 288.

20. Below I will present a conversation among ten- and eleven-year-olds that supports this premise.

21. For a more detailed discussion of this problem, see chap. 7 of my *On Becoming Responsible*.

22. Lawrence, Kohlberg, "The Child as a Moral Philosopher," *Psychology Today* 2:4 (1968): 27.

23. I say some renderings, for utilitarians present several possible readings of the principle of utility. Some couch it in terms of maximizing happiness, others in terms of maximizing the satisfaction of preferences, still others in terms of rules that have maximum utility (however defined).

24. Reid, *Essays*, p. 642.

25. Ibid.

26. The children to whom Gareth Matthews read his story about Ian ("Why is it better for three people to be selfish than one?") seemed to have little interest in fitting their views into a geometric model. (This example is discussed in Chapter 1.) See Matthews, *Dialogues with Children* (Cambridge, Mass.: Harvard University Press, 1984), pp. 92–93.

27. R. M. Hare, *Moral Thinking* (New York: Oxford University Press, 1981). I discuss Hare's position in greater detail in *On Becoming Responsible*, especially pp. 26–29.

28. See, for example, Douglas Seanor and N. Fotion, eds., *Hare and Critics* (Oxford: Clarendon Press, 1988), especially J. O. Urmson, "Hare on Intuitive Moral Thinking." See also my *On Becoming Responsible*, pp. 26–29 and chaps. 9 and 11.

29. Reid, *Essays*, p. 594.

30. Ibid., p. 643.

31. Thomas Reid, *Practical Ethics*, edited with commentary by Knud Haakonssen (Princeton, N.J.: Princeton University Press, 1990), p. 110.

32. Ibid.

33. Judith Lichtenberg, "Moral Certainty," *Philosophy* 69: (1994): 181.

34. Honesty will be discussed in more detail in the next chapter.

35. Forrest Carter, *The Education of Little Tree* (Albuquerque: University of New Mexico Press, 1976).

36. Ibid., p. 97.

37. Ibid.

38. Ibid., pp. 97–98.

CHAPTER 9. CASE BY CASE REASONING

1. Robert Fullinwider, "Science and Technology Education as Civic Education," in Paul T. Durbin, ed., *Europe, America, and Technology: Philosophical Perspectives* (Netherlands: Kluwer Academic Publishers, 1991), p. 207.

2. Robert Fullinwider, "Moral Conventions and Moral Lessons," *Social Theory and Practice* 15:3 (fall 1989): 325.

3. Albert Jonsen and Stephen Toulmin, *The Abuse of Casuistry: A History of Moral Reasoning* (Berkeley: University of California Press, 1988).

4. This was discussed briefly in Chapter 2.

5. *Webster's New Collegiate Dictionary.*

6. *American Heritage Dictionary.*

7. David Boeyink, "Casuistry: A Case-Based Method for Journalism," *Journal of Mass Media Ethics* 7:2 (summer 1992): 112–13.

8. Robin Levin Penslar, ed., *Research Ethics: Cases and Materials* (Bloomington: Indiana University Press, 1995).

9. This is described by Carl Taeusch, *Professional and Business Ethics* (New York: Henry Holt, 1926).

10. Fullinwider, "Moral Conventions and Moral Lessons," p. 325.

11. Gareth Matthews, "Concept Formation and Moral Development," in James Russell, ed., *Philosophical Perspectives on Developmental Psychology* (Oxford: Basil Blackwell, 1987), p. 185.

12. He is certainly not alone in this. In fact, Mark Johnson argues that this is just what we should expect. Moral concepts, he says, are open-ended. There are prototypical instances of, say, lying, which give the concept a stable core but do not yield a set of necessary and sufficient conditions that define it. The open-endedness of moral concepts makes room for the exercise of moral imagination, especially when novel circumstances arise. See *Moral Imagination* (Chicago: University of Chicago Press, 1993), especially pp. 91–107.

13. Plato, *The Trial and Death of Socrates*, trans. G. M. A. Grube (Indianapolis, Ind.: Hackett Publishers, 1975), p. 20.

14. See Martin Benjamin, *Splitting the Difference: Compromise and Integrity in Ethics and Politics* (Lawrence: University Press of Kansas, 1990), for an excellent discussion of both the need for compromise and how it may be successfully undertaken without compromising one's integrity.

15. Matthews, *The Philosophy of Childhood*, pp. 65–66.

16. See Janet Wilde Astington, *The Child's Discovery of the Mind* (Cambridge, Mass.: Harvard University Press, 1993), pp. 125–37.

17. Although this may seem puzzling, it is no more so than the deceptive behavior of nonhuman animals, which often is quite clever even though it does not involve lying.

18. Astington, *The Child's Discovery*, p. 127.

19. H. Wimmer, S. Gruber, and J. Perner, "Young Children's Conception of Lying: Lexical Realism—Moral Subjectivism," *Journal of Experimental Child Psychology* 37 (1984): 1–30; cited in Astington, *The Child's Discovery*, p. 129.

20. "George Washington and the Cherry Tree," adapted from J. Berg Esenwin and Marietta Stockard, in William Bennett, ed., *The Book of Virtues* (New York: Simon and Schuster, 1993), pp. 605–6.

21. Ibid., p. 606.

22. It is interesting to compare the readings on honesty in Bennett's *Book of Virtues* with those of a book of readings published shortly after Bennett's. Colin Greer and Herbert Kohl's *A Call to Character* (New York: Harper Collins, 1995) does not include the George Washington story. Instead, it offers Alice Walker's "Fathers." In this story, Alice confesses to her father that she has broken a fruit jar. There is no pronouncement, "I cannot tell a lie." Instead, Alice reflects on what she thinks her father wanted from her and the importance being truthful with him had for their relationship at that moment. Like young George, she was not punished. The story concludes, "I think it was at that moment that I resolved to take my chances with the truth, although as the years rolled on I was to break more serious things in his scheme of things than fruit jars" (p. 237). These are

Alice Walker's recollections of a dramatic moment in the life of a three-year-old—a moment that called for courage, responsibility, and truthfulness.

23. Philip Hallie, *Lest Innocent Blood Be Shed* (Kansas City, Mo.: Harrow, 1979), pp. 126–28.

24. Gloria Skurzynski, *Honest Andrew* (New York: Harcourt Brace Jovanovich, 1980). This delightful story was brought to my attention by David Nyberg, *The Varnished Truth* (Chicago: University of Chicago Press, 1993).

25. Skurzynski, *Honest Andrew*, pp. 6–7.

26. Ibid., pp. 8–9.

27. Ibid., p. 13.

28. Ibid., p. 14.

29. Ibid., p. 23.

30. Ibid., p. 24.

31. Ibid.

32. Ibid., p. 27.

33. Kohlberg's unpublished commentary is entitled, "On Philosophy for Children by Weinstein and Pritchard." Mark Weinstein brought my chapter to Kohlberg's attention, and apparently their conversation about the chapter prompted him to write the commentary. Shortly before his death, Kohlberg and I planned to have further exchanges. Unfortunately, this never materialized, so what follows has not benefited from Kohlberg's further response. The next several pages are taken from my "Reciprocity Revisited," *Analytic Teaching* (spring 1989): 54–62.

34. *Lisa*, an IAPC novel that focuses on moral inquiry, is written for junior-high students. However, I selected a passage suitable for younger children. This is the same passage discussed in Chapter 2, pp. 23–24.

35. Ibid., pp. 11–12.

36. This is basically a summary of Kohlberg's analysis in his commentary.

37. For further discussion of the notion of "preventive ethics" (as somewhat analogous to "preventive medicine"), see James A. Jaksa and Michael S. Pritchard, *Communication Ethics: Methods of Analysis*, 2d ed. (Belmont, Calif.: Wadsworth Publishing, 1995), pp. 12–15.

38. Robert Fullinwider, "Moral Convention and Moral Lessons," *Social Theory and Practice* 15:3 (fall 1989): 321–37.

39. Ibid., p. 333.

40. Marie Winn, *Shiver, Gobble, and Snore* (New York: Simon and Schuster, 1971). I was introduced to this story some years ago by our daughter's fourth grade teacher. She suggested I share this story with her students when making weekly visits to her classroom. Interestingly, Marie Winn calls her little book a "concept story."

41. Actually, the story makes a strong case for the need for social cooperation, but it makes no distinction among ways of accomplishing the needed cooperation. For example, Shiver, Gobble, and Snore find that when they do whatever they want without regard to its effects on one another, they eventually all end up unhappy. But does this mean that friends can get along with each

other only if they abide by certain rules concerning how they treat each other? This seems like just the sort of question young children might be able to discuss fruitfully, thus laying the groundwork for a little critical analysis of some of *Shiver, Gobble, and Snore* itself.

42. Fullinwider, "Moral Convention and Moral Lessons," p. 333.

43. Ibid., p. 323.

44. Ibid., p. 332.

45. Ibid., p. 334.

46. That there is a distinction between being a philosopher and engaging in philosophical reflection is obvious at the college level. Students who take philosophy courses engage in philosophical thinking. This does not mean that they are "philosophers and metaphysicians" in Reid's sense. The same, I have been maintaining in this book, can be true of children.

CHAPTER 10. CONCLUDING THOUGHTS

1. R. M. Hare, *Essays in Religion and Education* (Oxford: Clarendon Press, 1992), p. 140.

2. Ibid., p. 142.

3. See page 63 of *Philosophical Inquiry*, the teacher's manual for *Harry Stottlemeier's Discovery* by Matthew Lipman (Upper Montclair, N.J.: Institute for the Advancement of Philosophy for Children, 1974). Although the account that follows is based on responses by fifth graders, there is little reason to think that this story cannot be meaningfully discussed by those in the third or fourth grade.

4. The comments that follow are based on chap. 5, "Fairness," in my *Philosophical Adventures with Children* (Lanham, Md.: University Press of America, 1985).

5. See the workbook for *Mark*, which concentrates on issues in civic education and political philosophy. *Mark* is another IAPC children's novel, authored by Matthew Lipman.

6. David A. White and Sheila Schlaggar, " 'I wonder . . .': Primary Source Philosophy and Gifted Sixth Graders," *Teaching Philosophy* 16:4 (December 1993): 335–46.

7. Hare, *Essays on Religion and Education*, p. 130.

8. From Samuel Butler, *Ernest Pontifex, or the Way of all Flesh*, cited in Richard M. Hare, "Value Education in a Pluralist Society," in Matthew Lipman and Ann M. Sharp, eds., *Growing Up with Philosophy* (Philadelphia: Temple University Press, 1978), pp. 378–79.

Selected Bibliography

Adler, Jonathan. 1989. "Particularity, Gilligan, and the Two-Levels View: A Reply." *Ethics* 100:149–56.

Aristotle. 1980. *Nicomachean Ethics.* Translated by W. D. Ross. Oxford: Oxford University Press.

Astington, Janet Wilde. 1993. *The Child's Discovery of the Mind.* Cambridge, Mass.: Harvard University Press.

Benjamin, David and Jeremy Scott. 1989. "Review of Nagel's *What Does It All Mean?" Thinking* 7(4): 29–31.

Benjamin, Martin. 1990. *Splitting the Difference: Compromise and Integrity in Ethics and Politics.* Lawrence: University Press of Kansas.

Benninga, Jacques S., ed. 1991. *Morality, Character, and Civic Education in the Elementary School.* New York: Teachers College Press.

Black, Max. 1972. "Reasonableness." In *Education and the Development of Reason,* edited by R. F. Dearden, P. H. Hirst, and R. S. Peters, pp. 194–207. London: Routledge and Kegan Paul.

Blum, Lawrence A. 1980. *Friendship, Altruism and Morality.* London: Routledge and Kegan Paul.

———. 1994. *Moral Perception and Particularity.* New York: Cambridge University Press.

Boeyink, David. 1992. "Casuistry: A Case-Based Method for Journalism." *Journal of Mass Media Ethics* 7(2): 112–13.

Bok, Sissela. 1978. *Lying: Moral Choice in Public and Private Life.* New York: Pantheon.

———. 1983. *Secrets.* New York: Pantheon.

Callahan, Daniel, and Sissela Bok, eds. 1980. *Ethics Teaching in Higher Education.* New York: Plenum.

Carter, Forrest. 1976. *The Education of Little Tree.* Albuquerque: University of New Mexico Press.

Damon, William. 1988. *The Moral Child.* New York: Free Press.

Donaldson, Margaret. 1979. *Children's Minds.* New York: Norton.

Dworkin, Ronald. 1977. *Taking Rights Seriously.* Oxford: Oxford University Press.

Ennis, Robert. 1984. "Problems in Testing Informal Logic Critical Thinking Ability." *Informal Logic* (January).

———. 1987. "A Conception of Critical Thinking—With Some Curriculum Suggestions," American Philosophical Association, *Newsletter on Teaching Philosophy.* (summer): 1–5.

Ennis, Robert, and Stephen P. Norris. 1989. *Evaluating Critical Thinking.* Pacific Grove, Calif.: Midwest Publications.

Facione, Peter, ed. 1989. "Report on Critical Thinking." American Philosophical Association Subcommittee on Pre-College Philosophy, University of Delaware.

Flanagan, Owen. 1992. *Varieties of Moral Personality.* Cambridge, Mass.: Harvard University Press.

Fullinwider, Robert. 1989. "Moral Conventions and Moral Lessons." *Social Theory and Practice* 15:3 (fall 1989): 321–37.

_____ . 1991. "Science and Technology Education as Civic Education." In *Europe, America, and Technology: Philosophical Perspectives,* edited by Paul T. Durbin, pp. 197–215. Netherlands: Kluwer Academic Publishers.

_____ . 1994. "Ethnocentrism and Education in Judgment." *Report from the Institute for Philosophy and Public Policy* 14(1/2): 7–11.

Gilligan, Carol. 1982. *In a Different Voice: Psychological Theory and Women's Development.* Cambridge, Mass.: Harvard University Press.

Gutmann, Amy. 1993. "The Challenge of Multiculturalism in Political Ethics." *Philosophy and Public Affairs* 22(3): 171–206.

Hallie, Philip. 1979. *Lest Innocent Blood Be Shed.* Kansas City, Mo.: Harrow.

Hannaford, Robert V. 1993. *Moral Anatomy and Moral Reasoning.* Lawrence: University Press of Kansas.

Hare, R. M. 1981. *Moral Thinking.* New York: Oxford University Press.

_____ . 1992. *Essays in Religion and Education.* Oxford: Clarendon Press.

Hirsh, E. D. 1987. *Cultural Literacy: What Every American Needs to Know.* New York: Houghton Mifflin.

Hoffman, M. L. 1970. "Moral Development." In *Carmichael's Manual of Child Psychology,* vol. 2, edited by P. A. Mussen, pp. 261–369. New York: Wiley.

Hume, David. (1740) 1888. *A Treatise on Human Nature,* edited by L. A. Selby-Bigge. Oxford: Clarendon Press.

Johnson, Mark. 1993. *Moral Imagination.* Chicago: University of Chicago Press.

Jonsen, Albert, and Stephen Toulmin. 1988. *The Abuse of Casuistry: A History of Moral Reasoning.* Berkeley: University of California Press.

Kagan, Jerome, and Sharon Lamb. 1987. *The Emergence of Morality in Young Children.* Chicago: University of Chicago Press.

Kohlberg, Lawrence. 1981. *The Philosophy of Moral Development: Essays on Moral Development,* vol. 1. San Francisco: Harper and Row.

_____ . 1984. *The Psychology of Moral Development: Essays on Moral Development,* vol. 2. San Francisco: Harper and Row.

Lichtenberg, Judith. 1994. "Moral Certainty." *Philosophy* 69:181–204.

Lickona, Thomas. 1991. *Educating for Character.* New York: Bantam.

Lickona, Thomas, ed. 1976. *Moral Development and Behavior.* New York: Holt, Rinehart, and Winston.

Lipman, Matthew. 1974. *Harry Stottlemeier's Discovery.* Upper Montclair, N.J.: Institute for the Advancement of Philosophy for Children. (Also author of *Kio and Gus, Pixie, Lisa,* and other K–12 novels and accompanying teachers' manuals, which are all available through IAPC.)

———. 1988. *Philosophy Goes to School.* Philadelphia: Temple University Press.

———. 1991. *Thinking in Education.* New York: Cambridge University Press.

Lipman, Matthew, ed. 1993. *Thinking Children and Education.* Dubuque, Iowa: Kendall/Hunt.

Lipman, Matthew, Ann M. Sharp, and Frederick Oscanyan, eds. 1978. *Growing Up with Philosophy.* Philadelphia: Temple University Press.

Lobel, Arnold. 1971. *Frog and Toad Together.* New York: Harper and Row.

McPeck, John. 1985. "Critical Thinking and the 'Trivial Pursuit' Theory of Knowledge." *Teaching Philosophy* 8:4 (October): 295–308.

Martin, Michael. 1985. "The Goals of Science Education." *Thinking* 4(2): 19–22.

———. 1986. "Science Education and Moral Education." *Journal of Moral Education* 15(2): 99–108.

Matthews, Gareth. 1980. *Philosophy and the Young Child.* Cambridge, Mass.: Harvard University Press.

———. 1984. *Dialogues with Children.* Cambridge, Mass.: Harvard University Press.

———. 1987. "Concept Formation and Moral Development." In *Philosophical Perspectives in Developmental Psychology,* edited by James Russell, pp. 175–90. Oxford: Basil Blackwell.

———. 1994. *The Philosophy of Childhood.* Cambridge, Mass.: Harvard University Press.

Matthews, Michael. 1994. *Science Teaching: The Role of History and Philosophy of Science.* New York: Routledge.

Murphy, Arthur. 1965. *The Theory of Practical Reason.* LaSalle, Ill.: Open Court.

Paul, Richard. 1992. *Critical Thinking: What Every Person Needs to Survive in a Rapidly Changing World.* Sonoma, Calif.: Center for Critical Thinking.

Peters, R. S. 1974. *Psychology and Ethical Development.* London: George Allen and Unwin.

Piaget, Jean. 1929. *The Child's Conception of the World.* London: Kegan Paul.

———. (1932) 1965. *The Moral Judgment of the Child.* New York: Free Press.

Plato. 1981. *Five Dialogues.* Translated by G. M. A. Grube. Indianapolis, Ind.: Hackett Publishers.

Pritchard, Michael S. 1985. *Philosophical Adventures with Children.* Lanham, Md.: University Press of America.

———. 1991. *On Becoming Responsible.* Lawrence: University Press of Kansas.

Raths, Louis E., Merrill Harmin, and Sidney Simon. 1966. *Values and Teaching.* Columbus, Ohio: Charles E. Merrill.

Rawls, John. 1993. *Political Liberalism.* New York: Columbia University Press.

Reed, Ronald, and Ann M. Sharp, eds. 1992. *Studies in Philosophy for Children: Harry Stottlemeier's Discovery.* Philadelphia: Temple University Press.

Reid, Thomas. (1788) 1895. *Essays on the Active Powers of the Mind,* in *Philosophical Works,* vol. 2, with notes by Sir William Hamilton. Hildesheim: Gekorg Olms Verlagsbuchhandlung.

Sharp, Ann M. 1991. "The Community of Inquiry: Education for Democracy."
  Thinking 9(2): 31–37.
Shweder, Richard A., Elliot Turiel, and Nancy C. Much. 1981. "The Moral Intu-
  itions of the Child." In *Social Cognitive Development: Frontiers and Possible
  Futures,* edited by John H. Flavell and Lee Ross. Cambridge: Cambridge Uni-
  versity Press.
Sibley, W. H. 1953. "The Rational and the Reasonable." *Philosophical Review*
  62:554–60.
Sichel, Betty A. 1988. *Moral Education.* Philadelphia: Temple University Press.
Simon, Caroline. 1989. "Judgmentalism." *Faith and Philosophy.* 6(3): 275–87.
Skurzynski, Gloria. 1980. *Honest Andrew.* New York: Harcourt Brace Jovanovich.
Splitter, Laurance J., and Ann M. Sharp. 1995. *Teaching Better Thinking: The Class-
  room Community of Inquiry.* Melbourne: Australian Center for Educational
  Research.
Thomas, John C. 1992. "The Development of Reasoning in Children Through
  Community of Inquiry." In *Studies in Philosophy for Children: Harry Stottle-
  meier's Discovery,* edited by Ronald Reed and Ann M. Sharp, pp. 96–104. Phila-
  delphia: Temple University Press.
Thomas, Laurence. 1989. *Living Morally: A Psychology of Moral Character.* Philadel-
  phia: Temple University Press.
Varga, Judy. 1961. *The Dragon Who Liked to Spit Fire.* New York: William Morrow.
Weinstein, Mark. 1989. "Critical Thinking and Moral Education." *Thinking* 7(3):
  42–49.
Winn, Marie. 1971. *Shiver, Gobble, and Snore.* New York: Simon and Schuster.

Index